KU-845-190

People in Politics

also by Richard Rose

INFLUENCING VOTERS

POLITICS IN ENGLAND

POLICY-MAKING IN ENGLAND
(editor)

STUDIES IN BRITISH POLITICS
(editor)

MUST LABOUR LOSE?
(with Mark Abrams)

THE BRITISH GENERAL ELECTION OF 1959
(with D. E. Butler)

*Civis Romanus Sum**

PEOPLE IN POLITICS

Observations Across the Atlantic

by

RICHARD ROSE

University of Strathclyde
Glasgow

FABER AND FABER
London

First published in 1970
by Faber and Faber Limited
24 Russell Square, London, W.C.1
Printed in Great Britain
by Ebenezer Baylis and Son, Limited
The Trinity Press, Worcester, and London
All rights reserved

SBN 571 08828 7

UNIVERSITY
LIBRARY
NOTTINGHAM

*Cicero, *In Verrem*, V.lvii, 147
Cf. Lord Palmerston, House of Commons, June 25, 1850
Free translation: What's good enough for
Don Pacifico is good enough for me?

© *Richard Rose 1970*

TO ROSEMARY
who helped me to learn English
and
was willing to learn American

Acknowledgments

Full acknowledgments to all who have been accessories before the fact of this book would require an autobiography. The following list is much abridged. First of all, I would like to acknowledge the stimulation of many comments, written and oral, by Professor W. J. M. Mackenzie through the years; his remarks combine a canny eye for essentials with a direct and clarifying literary style. Secondly, I wish to thank the American Social Science Research Council and the Institute of Political Studies, Stanford University, for a three-month sojourn in Palo Alto, California, immediately before preparing this work. The pleasure of giving up England for Lent was matched only by the stimulation of a company of lively and cosmopolitan scholars. Chapter VIII is based directly upon work done at Stanford then. Thirdly, I would like to pay tribute to the nerve, if not the caution, of Matthew Evans of Faber and Faber, who enthusiastically welcomed the prospect of a book based upon the roughest draft manuscript that I hope he will ever have to see. His care and efficiency have made publishing this book the pleasure that any pregnancy ought to be, but rarely is. Martin Kessler brought exactly the right qualifications to the task of considering an American edition of this book: Viennese birth, English education, and residence in New York City. Mrs Alastair Ward valiantly struggled with the task of typing the first draft from a tape-recording of lectures delivered in a dialect very remote from that of Lanarkshire. Mrs J. McGlone typed later drafts from manuscript prepared by an author whose hand had never been disciplined by the Scottish tawse. Those who read the manuscript in whole or in part include Terry Clark, James Curran, Nicholas Deakin, James Douglas, Fred Greenstein, Hugh Heclo and Dennis Kavanagh. The late Peter Nettl read and reacted to an early draft of the manuscript with characteristic generosity and incisiveness. Dennis Sandole did the calculations for the tables in Chapter 7. Those who have commented have saved me from much over-exuberance inappropriate to the printed page, as well as from many faults of analysis and detail.

Last and far from least, I wish to thank the Faculty of Economics at Cambridge University for their invitation to deliver eight lectures reviewing the state of political sociology in the summer term, 1967. The Secretary of the Department of Applied Economics, Mr A. T. K. Grant, and various Cambridge friends provided hospitality that more than offset the weather. The knowledge that my audience was about to sit examinations concentrated my mind and, I hope, theirs. The fact that it consisted of students of considerable intelligence but limited formal instruction in politics and sociology gave the lectures an obvious purpose. In the words of the King's College carol service, this was to provide, in some small way, 'a light to lighten the Gentiles'.

Richard Rose
Bennochy
Helensburgh, Scotland

14 April 1969

Contents

Introduction

Politicians are people. Yet many seemingly educated individuals resist the idea that politicians have recognizably human desires for affection, esteem, security and money. Instead, they treat politicians as if they ought to be super-human. Ordinary citizens are people too. Sometimes they choose a political party to avoid controversy between husband and wife, rather than do an elaborate calculus of benefits to be derived from each party. Neither politicians nor citizens are the one-dimensional characters of mathematical models of the social sciences, nor are they the witless prisoners of television sets depicted in pseudo-liberal journalism. While few of us can imagine ourselves President or Prime Minister, or as one of the dimmest members of the electorate, at least we can try to understand these individuals for what they are.

Politics is much more than a matter of pleasing people. It involves hard choices about very human concerns: who will bear the burden of unemployment or military service? Should children or old people benefit more from the welfare state? Carrying out decisions requires skill in working institutions. That is why politicians who are good at handling people often make a mess of government. When a politician tries to reduce urban congestion or encourage economic growth, he is no longer working with single individuals. He is enmeshed in a large, imperfectly co-ordinated set of bureaucratic institutions in which the human element is the least of his problems. In the classic phrase, he is fighting the system. To understand how people act politically, we must also understand the institutions and environment which constrain and shape them as individuals.

In scope, this book could embrace all mankind. Some social scientists would claim that their knowledge stretches to such lengths; I would not claim this. When generalizations can embrace a wide range of countries, they are likely to be trivial or tautological. This book is about the people of America and the British Isles, the two lands I know best, as a native of the former and a resident of the latter. It is emphatically not a book about that familiar but artificial entity, the Anglo-American people. One of the themes of the study is that Americans are significantly different from people in Britain, whether viewed as citizens, politicians or as social scientists. A subordinate theme is that Americans often differ from each other in important ways, as do British people. Sometimes, these differences are very important politically. For example, the civil rights movement divides Americans on basic questions: Is a Negro an American? And is a Mississippian? To answer yes to both questions is not to equate Martin Luther King with the man who shot him. To be British is not the same as being English. Even a Dubliner educated on Shaw and classical sophistry would hesitate to argue that because an Englishman, a Scot, a Welshman, and someone from County Tyrone were all legally British, each was therefore the same as the other. As a former resident of Manchester, I sometimes wonder whether those who live north of Banbury Cross are English in the same sense as the people of the island's deep South.

It is important to raise these questions of cultural and geographical perspectives, because so much of our thinking nowadays is airborne. We can move our minds from continent to continent at the turn of a phrase, or move our bodies between continents between lunch and dinner. Knowing where we are when we arrive—or what our point of departure was like—is a more difficult matter. The founders of American society had a healthy scepticism of the political institutions of George III. Americans from the time of Woodrow Wilson through Senator Eugene McCarthy have romanticized them, because of the presumed efficiency of Cabinet government or the emotional effect of medieval ceremonials lacking in the United States. Some new American radicals, following Marx, are inclined to believe that the revolution is likely to come first in England, and migrate to London to give it a push. Then, like T. S. Eliot in an early letter to Ezra Pound, they complain about the resistance of the natives to change, and the badness of the cooking.

In times past, Englishmen visited America to complain about the manners and food of the natives, or in search of heiresses to replenish aristocratic fortunes. In universities, there arose a tradition of studying the anthropology of tribes in exotic places in Africa and Asia, and the Prince of Wales has continued this. Yet there are equally exotic places in Lancashire, offering to conventionally educated people such as George Orwell, challenges almost as great as Africa in terms of language and environmental hardships. The new English fashion seems to be to avoid the Dark Continent and turn to the light that shines forth from American universities. There are now Englishmen who have studied at Yale or Berkeley and there found God; they may then analyse their native country as some Americans study foreign societies, from the perspective of a radio hero of my youth, Jack Armstrong, the All-American Boy. One can still meet Englishmen, for want of a better word called educated, who have read American books only to confirm their worst cultural prejudices.

It is not the intention of this book to argue to American or British readers that the grass is always greener on the other side of the Atlantic. In fact, the grass *is* greener in England, but the mechanical devices to care for grass are superior in America. The aim of this book is to illustrate, concretely and practically, the insights that can be gained from looking at two industrial societies simultaneously from the inside and from afar. British and American ideas and illustrations have been chosen depending upon which seemed most apt for the purpose at hand.

In addition to describing two countries, this book depicts two very different points of view: that of the man of affairs and that of the academic social scientist. The reason for this is straightforward: I have had some experience of both worlds, and think that both are important. Unless a social scientist enjoys some imaginative empathy with men whose lives and emotions are invested in concrete political events, his comments, however logical, are likely to be weak in understanding. Unless a politician is prepared to test his intuitions and aspirations against logic and empirical evidence, then his actions may have very different consequences from those he intends. Politicians today, as in generations past, tend to be men who have difficulty in understanding statistical aggregates, even the thousands or millions of votes that can turn them out of office. Instead, they prefer to think about voters individually or even idiosyncratically, as if one could get to know each of them. Yet if a hard-working New York Senatorial candidate tried to spend one minute with each voter needed to guarantee victory, it would take him more than fifteen years to accomplish his aim. A new generation of social scientists suggests that it is not so difficult to take the politics out of the social scientist. Just as one needn't know anything about statistics to win elections, so one need not know anything about politicians to analyse election statistics. The experiences that academics have as citizens, tax-payers, promoters of research grants, or as victims of student revolts often seem unrelated to the universe described in their books. Something is lost in all this.

Throughout I have tried to illustrate what can be gained by running general concepts and specific examples in tandem. A generalization that cannot fit the first example that comes to mind is of limited use, just as an anecdote which does not imply some generalization is a diversion rather than a stimulus to thought. For example, whenever I read a book that assumes all politicians are rational, I think of the confusion in the Imperial Hotel at Blackpool in October, 1963, shortly after Harold Macmillan announced his retirement as Prime Minister. This act decapitated the Conservative Party and left his inheritors with the rationality of a band of chickens in the same situation. As is usual in British politics, blood was spilt only in the metaphorical sense. There was literally bloodletting around the Hilton Hotel in Chicago for one wondrous week in 1968, when Democrats assembled to nominate a potential President of the United States. Any social scientist who can find the hidden hand of rationality at work, guiding events in that riot within a convention within a circus, has better eyesight or greater faith in things unseen than this author.

The style of this book is straightforward enough. Most of the ideas have been developed in lectures over the years. The material has gone through considerable revision since then. The questioning tone of the lecture hall remains: to quote Lord Poole, 'It is much easier to see the problem than the solution. This is because there is no solution.' In addition, I have followed my standard lecturing practice of assuming that there is no point in saying things unless the lecturer and, hopefully, his listeners enjoy the subject.

The language of the book is polyglot. Mr Eliot's well-known dictum—a man should write with a sense of the past as well as of the present in his bones, so that both may have a simultaneous existence—has much to recommend it to social scientists, especially those involved in comparative studies. It could be argued that one should know the language of Bagehot and of Oxford philosophy, of Lincoln and of Talcott Parsons, and, perhaps, the language of Hyman Kaplan. Some ideas are best expressed in one idiom, and some in another. Inside every Irishman, there is a German philosopher struggling to get out; less certainly, inside every user of the natural language of social scientists, German-American, there is a Celtic poet with a vision to express in alien words. It will be interesting to see how many readers and how many reviewers—not always the same people—regard this volume as a work of social science, and how many regard it as a literary essay. For what it is worth, the author regards it as something of both.

One reader of the manuscript suggested that more attention should be given to the place of values in the study of politics. This comment surprised me, as the values of an author are usually discernible, either on the surface or just below. Certainly, no claim is made that this book is value-free. No section is devoted specifically to the values of social scientists, for such discussions have always been suspect ever since I heard the term defined, with reference to a social scientist who wrote much about values, as: 'Something that guy hasn't got.' Liberals may find some of their optimistic assumptions affronted by the discussion of awkward social science findings and recent unpleasant events in British and American history. For this, no apology is offered: the history of man and of government has been a history of conflict and even tragedy, at least since the days of the House of Atreus. To ignore this fact runs the risk of turning the literature of social science into science fiction.

People in Politics

I said to a friend in Dublin one day, 'There's nothing wrong with social science, you know. The only trouble is that if you ask a stupid question, then you get a stupid answer.'

'Ah, that's true,' he replied. 'But I think the Talmud says it better now: "A wise man's question is half the answer".'

One

Looking at Politics

The conventional public picture of a politician is of a servant of the common good. The private candid snapshot often shows a self-seeking man. Students of politics used to portray politicians in ways consistent with the public portrait. Increasingly, however, writers stress those things that make politicians appear self-centred and self-regarding men. It is pointless to argue which perspective offers the best or truest picture, for these and other views are each sometimes true. The simplest approach is to visualize a political figure as a cubist portrait—two faces, three eyes and all. The result may be less inspiring than a schoolroom painting of George Washington crossing the Delaware or of the Queen at the state opening of Parliament. It is, however, likely to comprehend more of the several faces of reality.

However described, politicians are at least familiar and tangible objects. While the activity of politics is familiar, because it is an abstraction, it is difficult to define and impossible to represent by visual images, even those of an abstract painter. Many definitions have been offered. Max Weber, for instance, defined politics as 'striving to share power or striving to influence the distribution of power, either among states or among groups within a state'. The definition of Michael Oakeshott gives less emphasis to power and more to patterns of life; politics, to him, is 'the activity of attending to the general arrangements of a set of people'. Values are especially important to David Easton; to him, politics is 'the authoritative allocation of values for a society'.[1] There is something to be said for each of these definitions of politics. To say it properly requires a book; many such books exist. Hence, there is no need here to settle definitions by debate in the abstract. The core and the fuzzy boundaries of things political should emerge in the discussion of specific topics that follows. It is far easier to point to what is politically relevant in a context than to define it *in vacuo*.

Inevitably, each person has notions about politicians and what politics is about. Conceptual frameworks are to students of politics what prose was to Monsieur Jourdain. We have been using them all our life, or at least, ever since we began to classify and relate objects around us as infants. Without some sense of what objects signify and how they are related, we could neither catch a bus nor cast a ballot. One can, of course, graduate from university without becoming conscious of major terms used in analysing politics. This does not mean that a person is innocent of preconceptions about politics, but rather that his picture of what politicians do is made up of inarticulate or simplistic beliefs.

Looking at the different ways in which people write about voting and elections illustrates concretely how different conceptual frameworks affect what we see in seemingly familiar political phenomena. At least eight different points of view can be identified.

In the eyes of candidates, elections might appear to be terrible ordeals. The results of years of effort are judged in a single day's balloting. In an election, unlike a marriage, one of the candidates is certain to emerge the loser and in the case of the Liberal Party in Britain, the great majority of candidates begin their campaign with defeat nearly certain. In such circumstances, one might expect politicians to view elections with distaste. A survey of candidates at the 1966 British general election found that the opposite was the case.[2] Candidates spent an average of about ten hours a day campaigning, whether their seat was safe, marginal or hopeless. Notwithstanding the importance of the result to their future, two-thirds of the candidates made no reference to the result in replying to a questionnaire; only a handful were depressed by defeat. Instead of showing post-election depression, two-thirds were elated by their experience as a centre of attention for a few brief weeks. One Liberal candidate in a permanently Conservative seat called campaigning 'the only thing really worth doing in life'. A Labour candidate facing an enormous Conservative majority wrote, 'I look forward eagerly to the next time.' The campaign, not the result, was their consummation, an act as gratifying emotionally as it was exhausting physically.

The journalist's approach to elections is based upon the assumption that the only things that count are the things he can see, hear and feel himself. The most immediate and visible objects in a campaign are the candidates: hence, a journalistic account of an election is usually an account of what the candidates do. At best, this approach can be only half right, for an election involves voters too. The vastness of an electorate makes it impossible to describe voters in the same detail as campaigners. This limitation of resources makes an account of what a few candidates do the most appropriate framework for a one-man description of an election. Theodore White exemplifies the technique in his studies of *The Making of the President*. Since it is hardly natural to describe an election without any reference to voters or to the effect of campaign activities upon the electorate, at times White attempts to fathom, by introspection or intuition, the views of masses of voters. In his study of the 1960 presidential election, for instance, he places at a strategic point in his book a large mass of census data, carefully wrapped in purple prose, implying that John F. Kennedy's victory in 1960 was the result of long-term social changes in America. Yet the fact is that John F. Kennedy nearly lost the election, notwithstanding all the social changes that White refers to. The evidence presented 'over-explains' the result.[3]

In many respects, the historian's approach to elections is similar to that of the journalist. Both concentrate upon describing the behaviour of campaigners. Journalists work among the quick, and historians among the dead, especially those who leave large files of private correspondence. Unfortunately, as literacy increases, so the tendency of politicians to commit their views to private correspondence decreases. One can also assume that at every election, especially those in the heyday of corruption, there are some things that no candidate would ever put in writing. Historians, unlike journalists, have a better chance to study individual voters, for early electorates were small, and with time and patience, considerable and detailed statistical knowledge may be acquired concerning who voted for whom in 1844 in upper New York state, or how the development of suburbs around London in the late 19th century affected the Conservative Party.[4] When doing this, historians are still writing about the past, but they are no longer writing in the literary tradition of historical scholarship.

A student of political institutions—whether historian, lawyer or political scientist—is likely to see an election in impersonal terms; his attention is caught by such things as the machinery for registering voters, nominating candidates and counting votes. Even in Britain, where the mechanics of elections are relatively simple, the institutions of elections are sufficiently complex to merit description and analysis at book length.[5] A comparative view reminds us that there is nothing sacrosanct about the way in which British and American people conduct elections. In most European countries, seats in Parliament are awarded by formulas intended to make representation proportional to votes. Elucidating the consequences of the particular institutions used in elections is a considerable and difficult task. The difficulty is exemplified by the fact that a scholar such as Maurice Duverger could err in asserting that the British and American practice of giving victory to whichever candidate was 'first past the post', regardless of his plurality, caused a two-party system.[6]

Because election results are one of the few types of political data to appear in numerical form, they are naturally suited to statistical analysis. Some boys and men seem to devour election statistics as others may study *Wisden* on cricket or *Who's Who in Baseball.* Extracting meaning from these figures does not necessarily require specialized statistical knowledge. The detailed appendices of the Nuffield election studies examine British voting trends in a way that requires no knowledge of algebra to comprehend. The use of complex statistics and large computers permits the extraction of much more detailed material from election results than might at first seem discernible to the untutored eye.[7] The real limitation upon the purely statistical approach to elections is, strictly speaking, that it is the analysis of votes and of aggregations of votes rather than of the people who vote.

The techniques of the psychologist are appropriate to study voters at first hand. The best known is the use of sample surveys to collect much detailed information from a carefully selected cross-section of the electorate. The findings suggest that the deep psychological drives attributed to the general public by those who psychoanalyse the public from Fleet Street or Washington, D.C. bars are unfounded. For instance, great or even super-human powers are often attributed to the personality of individual candidates. This was notably the case in the election of Dwight D. Eisenhower as President in 1952. The circumstances of the time, involving potentially deep anxieties about the Korean War, Communism, and corruption in Washington, created a situation in which one would expect many voters to regard Eisenhower as a charismatic leader, that is, a man to follow without regard to conventional restraints. A careful analysis of a sample of 1800 voters, carried out by James C. Davies and two colleagues, found that less than two per cent described Eisenhower in terms indicating a strong psychological attachment to the man.[8] Repeated surveys in America and in Britain emphasize that the involvement of most voters in an election is limited, rather than intense. Insofar as voters are psychologically involved in voting, this arises from the indirect linkage of partisan phenomena with a variety of face-to-face personal relationships. In short, the candidates rather than voters are more apt subjects to psychologize.[9]

Economists usually approach the study of voting by building elaborate superstructures of rational calculation upon extremely dubious psychological foundations. Economists are inclined to assume that each individual seeks to maximize the utility of his vote, and that each candidate or party tries to maximize the probability of victory. Anthony Downs has most elegantly shown the consequences of these assumptions in *An Economic Theory of Democracy*. It is unclear what Downs is attempting to maximize—perhaps aesthetic satisfaction—since the single-attribute characters portrayed there are very different from politicians and voters viewed in the flesh. When a politician does show that he is extremely power-oriented, this tendency toward monomania may even strike his 'normal' political colleagues as a bit peculiar. For example, Woodrow Wilson's desire to dominate his government and latterly, the Allies, led associates innocent of Freudian concepts to speculate greatly about his unconscious drives.[10] In politics, very few politicians consistently persist in trying to maximize electoral advantages. Politicians are more likely to attack or abuse market research than to use it intelligently in political campaigns.[11] Similarly, the attachment of voters to their parties does not show the calculating mentality that is applied to supermarket shopping; attachments to parties tend to be formed over long periods of time and to involve little explicit calculation.[12]

Sociologists are likely to see elections as yet another arena in which class conflicts can be expressed; in words that S. M. Lipset quotes approvingly, elections are 'the expression of the democratic class struggle'.[13] This remark illustrates the persisting tendency of sociologists to regard political phenomena as the consequence of social structure and, more particularly, of class structure. In Britain, there was ground for believing (or hoping) that elections turned on class identifications, at a time when sociology and Socialism were close. In New Deal America there was also ground for such a belief. Increasingly, however, research has shown that class is a limited influence upon voting in Britain, and even less in America.[14] One of the major growth industries in political sociology today is the explanation of why class counts for so little, rather than so much, in voting behaviour.

It is pointless to argue about which of the above mentioned approaches is the best approach to the study of politics in general or to elections in particular. One doesn't need much philosophical training to see how easy it is to rig the answer; all you have to do is specify the definition of what is best when you choose your side. It is equally pointless to claim that all approaches are equal for this begs the question: equal in what way? They are certainly not identical or interchangeable. Each involves specialized concerns in posing questions, and often specialized techniques in seeking answers. A political scientist is better suited to relate shifts in votes to shifts in Congressional or Parliamentary seats than is a psychologist or an economist. A depth psychologist is likely to be more competent than a statistician in telling us whether a voter inside the polling booth feels a latent sense of claustrophobia or even a sense of return to womb-like security.[15] My own approach to the problem is that of a C.I.O. industrial unionist rather than that of an A.F.L. defender of ancient craft union privileges. The industrial unionist gains scope and relevance by bringing several disciplinary approaches together. To say this is not to deny the value of good craftsmanship, whether the problem at hand is painting a word-picture of candidates or cooking statistics. In the field of voting studies, the greatest enemy is not the member of a rival union but the unqualified scab.

To grant that elections can be a proper subject for non-political study is not to suggest that such events are without any political significance. In America, the candidacy of Governor George Wallace at the 1968 election, even more than the candidacy of Barry Goldwater in 1964, was a reminder that contrasts between parties can have black and white intensity. In Britain, continuing economic difficulties remind people that the relative competence with which elected representatives manage the economy is a matter that immediately affects their pocketbooks. In France, Italy and especially in the Germany of the Weimar Republic, the choices offered voters at elections have been very real ones about the future of their societies.

Like any political event, an election is *both* a political phenomenon *and* an activity embedded in a larger society. Men we describe as politicians are simply members of society performing certain more or less specifically political tasks. In order to understand what they are doing, we need at a minimum some basic understanding of human nature and, more to the point, knowledge of how people in the society concerned are expected to behave. In looking at the government of a country, we need to recognize the many extra-legal conventions that affect how it works, and the scope and character of its relations with its subjects. Any catalogue of the many different things fit for study under the heading of politics suggests that there ought to be a variety of ways of conducting inquiries, just as there are many different kinds of people who write about politics. Some of these can be illustrated briefly. The important point is that techniques of study are neither good nor bad in themselves; they are only more or less useful as methods for gaining a better understanding of substantive political problems.

The narrative is the conventional conceptual framework for the study of politics. Events are described in the order in which they occur, or in an order deemed convenient for purposes of description. The Nuffield studies of general elections in Britain are a well-known example of this genre.[16] Each volume sets out a chronological account of the campaign and the events leading up to it, and a summary description of topics that cannot conveniently be fitted into a chronological framework. There is a minimum of description of cause and effect. Yet some sort of relationship must be implicit in the selection of subjects for emphasis. If one-quarter of a book is devoted to a discussion of features of constituency campaigning, it is, to say the least, surprising to learn in an appendix that the party organization and candidates' activities described in so much detail are usually worth much less than a thousand votes. The fact that the authors commit themselves to generalization in the concluding chapter may be logically inconsistent, but it is nonetheless desirable. After all, people who have invested time (and sometimes money) to read a book have a right to expect an author to come to some sort of conclusion. The alternative is to publish what I call a 'postcard' book. This is a volume which should conclude with a postcard addressed to the author, and a request that if any reader can figure out what it all adds up to, for heaven's sake drop him a line.

Newer approaches, by contrast, seek to explain general phenomena rather than describe or chronicle a particular set of incidents. This should involve setting out a considerable amount of empirical information about politics somewhere in a study, even if the information is only hearsay or third-hand newspaper accounts. The real value of the case material is thought to be in its implications, rather than intrinsic. Even if an author is convinced that his subject, say, a political party, is absolutely unique in the world, there is the expectation that he will adduce a typology of all possible parties in order to demonstrate just those points wherein the uniqueness of his subject rests. Since a single case is a dangerous basis for generalization, students of politics are increasingly concerned with comparative analysis, whether the things compared are individuals, cities, societies, or events in time. To compare all is not to confound all. Elections in Russia are not the same as those in America, just as elections in Northern Ireland are not the same as those in England. The simplest paradigm of comparison involves three questions: To what extent and under what circumstances are the things compared similar? To what extent and under what circumstances are they different? Are the chief findings applicable or irrelevant elsewhere? In an era in which high-speed airplanes and computers enable an individual to run through countries at a speed greater than his powers of comprehension, there is a danger that the comparative approach may lead to facile generalization. This is especially true if a comparison is intended to test a hypothesis which the formulator has already decided is true. In America, confident exponents of certitudes seem most frequently found among post-graduate students and in Britain, among undergraduates. I am not sure whether this is proof of the superiority of English or American education.

One reason why voting studies are popular in universities is that they are specially amenable to scientific treatment. Voting is a clearly identifiable 'dependent variable', i.e., thing to be explained. The term is not a phrase that one would expect to find on the lips of a Jane Austen figure, for it belongs to an explicitly anti-narrative mode of thought. More interestingly, it is not a word that one would find on the lips of a politician either. A former American Secretary of State, Dean Acheson, once ironically remarked, after reading an academic study of a crisis in which he was involved, that he could now write his memoirs under the title: *I Was a Dependent Variable*. To a social scientist, anyone or anything can be a dependent variable, an object to be explained by reference to a set of independent variables, which, as they change, cause the dependent object to alter. In aspiration, these variables are meant to be derived from a theory of society which will—tomorrow if not today—explain everything. For reasons grounded more in the psychology of academics than upon common sense, the idea of a general theory of society attracts many able minds on both sides of the Atlantic. Americans seem to prefer announcing that they have just found the Grail, whereas Englishmen prefer demonstrating that the object unveiled does not conform to the rigid specifications of the platonic idea of the Grail. Since Americans often use the word 'theory' to refer to an imperfectly integrated collection of abstractions, without regard to the proper (i.e., *Oxford English Dictionary*) definition of the term, the activities of the one group are little affected by the criticisms of the other. The English critics win in logic, but lose in real world terms, since the formally incomplete collation of concepts and hypotheses that Americans use often leads them to develop useful generalizations, aptly described by Robert Merton as 'theories of the middle range',[17] about such things as status anxieties, or the transmission of political attitudes from generation to generation.

My own recipe for studying a problem begins with a motto

adapted from Mrs Beeton's cookbook: 'First, catch your dependent variable.' Then one can try to explain changes in the dependent variable in terms of independent variables of relatively high generality, such as industrial society, and in terms of intervening variables of a relative specific character, such as national, regional or local variations in class structure, or even, variations in political structure. There are two dangers in formalizing research in this manner. One is that people may get so wrapped up in elaborating theories that they lose the time and inclination to test them against reality. The other is that the internal logic and elegance of the theories may take on a life of their own and lead the propounders to conclude that the only value of empirical research is to verify what they have already deduced. Such social scientists at least have one advantage over the explorer who sails mapless across an ocean, hoping he will some day get somewhere. The latterday explorers at least know what they are looking for—even if it is not what they will find upon arrival.

There is much to be said for spreading one's risks in research by starting an investigation with several plausible hypotheses in hand, each derived from some sort of theory. The object of the research is then to see which of several competing hypotheses is best supported by the evidence, and how many can be disproved. For instance, it is 'common sense' that voters in Scotland have been disproportionately Labour because of the centuries-old hatred of Anglophile Conservatives. It is equally common sense that voters in Scotland have been disproportionately Labour because so many electors are Catholics of Irish descent, reacting against the Conservatives as the party that dominated Ireland. A third reasonable hypothesis is that Scotland is disproportionately Labour simply because it has a relatively high proportion of manual workers. These three plausible generalizations can be tested with survey data of voting behaviour. Gallup Poll data from the 1964 election supports the second hypothesis but not the other two.[18] This finding may seem of little significance, but it can be related to problems of ethnic solidarity within the United Kingdom and America, and to general theories of the importance of class, religion and nationality as causes of divisions within society.

Any effort to test hypotheses with something approaching scientific rigour presupposes that the data for one or all of the variables are easily amenable to measurement and manipulation. Voting behaviour meets these requirements very well. Voting is a relatively common unit of measurement across time and across national boundaries. It is now a straightforward although hardly inexpensive task to interview and analyse information about a nation-wide sample of several thousand members of the electorate. The product is an enormous amount of material which can be assessed for reliability by statistical methods, and for validity by reference to election returns and census materials. In its final form—magnetic tape or IBM cards suitable for computer input—the data is ideally suited for intensive and extensive analysis. One should never underestimate the importance of physical convenience. In research terms, it is now easier to analyse civil disorders by feeding into a computer data relating gross national product and political upheavals reported in the *New York Times*, than it is by the old-fashioned and more dangerous method of participant observation. I once met a tidy-minded social scientist whose perspective had become so narrow that he thought the only messy data in politics was that caused by individuals not knowing how to punch holes correctly in IBM cards. What I had in mind was some information I had collected about race relations in a Middle Western American city in 1964. After interviewing a number of whites and Negroes chosen in a technically unscientific but far from irrelevant manner, I concluded that a court decision jailing Negro civil rights leaders had been rigged. The data was messy because my white sources were adamant that they would repudiate what they said if ever I printed their statements or fed them into a computer.

When confronted with messy problems, the instinct of a modern social scientist is to abstract every element that is capable of measurement in a reliable and objective fashion, i.e. one in which different researchers operating independently of each other can at least agree on the 'facts' of a problem, if not on the interpretation of these facts. For example, the traditional student of politics might write an essay trying to answer the seemingly straightforward question: Was Ramsay MacDonald a successful Prime Minister? His latterday counterpart will not begin to give an answer until some attempt is made to define 'success' in reliable and objective terms. Success might be measured in a variety of ways. One might simply conduct an opinion survey of a sample of journalists or of academic political scientists, asking them to rank each modern Prime Minister on a scale ranging from 'very successful' to 'very unsuccessful'. This at least may provide some consensus of opinion. Alternatively, success might be defined in terms of length of stay in Downing Street, since many politicians, as well as students of politics, seem to define success in terms of holding on to office. Given this gloss on the term, it is a simple matter to measure the relative degree of success of each 20th-century British Prime Minister.

TABLE I.1. LENGTH OF OFFICE, 20TH-CENTURY BRITISH PRIME MINISTERS

	Name	*Party*	*Tenure*	
			Years	*Days*
1.	3rd Marquis of Salisbury	Con.	13	256*
2.	H. H. Asquith	Lib/Coalition	8	243
3.	Sir Winston Churchill	Coalition/Con.	8	238
4.	Stanley Baldwin	Con.	7	72
5.	J. Ramsay MacDonald	Lab./Coalition	6	289
6.	Harold Macmillan	Con.	6	280
7.	Clement Attlee	Lab.	6	92
8.	David Lloyd George	Coalition	5	320
9.	Harold Wilson	Lab.	5	0
10.	A. J. Balfour	Con.	3	146
11.	Neville Chamberlain	Con.	2	346
12.	Sir H. Campbell-Bannerman	Lib.	2	125
13.	Sir Anthony Eden	Con.	1	278
14.	Sir Alec Douglas-Home	Con.	0	363
15.	A. Bonar Law	Con.	0	212

*Includes 19th-century period as Prime Minister.
**Total time in office, October 6, 1969.

The table of longevity in office places MacDonald fifth among fifteen 20th-century Prime Ministers. David Lloyd George is the median figure, with a tenure of almost six years in Downing Street. The table does not prove that Ramsay MacDonald was more successful than Lloyd George in any sense other than office-holding. The object of the exercise is not to prove success but to measure it in terms of a single characteristic which is, at the least, not entirely irrelevant to political success. On almost any reckoning, all of the six Prime Ministers with the shortest tenure in office were unsuccessful Prime Ministers.

A comparable test cannot be undertaken of American Presidents, because of fixed terms of office; many men, from notorious failures such as U. S. Grant to very formidable successes, such as Andrew Jackson and Woodrow Wilson, succeeded in serving the customary limit of two terms. The attention given John F. Kennedy's wealthy background and style of behaviour might suggest the hypothesis that a man must be wealthy and of high social status to become President nowadays. High social status can be indicated by an Ivy League education. The wealth that goes with breeding is inherited wealth, not the vulgar riches of the self-made man. It is a straightforward matter to classify 20th-century Presidents on each of these counts.

TABLE I.2. SOCIAL STATUS AND WEALTH OF 20TH-CENTURY AMERICAN PRESIDENTS

	President	*Party*	*Born Wealthy*	*University (BA)*
1.	William McKinley	Republican	No	Allegheny
2.	Theodore Roosevelt	Republican	Yes	Harvard
3.	William Howard Taft	Republican	No	Yale
4.	Woodrow Wilson	Democrat	No	Princeton
5.	Warren Harding	Republican	No	Ohio Central
6.	Calvin Coolidge	Republican	No	Amherst
7.	Herbert Hoover	Republican	No	Stanford
8.	Franklin D. Roosevelt	Democrat	Yes	Harvard
9.	Harry Truman	Democrat	No	None
10.	Dwight D. Eisenhower	Republican	No	US Military Academy
11.	John F. Kennedy	Democrat	Yes	Harvard
12.	Lyndon B. Johnson	Democrat	No	Southwest Texas
13.	Richard M. Nixon	Republican	No	Whittier

The hypothesis is disproven on both counts. Only three of the thirteen American presidents in this century inherited substantial sums of money, and only five of the thirteen went to the 'Big Three' schools, Harvard, Yale and Princeton. What is most striking is the character of the five American Presidents since the end of the Second World War: four of them were born west of the Mississippi, raised by respectable but hardly well-to-do parents, and educated in very

3

ordinary ways. In this grouping, John F. Kennedy was very much the odd man out.

At most, and at least, trying to measure success illustrates the problems and implications of judging politicians. The traditional scholar might argue that a concept badly defined is worse than a concept lacking any empirical referents. A modern social scientist could reply that his critic is a woolly-minded philosopher who would rather talk about a question than look for answers. A sensible judgment is that the exercise at least provides one measure, although hardly the only one, of a term that is capable of many definitions, some empirical and some referring to matters of taste.

The foregoing evaluations illustrate the bias toward quantitative measurement in the social sciences today. The exercises employ numerical data as an index of success, without purporting to claim that the indicator is identical with the thing itself. In this, social scientists can quote the authority of the noted mathematician, John Tukey: 'Far better an approximate answer to the right question, which is often vague than an *exact* answer to the wrong question, which can always be made precise.'[19] The illustration is also apt in that it does not require specialized reference materials. The calculations can be made or verified by anyone with access to an Almanack. Furthermore, it does not require a knowledge of complicated mathematical or statistical skills. Many calculations simple enough to be done on the back of an envelope can dispel great clouds of generalization hanging heavy over political discourse in Britain and America today.

Whether expressed in numbers or in words, the answers that social scientists provide are not scientific in any mechanical sense; like bookmakers, they live by probabilities rather than certainties. Within the social sciences, politics is the least scientific subject, since infrequent or unique events, such as wars, or assassinations, can be of major importance. Yet even in the case of a unique event, such as the choice of Sir Alec Douglas-Home as Prime Minister in 1963, one can ascertain influences that are general as well as factors that were unique. For example, it was highly probable that someone with an exclusive social background would become party leader. Etonians particularly turn up in leading Conservative positions thousands of times more often than would occur by chance. The concept of probability is crucial. There are many people who think that if one cannot be 100 per cent certain in politics, then the only alternative is to assume 100 per cent uncertainty. For instance, as the last few results of the 1966 British general election were being awaited, I asked a seemingly educated young journalist what he thought. 'It still looks very interesting,' he replied. 'You know, these things are never over till the last result is in.' I offered to bet him £10 against 10 shillings on a Labour victory. Unfortunately, his faith in the unpredictability of political events vanished at this point; he refused the wager.

The answers that social scientists offer are usually tentative and incomplete. They are most appropriate if evaluated instrumentally, as things that may or may not increase our knowledge rather than philosophically. Anyone can criticize the conceptual framework of *The Annual Register* or a statistical analysis of data in the *UN Yearbook*. Such criticism does not solve the problem of how one is to summarize succinctly a multitude of events occurring in twelve months, or a vast amount of information gathered from the four corners of the earth. Waiting for a group of philosophers to agree on a perfect framework is as futile as trying to breed twins from a pair of mules. When confronted with a concrete political situation for analysis, it is most economical to consider the relative difficulties and promise of alternative means of ordering knowledge. This approach could be called pragmatic, but for the fact that the term has a bad odour in England. It is defined in the *Pocket Oxford Dictionary* as 'Meddlesome, positive, dictatorial'. (This definition also appears in the American *Webster's Dictionary* but is there labelled archaic.)[20] This problem-solving approach requires that an individual have a wide, even eclectic knowledge of social science concepts and techniques. It also helps if he has a knowledge of politics of the sort that can be soaked up in Westminster, Washington or in his local town hall or party headquarters. This last advantage is subject to the usual exhortation to practise moderation, rather than abstinence, in drinking in knowledge. A scholar drunk on the day-to-day trivia of gossip columnists or statistics is as incapacitated as the politician who thinks he can take every decision without any information.

Solving an intellectual problem is not the same thing as solving a politician's problem. An academic may conclude from a study of American race relations or of social inequalities in English society that there is no political solution to the particular troubles at the centre of political controversy. A politician cannot admit that he is dealing with insoluble problems. One of his functions is to provide reassurance to the populace; another is to act, insofar as possible, to alleviate difficulties and to realize new goals. An academic may gain a certain pleasure from asserting forthrightly that a society faces insuperable problems, just as a politician gains plaudits if he can, even temporarily, appear to be solving a major difficulty. In the last resort, both strive for more than it is possible to attain. Their work is to be judged by relative not absolute standards. While the things that politicians and social scientists do are very different, the ways in which both act can be labelled by the same terms; good, bad and indifferent.

NOTES—CHAPTER I

1. Cf. *From Max Weber*, edited by H. H. Gerth and C. Wright Mills (London: Routledge 1948), pp. 78ff.; Oakeshott, *Political Education* (Cambridge: Bowes & Bowes, 1951) p. 8, and Easton, *A Framework for Political Analysis* (Englewood Cliffs, N.J.: Prentice-Hall, 1965) p. 50.
2. See Richard Rose and Dennis Kavanagh, 'Campaigning for Parliament', *New Society*, July 28, 1966.
3. Cf. Philip E. Converse, chapters 2 and 6 in Angus Campbell *et. al.*, *Elections and the Political Order* (New York: Wiley, 1966). On more general problems of White's values, see the review by Richard Rose of his 1964 study, 'Change of Style at the White House' *New Society*, August 5, 1965, and Paul Foot, *The Politics of Harold Wilson* (Harmondsworth: Penguin, 1968) pp. 9–20.
4. See Lee Benson, *The Concept of Jacksonian Democracy* (New York: Atheneum edition, 1964) Ch. 7, and James Cornford, 'The Transformation of Conservatism in the Late 19th Century', *Victorian Studies* VII:1 (1963). More generally, see Lee Benson, 'An Approach to the Scientific Study of Past Public Opinion', *Public Opinion Quarterly* XXX:4 (1967).
5. See Richard Leonard, *Elections in Britain* (Princeton: Van Nostrand, 1968), and D. E. Butler, *The Electoral System in Britain Since 1918* (Oxford: Clarendon Press, 2nd edition, 1963). For a comparative analysis, see W. J. M. Mackenzie, *Free Elections* (London: Allen & Unwin, 1958).

6. Cf. *Political Parties* (London: Methuen, 1954 edition), and e.g. Douglas Rae, *The Political Consequences of Electoral Laws* (New Haven: Yale, 1967).
7. See e.g., Donald Stokes, 'Parties and the Nationalization of Electoral Forces', in W. N. Chambers and W. Dean Burnham, *The American Party Systems* (New York: Oxford, 1967).
8. 'Charisma in the 1952 Campaign', *American Political Science Review* XLVIII:4 (1954). Davies might be expected to err, if at all, in over-estimating deep psychological motives. Cf. his *Human Nature in Politics* (New York: Wiley, 1963).
9. Cf. the discussion in Ch. 3.
10. See Alexander and Juliette George, *Woodrow Wilson and Colonel House* (New York: Dover edition, 1964) pp. xviii–xxii, and Alex Gottfried, 'The Use of Socio-Psychological Categories in a Study of Political Personality', reprinted from the *Western Political Quarterly* in Heinz Eulau *et. al.*, *Political Behavior* (Glencoe, Illinois: Free Press, 1956).
11. See Richard Rose, *Influencing Voters: a study of campaign rationality* (London: Faber, 1967), for evidence from both Britain and America.
12. See Angus Campbell *et. al.*, *The American Voter* (New York: Wiley, 1960), especially Chs. 7 and 10. Downs, it should be noted, argues that it is irrational for voters to calculate their vote on the basis of more than very limited knowledge, *An Economic Theory of Democracy* (New York: Harper, 1954) Part III.
13. *Political Man* (New York: Doubleday, 1960) p. 220.
14. See particularly Robert Alford, *Party and Society* (Chicago: Rand, McNally, 1963) and Richard Rose and Derek Urwin, 'Social Cohesion, Political Parties and Strains in Regimes' *Comparative Political Studies* II:1 (1969).
15. For interesting quotations from people about their emotions when voting, see G. A. Almond and S. Verba, *The Civic Culture* (Princeton: University Press, 1963) pp. 145ff.
16. See e.g., D. E. Butler and Anthony King, *The British General Election of 1966* (London: Macmillan, 1966).
17. See *Social Theory and Social Structure* (Glencoe, Illinois: Free Press, 1957 edition).
18. See Richard Rose, 'Class and Party Divisions: Britain as a Test Case', *Sociology* II:2 (1968) pp. 140–41.
19. Quoted at p. 7 of Arthur Banks and Robert Textor, *A Cross-Polity Survey* (Cambridge, Mass.: MIT Press, 1963). See also, Heinz Eulau, 'From Utopia to Probability: Liberalism and Recent Science', *The Antioch Review* (Summer, 1966).

20. Harold Wilson has claimed to be a pragmatist, in the contemporary American sense of evaluating goals in the light of empirical considerations. In practice, he has more nearly resembled Michael Oakeshott's 'mere empiricist', a practitioner of 'politics without a policy, the politics of the proverbial oriental despot' or of 'the wall-scribbler and the vote-catcher'. *Op. cit.*, p. 10.

Two

National Identities

What is an Englishman? The question is rarely asked, even though it is certainly fundamental to an understanding of political life. Many who would reject the British Israelite doctrine that the English are God's chosen people believe that in arts of government at least, Englishmen are special if not unique. Bagehot's view was less exalted: 'Are they not above all nations divided from the rest of the world, insular both in situation and in mind, both for good and for evil?'[1] His backhanded tribute is equally apposite to other nations. Americans, French, Germans and Irish, each in their own way, tend to think that the character of their national politics is unique if not blessed in its differences from all other nations.

Describing the specific things that make Englishmen different is no easy task. Notwithstanding a tradition of classical instruction, the Greek motto—Know thyself—is hardly applied in the study of British government. The very absence of a written constitution has long been a subject of congratulation, not only because it permits flexibility, but also because it veils the sources and limits of political authority in mystery. Upon close examination, the constitution may turn out to be as intangible as the mystical contents of Joanna Southcott's box.[2] Most Englishmen would be hard put to say exactly what the box ought to contain. The Constitution, like national identity, is taken for granted as an unexamined and easy inheritance from one's forbears. By contrast, describing things that make Americans distinctive is a relatively easy task. America has a written Constitution because the people who made a successful revolution found themselves, of necessity, forced to make a state. Once the state was founded, its leaders then faced the task of making Americans. The job was easier in the late 18th century among a small and relatively homogeneous population than it is today, after the receipt of many polyglot waves of immigrants, such as English fugitives from 17th-century religious persecutions, Jewish fugitives from 20th-century Russian and German persecution, and Africans carried into slavery. The resulting uncertainty about identity—individual and national—gives a perennial sense of personal urgency to Crevecoeur's rhetorical question: What is an American?[3] The authors of successive citizenship acts tried to give a straightforward answer. Laws specify the simple steps that any immigrant or his children can take to become an American. By hard work and a little striving, anyone can become an American, whereas Englishness, at bottom, has always remained a matter of the correct choice of parents.

Distinctive national characteristics are often difficult to explicate to people who live in a society, because the things that make them different are what they have come to regard as normal. For example, Englishmen think a monarchy is the normal form of democratic government, just as Americans assume that a Republic is normal. People who grow up in a society learn—implicitly as well as explicitly—how to recognize and handle things that may have no counterpart elsewhere. The peculiarity of such phenomena as violence in America or discrimination between Oxford colleges only becomes apparent when one tries to explain or justify such practices to persons from another country. Emotional responses are much more readily recognized as nationally distinctive. Few Americans would expect foreigners to regard 'The Star-Spangled Banner' as a notable work of music. The emotional symbol that most puzzles me is English. Why should so profoundly non-Semitic a race respond to choral renderings of William Blake's 'Jerusalem'?

Because intelligent men often are obtuse when confronted with an idea alien to them, social scientists have good reason to probe the 'mysteries' of national identity. In an older and less self-conscious era, a person who thought that he had some insight into his own or another nation's character simply sat down and wrote out his ideas in as compelling a literary manner as possible. Walter Bagehot's *The English Constitution* is the best known British example; for every Bagehot, the nation has produced hundreds of writers whose books are now overpriced at a shilling on the secondhand racks. In the English fashion, Bagehot's strength and limitation was to use epigrams instead of logical analysis. In the French fashion, Alexis de Tocqueville combined the two. His great *Democracy in America* is intended to describe systematically the social and political consequences of the primacy of democracy and equality as values in early 19th-century America.[4] Among American writers, cultural anthropology was initially fashionable; it provided literary and systematic social science insights into milieux as exotic as the South Seas or Muncie, Indiana. In the Second World War, some anthropologists wrote studies of national character about countries they had never visited, but that their compatriots were about to invade.[5] These studies, like their older equivalents, depend more on the power of an author's style and imagination than on the quality of his logic and evidence. The cautious reader of a stimulating book such as David Riesman's *The Lonely Crowd* can hardly avoid asking the crucial question: All this is very interesting, but is it true?[6]

To reduce individual and sometimes idiosyncratic insights to some kind of manageable form, social scientists have developed the concept of culture. It refers to the pattern of values, beliefs and emotions most widely shared among members of a society.[7] The term is not used in the aesthetic sense of 'high' culture or 'pop' culture. Culture concerns the attitudes that people have toward the world around them and their predispositions to action. It concerns the way in which they identify the things that confront them, the value they place upon things, and the emotional responses that they register. For instance, three people from different cultures, each confronted with a photograph of an Asian guerilla fighter, might each react in culturally distinctive ways, one seeing him as an outlaw, another as a yellow peasant, and the third as a kinsman or soul brother. When identifying things in the world about them, people may indirectly indicate their own sense of personal identity. A culture is not to be confused with institutions or the patterns of behaviour in a society; for people with the same outlook may nonetheless act differently in specific situations. A culture is that set of outlooks that gives these things meaning. In shorthand terms, a culture can summarize the identity of a nation, even though it includes views that every citizen would not accept.

Many values, beliefs and emotions of a culture are diffuse, rather than specifically political. Ordinary human beings do not segregate their thoughts into tidy boxes, labelled politics, economics and sociology, as easily as these classifications can be imposed upon them by strictly disciplined social scientists. For example, a Boy Scout official addressing his pupils about leadership and service, or a prosecutor asking a jury whether they would want their servants (or gamekeeper) to read *Lady Chatterley's Lover*[8] would not think of himself as 'talking politics', yet the attitudes expressed are of fundamental relevance to political ideas of equality and deference. To note this is not to try to reduce politics to sex or educational psychology, but rather, to stress the overlapping character of the things that different social science disciplines study. One must abstract basic political outlooks[9] from the totality of cultural attitudes in a society, in order to reduce disparate phenomena to a manageable size. Yet after doing this, it is important to exercise an intellectual form of peripheral vision, so that there is a continuing awareness of things that have been left out, but may unexpectedly emerge as important.

Identifying attitudes crucial in every political culture is a task that has occupied scholars for thousands of years: there is no sign of agreement yet. Traditional political theory provides many terms useful in trying to identify basic political outlooks. The nature of man and of the state, the duties and rights of its citizens, and the aims of government are all central to any discussion of collective political attitudes. This language is rarely used by modern social scientists, though analogous terms are often employed.[10] One reason may be ignorance of classical political theory. Another is that these terms have been used for so many generations without reference to empirical evidence that it would only be confusing to use the same label for empirically testable ideas and those that it would be inconceivable to test.

Contemporary political scientists have yet to agree among themselves about which attitudes should be regarded as fundamental in

UNIVERSITY LIBRARY

END OF TERM RECALL

Undergraduates and Education Year students are reminded that all books and pamphlets borrowed before March 9th 1983 are due for return by March 16th 1983.

A fine of 5p per book, per day, will be charged on overdue books.

Books may be renewed or borrowed for the vacation from March 9th 1983.

Prompt renewal will save time.

PLEASE BRING YOUR LIBRARY CARD.

any or every political society. Concepts are at an inchoate—some would say, incoherent—level. There is agreement that the things of most importance in a culture are often implicit, rather than explicit, because they are taken for granted by nearly everyone in a society. These underlying assumptions are very different from the opinions and attitudes measured by public opinion polls. The latter concern disagreements about policies, party preferences and political personalities. The former concern the nature of the political society within which disagreements can peacefully take place.

To note the importance of agreement about the fundamentals of a society is not to assume what remains to be explored: *whether* there is a consensus about basic political attitudes in a country. If the elements of consensus are defined at a very high level of abstraction, then it would be possible to conclude that all subjects within a state, even all mammals on this planet—and perhaps some vegetables and minerals too—are in fundamental political agreement. So indiscriminate a proposition has little meaning or value. Often, the fact that a state exists is taken to assume that there is some consensus among its nominal subjects. This does not necessarily follow. More than one outlook can co-exist within a single state. Differing 'sub-cultures' may take complementary forms that, in aggregate, sustain political harmony. This is the case in Switzerland, the Netherlands and several other pluralistic societies.[11] In the case of America in the 1860s and South Viet Nam in the 1960s, it would be more appropriate to speak of the co-existence of conflicting cultures within the boundaries of a single state, rather than impose a spurious unity by referring to each warring party as a sub-category of some notionally unified larger entity.

Among sub-cultural loyalties, the most important concern the political community, i.e., the proportion of people within a state who feel that they belong together. The use of the social psychological concept of community avoids confusing nationality as a state of mind with nationality as a legal status.[12] Sometimes a hyphen is the appropriate conjunction between the words 'nation' and 'state'. Sometimes the phrase is best written: 'nation *v.* state'. Giving a man a passport of the United Kingdom or the United States of America makes him a legal subject, but it does not guarantee that he thinks of that as his primary ethnic identification. He may prefer to regard himself as Irish, Italian, Polish or something else. Reciprocally, thinking of oneself as a Ukrainian or a Macedonian does not *ipso facto* entitle an individual to carry a passport in the name of the stateless community with which he identifies. The resulting incongruities between community identification and state boundaries involve substantial strains upon individuals and upon governments. The high-point of communal conflicts in European society occurred in the first half of this century, with the break-up of the multi-national Hapsburg and Ottoman Empires, and the succession of a large number of states nominally dedicated to the principle of self-government for every community. Unfortunately, communities were not neatly distributed for purposes of drawing boundaries. The aftermath of the 1919 Paris Peace Conference was yet more communal conflict. In Northern Ireland, difficulties have continued until today; for more than one-third of the people think of themselves as Irish, although their passports and their (*sic*) government say they are British.[13] Some writers argue that the presence or absence of a well defined sense of national identity is crucial in developing stable government. France is the great refutation of this proposition. However an Anglo-Saxon feels about the French, he cannot deny that they have enjoyed a common identity, even superiority, for centuries. With minor exceptions, the boundaries of the state and of the French community have long coincided. Yet, sub-cultural divisions have persistently shown a degree of intensity in French society that has made the country a byword for political instability.

Within Britain, and to a lesser extent the United States, the most persisting source of sub-cultural division is usually assumed to be class structure. This assumption owes more to the power of political ideologies than it does to the weight of empirical evidence. Repeated empirical studies in Britain, and even more in America, have shown that there is a limited statistical relationship between occupational class and party identification. Moreover, the fact of voting for a party that may be said to advance the interests of the working class or the middle class is *not* tantamount to endorsing class conflict. There is some evidence suggesting that position in the class structure may be more important as an influence upon non-political attitudes such as educational aspiration than it is upon political outlooks. In the United States, the most distinctive political sub-culture is defined by caste (i.e. skin colour) not occupation. A variety of studies have shown that religion, immigrant origin, and regional identifications can also be important influences upon the partisan groupings of Americans and, by implication, upon their sub-cultural outlooks.[14]

Neither class nor communal loyalties are the main source of political divisions in Western societies. A study of 76 parties in 17 Western countries shows that this 'honour' belongs to religion, in various forms ranging from the universalistic claims of Catholicism through sectarianism to anti-clericalism.[15] Among Western parties 54 per cent are based on religious or anti-religious support; by comparison, 42 per cent are based on some form of class support. Contrary to expectations, no country shows a party system neatly divided into working-class and middle-class parties. Where occupation is important within the non-Socialist sections of society, it relates to varied political outlooks—middle-class liberal anti-clericalism, middle-class clerical conservatism, middle-class reaction, and, agrarian interest group parties found in all four Scandinavian countries. Only eight linguistic or nationality parties are now identifiably active. Usually, communal identities parallel other loyalties. In the extreme case, the Creditiste Party in Canada draws 100 per cent of its votes from Catholics in Quebec and 97 per cent of its supporters are French-speaking. In all, eighteen parties lack any social basis for the things that divide them from others within society. In societies where religious, communal or regional sub-cultures are very strong, regimes have usually been subject to strains. The freedom of America from such challenges has perhaps owed as much to the fragmentation of subcultures in America as it has to agreement on fundamentals, given conflicts on race relations between Northerners and Southerners, and Negroes and black nationalists. In Britain, the failure of such sub-cultural groups to create political difficulties is as much a reflection of small numbers as of an all-embracing consensus. Where Catholics, Welsh-speakers, or peasant hill-farmers are numerous, there one also finds 'un-English' forms of party divisions.[16]

Use of partisan support as an index of sub-cultural divisions does not mean that all who vote for a party agree in their political outlooks or are equally committed to what are (or what they take to be) the programmatic aims of their party. Studies in America and Britain have emphasized that there is an imperfect agreement between the policy preferences of voters and the parties they support. The proportion of partisans who have a coherent political ideology meriting description as a separate Socialist or Tory sub-culture is a limited faction of the total electorate. Moreover, studies have shown that the sense of social distance between Republicans and Democrats and between Conservatives and Labour voters is small by comparison with Germany, Italy and Mexico.[17] To write of public opinion in terms of the ideas of political philosophers is to impute to the whole population the outlooks of a few intellectuals and political activists.[18]

Whether we regard information about ordinary voters or ordinary political philosophers as most important depends upon the answers given to the question: Whose views form the culture? The democrat's instinctive reply is, 'Why, the attitudes of everyone are important.' In its starkest form, this answer implies that the political outlook of an isolated farmer's wife should receive as much attention as that of a leading Cabinet minister. This can be justified on the ground that the outlooks of the subjects of government limit even very authoritarian authorities in what they can get their subjects to do. If a nation's population is selected for analysis, this suggests studying political cultures by nation-wide surveys. Unfortunately, surveys analysing a culture are hard to design. It is much more difficult to capture the implicit premises and the nuances of a *weltanschauung* than it is to collect information about voting. This is particularly true if one is interviewing people who are not accustomed to articulate the assumptions underlying behaviour, i.e., most adults in Britain, America and elsewhere. Because comparisons across cultures are necessary, further difficulties arise from the need to find cross-cultural equivalent measures for values, beliefs and emotions. There is, for instance, a tendency for questionnaires drafted in the United States to reflect the world in a red, white and blue mirror.

Rejecting survey techniques, Robert Lane studied the political culture of Americans by intensive and repeated tape-recorded interviews with sixteen residents of a single housing project in New Haven, Connecticut. The resulting book, *Political Ideology*,[19] contains many interesting speculative insights about these men. It would require inordinate time and language skills to undertake a cross-cultural study in this way. Moreover, one might suggest that such a study hardly begins to encompass the whole of the American political culture. This would also require interviews with 16 New Haven women, with 16 white men from Tupelo, Mississippi, and 16 Negroes; with 16 Jews and 16 Catholics; with 16 farmers and 16 prosperous professionals, and so forth and so on until one had listed enough categories to lose all hope of one person achieving a detailed and intimate understanding of these people as individuals.

In a country that Bagehot described as a place where 'certain persons are by common consent agreed to be wiser than others and their opinion is by consent to rank for much more than its numerical value',[20] there is much to be said for erring on the side of anti-egalitarianism. Unfortunately, there is no common consent about the categories of individuals who best articulate cultural attitudes. Conventionally, academics have solved this problem by assuming that the ideas of first-rank philosophers are of primary importance in characterizing national attitudes. This confuses academic distinction with political popularity. One cannot conceive that the ideas of a Wittgenstein would have gone down well at a meeting of back-bench MPs in the Conservative Party, and Bertrand Russell, after half a century of lecturing, has failed to make much impact upon the stolid back-benchers in the Parliamentary Labour Party. Given Hugh Dalton's dictum that a politician should be a man who got a good second-class degree at university, but not a first,[21] one might better seek cultural beliefs in the writings of men whose ideas are readily comprehensible to busy politicians who must, as it were, make speeches while they read. In the past decade, J. K. Galbraith has been pre-eminent as an expounder of theses that can be readily comprehended by any politician. Probably the best and least exploited source of information about the thought processes of politicians can be found in *Hansard* and in the *Congressional Record* and transcripts of Congressional committee hearings. They provide massive evidence about the implicit assumptions as well as the explicit ideas of our legislators.[22]

A contrasting approach is to infer individual values, beliefs and emotions from aggregate data about a society.[23] For instance, in order to locate countries where isolated persons with parochial outlooks are numerous, one selects all countries with census figures containing a substantial degree of error, on the assumption that the more uncertain a government is about the numbers of subjects it has, the greater the proportion of subjects likely to be unaware of the government's directives. This index of cultural outlooks suggests that 40 of 133 countries in the world have a substantial number of parochial subjects, for they report population figures with a margin for error of at least 10 per cent.[24]

Perhaps the most popular way to study political culture is that of conscious eclecticism. Information can be drawn from a melange of sources—personal experience, historical events, survey data and writings of politicians and philosophers—in order to illustrate a more-or-less coherent interpretation of basic political attitudes within a society. Such statements about culture are often empirically testable, but the interpretation goes well beyond existing evidence in an attempt to provide a comprehensive analysis.[25]

The best known attempt to grapple empirically with the concept of political culture is Gabriel Almond and Sidney Verba's *The Civic Culture*. It is based upon specially commissioned surveys in America, Britain, Germany, Italy and Mexico; the same questionnaire was administered to each nation-wide sample in 1959. As in any first attempt, difficulties arose. Originally, France was intended to be one of the countries subjected to a survey, but the Gaullist *coup* in 1958 made the French political situation so unpredictable that the authors decided not to do fieldwork there. In Italy, only a small proportion of persons who voted Communist at general elections admitted their party allegiance when interviewed. In Mexico, only persons living in cities of 10,000 or more people were included in the study. As a result, *The Civic Culture* findings do not concern societies where cultural conflicts are of near civil-war proportions. The unwillingness of Communists to identify themselves testifies to the intensity of sub-culture divisions in Italy, but makes it impossible to generalize about one of these groups. The exclusion of rural Mexicans from the study might be justified on the grounds that such persons may well be outside the ambit of Mexican government and would more appropriately be studied in a volume concerning the political culture of Central American Indians.

Intellectually, Almond and Verba were concerned with cultural attitudes concerning the popular demands made on government, the way in which its policies affect the lives of its subjects, and the obligations and rights of an individual as a member of a political system. From the many possible permutations of these attitudes, the authors selected three as specially significant. In a parochial political culture, individuals have virtually no awareness of a central government or of its demands, nor do they have a sense of obligation to it or a hope of influence. Today, such cultures are most likely to be found in the Afro-Asian world, where the recession of Imperialism has left a number of entities recognized as sovereign states by the United Nations, but not enjoying *de facto* recognition from all of their own populations. A subject political culture is one in which individuals are aware of government decisions and demands upon them, but lack an awareness of how government policy can be influenced, and the belief that they could or should influence policy. Such an outlook is fully consistent with an oligarchical or authoritarian regime. In a participant culture, not only is an individual aware of government and what it does, but also he sees government as open to influence from people like himself. This liberal-democratic outlook is familiar, because it most closely approximates the political culture of Britain and America, or, at the least, what we think the culture *ought* to be and how our governments ought to act.

The central feature of a civic culture is *competence*, the ability of individuals to influence government, and, *subjective competence*, an individual's belief that he could influence government—if he attempted to do so. The latter concept is of special importance to Almond and Verba. Because culture concerns psychological orientations rather than behaviour, what people think they can do is made more important than what they actually do do. There is, of course, a great disjunction between the two. While three-quarters of British and Americans thought that they could exert political influence if they tried, only one-third of the American and one-sixth of the British respondents said they had ever tried to exercise such influence, even at the lowly level of local government. The fact that only a small proportion of those who endorse liberal-democratic rights actually try to exercise these rights is a matter of some political importance. Because this group is small, Almond and Verba could not readily separate them out from other respondents in their surveys. Instead, they concentrated upon persons who were potentially capable of taking an active part in politics. Once one accepts the point of asking potentially active people how they would act in hypothetical situations, then it is possible to perform a number of interesting, even if conjectural, cross-cultural comparisons. For instance, Americans are more predisposed to favour group action to achieve political aims than are the British, who see themselves acting alone in trying to influence their MP or civil servants.[26]

On most tests of liberal civic virtues, America and Britain bunch together at the top, Germany and Italy follow in that order and Mexico lags in the rear. This does not reflect simple economic determinism for many findings depend upon the level of education within a society. It is the association of a higher standard of living with more education that tends to depress the position of the two Latin countries in the Anglo-Saxons' league tables. Occasionally, the pattern is broken in ways that are specially interesting. For instance, the Mexicans have a very high degree of pride in their government, by comparison with Germans and Italians. The finding is hardly surprising, given the comparative achievements in the three countries since the Mexican revolution of 1911. It is at least reassuring as a token of the validity of the interviews.

In drawing conclusions from their interviews, Almond and Verba emphasize the importance of a balanced disparity of individual attitudes within a given culture. The authors treat the inconsistency between what people say about politics and what they do as evidence of the tribute that hypocrisy pays to virtue, with the two balancing out. In this way, a person is able to maintain a commitment to democratic ideals without having to bear the burdens that constant political activity impose. In a large society, there is a mixing or balancing of disparities between individuals as well as within individuals. A civic culture is one with a very small number of people with parochial outlooks, but also a limited number of active political participants. Some are willing subjects, and a larger number are people who feel able to influence politics, but do not actually attempt to do so. They are said to provide the restraint necessary to prevent politics from becoming an arena in which large numbers of people seek major satisfactions, with all the possibilities for bitterness and frustration that defeat might involve. On strictly scientific grounds, it is unfortunate that no indication is given of the quantity of each outlook needed to secure the right mixture within individuals or within a national culture. On balance, this is probably desirable, for it avoids giving a false sense of precision. The substantive point is clear: acceptance of the myth of widespread political influence is the base on which liberal democracy immediately rests.

The emphasis upon the role of myth in the civic culture is reminiscent of Bagehot's concern with the dignified as well as the efficient parts of government.[27] The dignified parts are those by which a government gains authority. To Bagehot, these were monarchy and everything associated with the monarchy in the theatrical side of government. The myth of monarchical government was said to make the increasing importance of popular institutions in 19th-century Britain comprehensible and tolerable to the masses. From Almond and Verba one might infer that the myth of government by popular participation makes comprehensible and tolerable to the masses the existence of 'a free co-optative oligarchy', that is, government by a small number of people who choose their colleagues and successors from those who enter into free competition for influence. This kind of inference is supported by the late V. O. Key's conclusion to *Public Opinion and American Democracy*. This emphasizes that the dignified importance of public opinion in the American political culture has as its efficient corollary that 'a wide range of discretion exists for whatever wisdom leadership echelons can muster in the public service'.[28] Almond and Verba reject this implication. They stress the extent to which governors as well as governed can be influenced by the myth of popular participation, a myth reinforced by the institution of popular election. It can also be noted that when governors and governed share a common point of view, there is little chance that the discretion of leaders will exceed the limits of that which followers will accept.[29]

As long as governors and governed share the same values or believe the same myths, then it is difficult to prove that leaders are manipulating followers. If the latter were to exceed the bounds of that which was popularly approved or tolerated, then the ordinarily dormant majority would activate their sense of political competence and bring pressure to bear against such cultural deviants, whether men in high office or an unpopular political minority.[30] In a broad and metaphorical sense, one might then speak of the political culture controlling political behaviour, or at least operating as a kind of quasi-mechanical governor upon all persons in a society.

Explaining political phenomena in terms of a political culture is an uncertain and often unsatisfactory business. The fact that it can easily be done, as the preceding paragraph illustrates, makes it potentially dangerous. At best, the idea of a political culture can provide only short range explanations of behaviour. We can use it to explain why some people stand for 'God Save the Queen' while others stand for 'The Star-Spangled Banner'. But if we try to explain why the English always stand for whatever their government does, while the French often do not, it is hardly sufficient to say that this is because they have different political cultures. Such an explanation begs the question: What makes the French and English cultures so different? The simplest way to avoid this question-begging position is not to use political culture as the subject of an active verb. The political culture is not an actor in the sense that an individual or even an institution can be; it is an analytical abstraction. Moreover, a culture is an intervening variable, coming between the individual and his environment. Cultural values create neither the individuals nor the environment which they mediate. Sooner or later, we must look behind that bundle of abstractions and ask: how does political culture get to be the way it does?

The prevailing American answer is that the cultural outlooks of individuals are formed through a lengthy and diffuse process of political socialization, involving the overt and latent transmission of values, beliefs and emotions. Political socialization is a by-product of an individual's experiences, from which he learns how to fit into society. One might even say that an individual is taught how to 'adjust' to society, but for the fact that the verb has conservative overtones; moreover, some people, through intention or misfortune, fail to adjust to the prevailing cultural outlook. On balance, the great majority of people in Britain and America accept what they learn about political behaviour from generation to generation. Insofar as different outlooks are learned suiting people to contrasting stations of life, they are likely to be as complementary as leader and led can be. In Britain, for example, working-class people do not learn political outlooks differentiated in ways that would make them maladjusted.[31] In America, the pressures on Negroes to reject prevailing cultural outlooks are extreme, yet American research too indicates that there is more adjustment to the *status quo* than Black Power advocates or liberal white social scientists might wish. Among Negroes, maladjustment may show in non-political ways, such as family instability or addiction to non-political violence.[32]

Socialization into a political culture begins early in life, long before schools prescribe lectures on the American or British constitution.

Very few people nowadays wish to emphasize the importance of infancy in shaping adult political attitudes, but the shadow of Freud and of developmental child psychology can still be discerned, even when interest has shifted to the analysis of problems of personality development in relation to the problems of a society.[33] In America, such ideas are learned, as it were, at the mother's breast, just as class-oriented if not Marxian modes of thought are learned in Britain. Somehow it seems to me more appropriate to read Freud rather than Marx in adolescence. Starting with Marx can produce men such as the Oxford reviewer of a few years ago who argued that John Braine's novel *Room at the Top* demonstrated that satisfactory sexual relations were only possible in a Socialist society.[34] It may be symptomatic of Britain's reception of alien ideas, as distinct from refugee aliens, that while Marx and Freud were born and educated on the Continent, both died and are buried in England.

Studies of the influence of parents upon children's political outlooks have demonstrated that there is something to be gained by looking at the formation of attitudes *ab ovo*.[35] Except in a misleading metaphorical sense, a child is not nurtured by a nation or a class, but rather by two parents. Within the home he acquires his earliest knowledge about many things, some of which may be directly political—such as his parents' party identification—and some of which may be indirectly of political significance, such as parental attitudes toward authority. The strength of parental influence is most readily indicated by studies showing that children in both Britain and America tend to adopt the same party identification as their parents.[36] In both countries, the party identification of a voter's parents is a better predictor of his party choice than is an individual's current class position. In some instances, parents are capable of transmitting political and social outlooks that go against the general tendencies of most around them. Jackson and Marsden's study of *Education and the Working-Class* has shown how important a role a minority of working-class parents have played in stimulating their children to academic success.[37]

In point of time, educational institutions come next as potential moulders of cultural outlooks. The schools receive their pupils young and give them formal and informal instruction past puberty, when young people become aware of what social roles are open to them, and what attitudes are appropriate for adults in society.[38]

By the age of 15, most young people can satisfactorily answer a questionnaire about politics. In many cases, the school reinforces the influence of family, given the connections between family and schooling, whether a youth is at a slum school or at Eton. It is hardly surprising that persons with more education are more likely to favour the Conservatives or Republicans, for these parties are associated with social strata to which further education provides an *entrée*. What is particularly striking is that in Britain the small fraction of adults with a university education are less Conservative than those with an academic secondary education. A university education breaks standard patterns because it removes a young person from his home and sets him in a very cosmopolitan student environment, where he is exposed to far more different ideas about society than he would otherwise learn. Education does not seem to have the same impact in America. Even in 1964, when the Republican presidential candidate, Barry Goldwater, was noticeably non-intellectual, Republican voting strength rose with education at all levels.[39]

Experience at work tends to reinforce the influence of education, given the importance of formal educational qualifications for an increasing number of jobs. In Britain, the majority of young people have entered the labour market at the age of 14 or 15, thus spending up to seven years at work before enjoying franchise rights. In America, the importance of further education means that work experiences tend to affect the young adult rather than the young adolescent. Almond and Verba show that people who feel they can influence conditions at work are also more likely to feel competent to exert political influence.[40] One would expect individuals belonging to unions to feel that they have more say in their work, and probably in their government. Elizabeth Bott's study of *Family and Social Network* suggests that people who have held a multitude of jobs and moved around from place to place are much more likely to see politics in terms of a variety of finely distinguished groups, whereas people whose work has held them to their place of origin are likely to see politics in simple 'Us *v.* Them' relationships.[41] In the case, say, of a coal miner working in a mining village where his family has lived and worked for generations, work experience reinforces other clear-cut influences. A laundromat owner in Southern California, coming to his job from an Oklahoma farm after six years in the Marines, is an example of an individual whose views of the world are likely to be more complex and less predictably stable, because of the variety of influences to which he has been exposed.

In the classical literature of sociology, the cumulative consequences of socialization are often referred to as the influence of class structure. The term 'class' is a shorthand label with many of the advantages and disadvantages attached to such a term. It brings to mind a picture of manual workers or middle-class people with a whole cluster of attributes and, more arguably, with distinctive political outlooks. As long as the term is used in the abstract, few problems arise that cannot be solved in the abstract. There remains the nagging doubt that there is something logically dubious about explaining the past behaviour of an individual in terms of his current occupation. In empirical research, the disadvantages of referring to classes often outweigh the advantages. In Britain and America, people do not carry membership cards in the middle-class or the working-class, as they might to a club or a trade union. Conventionally, class is defined by an individual's occupation. It is, however, taken to imply a whole cluster of characteristics aptly summed up in the American phrase 'socio-economic status'. For example, a working-class man in Britain should also have a minimum of education, belong to a trade union, be a tenant and think of himself as a member of the working-class. Of course, he should also vote Labour. In practice, only 26 per cent of British manual workers have all four of these social characteristics and one-third lack two or more of these presumed correlates of occupational class.[42]

The relative importance of occupational class can best be assessed in situations in which other socialization influences are also at work. In societies such as Northern Ireland and the Netherlands, where religious divisions are deep and pervasive, the churches socialize people into sub-cultures as occupational influences are supposed to do in Britain. In America, the number of grounds for social division and the resulting complexity of the social structure makes it impossible to assign to any one agency of socialization the same importance for Anglo-Saxons and East European immigrants, for Catholics, Jews and Protestants, and for whites and Negroes.[43] In England, the relative simplicity of the social structure makes it possible to test the importance of influences such as family and schooling against class. An imaginative study by Ted Tapper has investigated influences upon the cultural outlooks of approximately 1500 14-year-olds. Tapper tested the importance of the father's occupation, parental attitudes, and of secondary school environment, which ranged from slum secondary modern institutions to Manchester Grammar School. The importance of each of these factors was assessed in relation to attitudes about politics, education, future occupation and social status. The statistical findings show that while parent's occupation was significantly related to an adolescent's outlook in two of the four tests, it was not related as strongly as the youth's current party preference. Moreover, in three of the four tests, secondary schooling was independently significant.[44]

Studies of the formation of political attitudes can concentrate upon one of four target groups: the mass of adolescents, adolescents being trained for potential political leadership, adults in politically peripheral positions, and adults in political leadership posts. Most of the findings discussed so far have concerned the mass of adolescents. Given the fact that so many things that happen to a person in adulthood are evaluated in the light of prior experience, this emphasis has some intellectual justification. The concern with large groups in the population can be defended not only on the grounds of research convenience, but also, in terms of egalitarian political beliefs. It is significant that in England, where egalitarianism is much less widespread, studies of adolescent political socialization have tended to concentrate upon youths at major public schools. Winchester leads Eton, for it has already been the subject of two books and a journal article by political sociologists.[45] Although these studies are often interesting, it should always be remembered that the data they provide do not concern directly adult political behaviour.

While many are socialized for political participation, few are called to public office. The exceptions may be insignificant numerically, but their location in government is politically crucial. No amount of youthful experience, including a university degree in politics or expulsion for radical activities, can prepare an individual —in a practical or an emotional sense—for the experiences he will encounter after becoming chairman of a local party, a lobbyist, or the recipient of lobbyists' demands. One might suggest that the more important an individual's political position, the harder it is to prepare for it prior to holding the office. Even a lifelong politician such as John F. Kennedy is supposed to have remarked that he had not really understood the job of the Presidency until after he came to the White House. The study of things that influence politicians early in life may give clues about personality characteristics that influence their later behaviour, as well as indicating when and how these individuals first became interested in going into politics. It does not follow that forty years on these influences will still be dominant. In fact, it would be surprising if this were the case. Careful cross-national studies by Lewis Edinger and Donald Searing have documented that background influences are of limited importance in determining current attitudes, by comparison with relatively recent adult experiences.[46] Once in active politics, individuals undergo intensive socialization experiences, for they join formal and informal groups that implicitly and explicitly provide them with cues for their behaviour and attitudes. Typically, this takes the form of socialization into an outlook appropriate to an office, whether it be that of town councillor or a Cabinet minister. Studies have found that differences in early backgrounds seem to have limited effect upon the way that people then define their current political roles.[47] In other words, while childhood can be important in shaping the political attitudes of most people, among active politicians the socialization that counts most is that experienced as an adult 'on the job'.

Whatever the political position of an individual, the socialization process may be considered the hyphen or buckle connecting him to the central beliefs of his society. This formulation puts prime emphasis upon the role of society in shaping the outlook of any given individual. It avoids the liberal fallacy that society is but the sum of the attitudes that each individual develops by himself. The values of a political culture antedate the birth of any particular individual, and the institutions that play so important a part in his political socialization usually exist prior to his birth too. Yet an individual is not to be conceived of as a purely passive recipient of what may seem in the abstract to be a highly efficient or mechanistic indoctrination process. Socialization is a reflection of probabilities, rather than a conspiratorially consistent set of experiences. One cannot speak of determinism in the absolute sense, for by adolescence, and even more by adulthood, an individual is likely to be exposed to some experiences which differ in the content and direction of their cultural cues. One must remember not only that there is a high probability that a middle-class person from a conservative middle-class home is likely to have a conservative political outlook, but also that there is a low probability of predicting accurately the cultural outlook of an American-born son of Jewish immigrant parents after he spends three years at Oxford studying poetry.

The study of socialization also joins the study of the subjective meaning of actions with the study of the material environment.[48] In terms of frameworks, students of political socialization ought to give as much attention to the objective features of a society as to the subjective manner in which individuals perceive it. Yet because students of political culture read the literature of social psychology more thoroughly than that of history, studies such as Almond and Verba's *The Civic Culture* give much more emphasis to the culturally determined perceptions of the individual than they do to the objects being perceived. The emphasis is justifiable insofar as ordinary people have imaginations capable of transforming seemingly simple, unambiguous phenomena into shadowy objects very different from what a sociologist would predict. To this extent, the concept of political culture can be useful explaining, as an intervening variable, why peoples in different societies respond so variously to relatively general experiences such as industrialization. Yet, since life is short and books are already long enough, there is always the danger that discussions of a political culture may be limited in the attention given to concrete forms of an environment. While early behaviourists erred by over-emphasizing the importance of environmental stimuli as predictors of individual responses, today's may err in over-estimating the importance of the cultural outlook of individuals, at the expense of ignoring both material stimulus and response.

Many features of the political culture of England and America cannot be studied solely in terms of an individual's contemporary environment and how he has perceived the experiences of his own lifetime. One must push inquiries further back in time, for 19th-, 18th-, and even 17th-century developments have had substantial influence upon basic political outlooks in both countries. Americans are fortunate in that the arrival of Columbus in 1492 and the settlement of Virginia in 1607 provides limiting dates for investigations back in time. Events happening to European forebears can be taken as given, though they should not be completely ignored.[49] In England, a case could be made for pushing analysis back to the Reformation or the early Middle Ages, though not in this secular age, to Genesis. From a contemporary point of view, it seems to me that 'modern' England can be defined as the society that followed the completion of industrialization by the 1850s.[50] Yet one must remember Lord Attlee's characterization of so recent a Prime Minister as Sir Winston Churchill: 'a layer of 17th century, a layer of 18th century, a layer of 19th century and possibly even a layer of 20th century.' Attlee went on to note: 'You were never sure which layer would be uppermost.'[51] Anyone familiar with Tocqueville's characterization of Americans in 1830 and Americans today, or Bagehot's of Englishmen in 1867 and their latterday heirs, will see that there is something to be said for the argument that past cultural outlooks still influence the contemporary culture, or even, that some norms today demonstrate the persistence of past values, beliefs and emotions.[52] It is difficult to test this proposition by survey research. Few useful answers are likely to be obtained by asking directly: 'What do you think are the most important political events that happened before you were born?' Rarely can one find a society such as Northern Ireland, where events in the distant past are still a subject of current slogans, e.g., Remember 1690.

Examining cultural values through time is immediately feasible in England and America, because many formal characteristics of government have remained remarkably stable for long periods of time. Although the radio, movies and television have developed and concentrated attention on the Presidency, Congress remains central in the political thoughts of Americans.[53] Horse-drawn carriages and penny-farthing bicycles have disappeared in England, but the Labour and Conservative parties still persist. The two countries also illustrate the importance of early historical solutions of such cultural problems as national identity and legitimacy. Once successfully solved, cultural harmony can then persist for generations. One might almost say that the culture is 'fool-proof' against rejection, given some of the people who have had their chance to govern Britain and America in the past century. Even the limiting groups—the American South and Northern Ireland—have their partial rejection of cultural norms explained in terms of the persistence of attitudes from past centuries. Certainly, knowledge of the peculiar solution of 1877, settling America's problem of civil war but not settling the problem of its ex-slaves, is essential to comprehend attitudes still salient in American race relations.[54] In Northern Ireland, when people are asked to explain how the things troubling society first occurred, almost one-third evoke events happening from 50 to 300 years ago.[55] These historical references do not demonstrate strict historical determinism, but rather emphasize things often overlooked. After all, standing still is something much more natural to an Englishman than trying to change. In America, there is nothing more traditional than the desire to produce something new.

In the majority of countries in the world, changes in politics have been so recent and intense that a middle-aged man's expression of values and beliefs learned in youth would be inappropriate or incongruous. For instance, a German born in Berlin in 1900 has been the object of recurring socialization. As a youth he would have been socialized into attitudes suited to the conservative character of the Kaiser's Reich, whether conservatism took the form of upholding the *status quo*, or the platform of the Social Democratic Party. No sooner did he reach adulthood, perhaps after brief wartime service, than the regime was scrapped, boundaries contracted, and a Republic substituted at Weimar, with as many democratic trappings as the Kaiser had Imperial ones. In his early adult years, problems of inflation, economic recovery, depression, and recurring street battles between Nazis and Communists would all have borne upon him. By the time this German reached the age of 33, a time when an Englishman or American might have fixed his political outlook for life, once again he had to start learning how to think about politics, to survive in Hitler's Reich. The penalties were severe for failing his intensive course in adult re-socialization. Assured that this Reich, at least, would last a thousand years, our German adjusted to the new ways. Twelve years later, after another round of military service, he had to undergo yet another radical revision in outlook. Defeat brought with it a short, but very intense experience in learning the arts of physical survival. By 1949, our paradigm German once again found himself the object of re-socialization by one of the two German governments then constituted. If an East Berliner, he may have fled later to the Western sector seeking re-socialization yet again. Each of these six changes was grave enough to make persistence of earlier attitudes awkward, if not actively dangerous, for only a morbid pessimist would argue that nothing of great significance had changed in German political culture from Hohenzollern

Berlin through Buchenwald to Dr. Adenaur's Bonn. The German case is an extreme example of changes in the political environment compelling cultural changes, yet it is an illustration appropriate to most of 20th-century Europe, given the intensity of political changes that Germany forced upon its neighbours in ten years of war.

In a laboratory experiment subjecting a rat to sharp and frequent disruptions in his environment, one would expect the animal to have the rodent equivalent of a nervous breakdown. Yet the majority of adult Germans have not been reduced to a pathological state by exposure to many conflicting cultural outlooks.[56] Many Germans have appeared equally able to learn the culturally appropriate response to Weimar, to Hitler, or to a Soviet or Americanized form of government. Given sufficient inducement or threats, large numbers of people can, for better or for worse, modify their political outlooks with great alacrity. Today we hope that the examples of totalitarian-induced cultural change are a thing of the past. One can change human nature, and change it quickly, but only at a price that few in Britain or America would ever wish to pay.

NOTES—CHAPTER II

1. Walter Bagehot, *The English Constitution* (London: World's Classics edition, 1955) p. 185.
2. Note the Act of Parliament depriving British subjects in Kenya (the Kenyan Asians) of full citizenship rights, and Anthony Lewis, 'The Need for a Written Constitution', *The Spectator*, March 8, 1968.
3. Cf. R. L. Merritt, *Symbols of Community* (New Haven: Yale, 1966), Will Herberg, *Protestant, Catholic, Jew* (New York: Anchor edition, 1960), and Leo C. Rosten, *The Education of H*y*m*a*n K*a*p*l*a*n** (New York: Harcourt, 1937).
4. Tocqueville also wrote incisively about the British Isles. See *Journeys to England and Ireland*, edited by J. P. Mayer (London: Faber edition, 1958).
5. See E. A. Hoebel, 'Anthropological Perspectives on National Character', *The Annals* Vol. 370 (March, 1967) and other articles in this special issue on national character.
6. Cf. David Riesman *et. al.*, *The Lonely Crowd* (New York: Anchor edition, 1955), S. M. Lipset and Leo Lowenthal, editors, *Culture and Social Character: the work of David Riesman* (New York: Free Press,

1961) and Nathan Leites, 'Psycho-Cultural Hypotheses about Political Acts', *World Politics* I (October, 1948).

7. The concept of culture is used in many different ways. The *International Encyclopedia of the Social Sciences* (New York: Macmillan and Free Press, 1968 edition) has seven separate articles listed under the heading Culture, and gives 11 further cross-references. For a general discussion in a political context, see G. A. Almond and S. Verba, *op. cit.*, Ch. 2. For examples of political applications, see Lucian Pye and Sidney Verba, editors, *Political Culture and Political Development* (Princeton: University Press, 1965). An early discussion by Alex Inkeles and Daniel Levinson also remains relevant: 'National Character: The Study of Modal Personality and Sociocultural Systems' in Gardner Lindzey, editor, *Handbook of Social Psychology* Vol. II (Reading, Mass.: Addison-Wesley, 1954).
8. Cf. C. H. Rolph, *The Trial of Lady Chatterley* (Harmondsworth: Penguin, 1961) p. 17.
9. The terms 'outlooks', 'orientations' and 'attitudes' are used interchangeably to refer to the sum of cultural values, beliefs and emotions within an individual or society.
10. Cf. William Bluhm, *Theories of the Political System* (Englewood Cliffs, N.J.: Prentice-Hall, 1965).
11. Cf. Arend Lijphart, 'Typologies of Democratic Systems', *Comparative Political Studies* I:1 (1968).
12. For a learned and clarifying discussion of this crucial distinction, see *State and Nation* (London: Hutchinson, 1964) by Benjamin Akzin, author of nine books in three languages.
13. Cf. a preliminary report of a study there by Richard Rose, 'Inside the Mind of the Ulster Voter', *Sunday Times*, February 8, 1969.
14. See e.g., A. Campbell *et. al.*, *The American Voter* and Robert Alford, *op. cit.*
15. The material in this paragraph is summarized from Richard Rose and Derek Urwin, 'Social Cohesion, Political Parties and Strains in Regimes'.
16. See Richard Rose, 'Class and Party Divisions: Britain as a Test Case', pp. 138–43.
17. G. A. Almond and S. Verba, *op. cit.*, pp. 100ff.
18. Cf. A. V. Dicey, *Law and Public Opinion in England* (London: Macmillan, 1914 edition).
19. (New York: Free Press, 1962).
20. *Op. cit.*, p. 141.
21. See Hugh (later, Lord) Dalton, *Memoirs*: Vol. I (London: Muller, 1953) p. 61–62. Dalton, needless to say, took a second-class degree at

Cambridge, as Attlee did at Oxford. One's imagination boggles at the thought of how Ernest Bevin *or* his examiners would have come out of an examination room.

22. For a classic example of drawing meaning from such documents, see Ralph K. Huitt, 'The Congressional Committee: a Case Study', *American Political Science Review* XLVIII:2 (1954).
23. For a sophisticated discussion of the uses and limits of such materials, see Erwin K. Scheuch, 'Cross-National Comparisons Using Aggregate Data; Some Substantive and Methodological Problems', in R. L. Merritt and Stein Rokkan, editors, *Comparing Nations* (New Haven: Yale, 1966).
24. Calculated from data in Bruce M. Russett *et. al.*, *World Handbook of Political and Social Indicators* (New Haven: Yale, 1964) pp. 15–21.
25. For examples, see the contributions to Lucian Pye and Sidney Verba, editors, *op. cit.*, including that of this author.
26. G. A. Almond and S. Verba, *op. cit.*, Ch. 7.
27. *Op. cit.*, pp. 44ff.
28. (New York: Knopf, 1961) p. 555.
29. Cf. Warren Miller and Donald Stokes, 'Constituency Influence in Congress', *American Political Science Review* LVII:1 (1963), and Herbert McCloskey *et. al.*, 'Issue Conflict and Consensus Among Party Leaders and Followers', *ibid.*, LIV:2 (1960).
30. Cf. Robert Dahl, *Who Governs?* (New Haven: Yale, 1961) Book VI.
31. See Eric Nordlinger, *The Working Class Tories* (London: MacGibbon & Kee, 1967) and R. T. McKenzie and Allan Silver, *Angels in Marble* (London: Heinemann, 1968).
32. Cf. Thomas Pettigrew, *A Profile of the Negro American* (Princeton: Van Nostrand, 1964) and A. Kardiner and L. Ovesey, *The Mark of Oppression* (New York: World Book edition, 1962).
33. See e.g., J. A. C. Brown, *Freud and the Neo-Freudians* (Harmondsworth: Penguin, 1961).
34. The implications of this idea for political propaganda have often been discussed, but never implemented—at least in Britain. Cf. Anthony Howard and Richard West, *The Making of the Prime Minister* (London: Cape, 1965) p. 130, and Richard Rose, *Influencing Voters*, pp. 76, 81.
35. See especially, Fred Greenstein, *Children and Politics* (New Haven: Yale, 1965) and David Easton and Jack Dennis, *Children in the Political System* (New York: McGraw-Hill, 1969).
36. See A. Campbell *et. al.*, *The American Voter*, Ch. 7. Cf. Philip Abrams and Alan Little, 'The Young Voter in British Politics', *British Journal*

of Sociology and Kent Jennings and Richard Niemi, 'The Transmission of Political Values from Parent to Child', *American Political Science Review* LXII:1 (1968).

37. (London: Routledge, 1962) p. 54.
38. See Erik Erikson, *Childhood and Society* (New York: Norton, 1950).
39. For British data, see Richard Rose, *Politics in England* (London: Faber, 1965) p. 69. Data on the 1956 and 1964 American presidential elections are from a re-analysis of survey data collected by the Survey Research Centre, University of Michigan.
40. *Op. cit.*, Ch. 12.
41. *Family and Social Network* (London: Tavistock, 1957) Ch. 6.
42. See Richard Rose, 'Class and Party Divisions: Britain as a Test Case', p. 151.
43. Cf. Gerhard Lenski, 'Status Crystallization: a Non-Vertical Dimension of Social Status', *American Sociological Review* XIX:4 (1954).
44. See E. R. Tapper, *Secondary School Adolescents* (Manchester: Faculty of Economics, Ph.D., 1968) Ch. 7.
45. Rupert Wilkinson, *The Prefects* (London: Oxford University Press, 1964), T. J. H. Bishop, in collaboration with Rupert Wilkinson, *Winchester and the Public School Elite* (London: Faber, 1967), and D. McQuail, L. O'Sullivan and W. G. Quine, 'Elite Education and Political Values', *Political Studies* XVI:2 (1968). On Eton, see Ron Hall, 'The Family Background of Etonians', in Richard Rose, editor, *Studies in British Politics* (London: Macmillan, revised edition, 1969).
46. 'Social Background in Elite Analysis', *American Political Science Review* LXI:2 (1967), and Donald Searing, 'The Comparative Study of Elite Socialization', *Comparative Political Studies* I:4 (1969).
47. See Kenneth Prewitt, Heinz Eulau and Betty Zisk, 'Political Socialization and Political Roles', *Public Opinion Quarterly* XXX:4 (1967). For a somewhat different point of view, see J. D. Barber, 'Classifying and Predicting Presidential Styles', *Journal of Social Issues* XXIV:3 (1968).
48. Cf. Percy Cohen, 'Social Attitudes and Sociological Enquiry', *British Journal of Sociology* XVII:4 (1966).
49. See e.g., Oscar Handlin, editor, *Immigration as a Factor in American History* (Englewood Cliffs, N.J.: Prentice-Hall, 1959), and Louis Hartz *et. al.*, *The Founding of New Societies* (New York: Harcourt, Brace, 1964).
50. Cf. Richard Rose, 'England; a Traditionally Modern Culture', pp. 84ff. in Lucian Pye and Sidney Verba, editors, *op. cit.*
51. *The Guardian*, April 21, 1963.
52. The more detailed discussion of the hypothesis that cultural attitudes

persists across centuries, see S. M. Lipset, 'A Changing American Character?' in S. M. Lipset and Leo Lowenthal, editors, *op. cit.*, and S. M. Lipset, *America—the First New Nation* (London: Heinemann edition, 1964).

53. See Robert Lane, *op. cit.*, 147–52.
54. Cf. C. Vann Woodward, *Reunion and Reaction* (New York: Anchor, 1956).
55. Figures from a yet unpublished study in Northern Ireland by the author.
56. Cf. Sidney Verba, 'Germany: the Remaking of Political Culture', in L. Pye and S. Verba, editors, *op. cit.*, and Lewis Edinger, *Politics in Germany* (Boston: Little, Brown, 1968) Chs. 3–5.

Three

The Whole Man in Politics

The idea of politics without television, without professors or even, of politics without government is entirely conceivable; some might even find it attractive. Yet the idea of a politics without people seems absurd. Unfortunately, politicians as well as professors repeatedly show that it is possible to view society *en masse* without any sense of the humanity of its constituent parts. Useful one-dimensional intellectual abstractions such as political man or economic man are employed as if they represented people in all their complexity, rather than serving as convenient but partial ways to refer to individuals in specific types of situations. A society consisting of the progeny of economic men and political women (or *vice versa*) would no doubt have the virtue of total calculability; I doubt if it would have many other virtues.

Only the *gestalt* school of psychologists has developed a technical social science term to refer to people 'in the round'. Economists justify the creation of a universe populated by economic men on the grounds that extreme abstraction permits them to concentrate attention upon the profit-maximizing aspect of human beings, just as political scientists might justify studies of power-maximizing individuals on the ground that power is the key attribute of political analysis. Inevitably, some abstraction of individual characteristics is necessary, for all attributes of an individual are not equally relevant politically. Even if one found a correlation between drinking tea with milk and approving of monarchs, and drinking Coca-Cola and approving of Presidents, it would be a spurious one.

Deciding what aspects of personal life to omit is difficult, for a wrong decision can easily fault analysis at its very foundations. Even something as apparently non-political as taste in music can sometimes be politically relevant. One can hardly understand the emotions driving participants in the Negro protest movement in America in the 1960s without some familiarity with music as different as religious spirituals and Charley Parker. Similarly, protest marches by Catholics in Northern Ireland in 1968 assume new meaning when the marchers abandon songs of the Irish Republic and instead start singing 'We Shall Overcome'. Yet approaching politics through music would be a circuitous method, for few politicians seem to love music.

The direct approach is to start with the simple questions: What part should we expect a citizen to play in politics? What part should politics play in the life of a citizen? Stating the problem explicitly in value-laden terms rejects the possibility of a completely scientific answer, but it also avoids the error of purporting to give a strictly scientific answer to what, inevitably, remains a value-laden question.

From the time of Plato until relatively recently, most political philosophers and practical men of politics took a dim view of the civic competence of the mass of the population. Politics was the occupation of a few; mob action was the only way that the majority might exert political influence. At the time of the Civil War in 17th-century England, as Peter Laslett points out, the literate few could believe that they were thinking for the whole population; the mass lived in an oral culture, and political society was run in writing.[1] A century later politics was still the affair of so few people as to constitute face-to-face government. Henry Fielding defined 'the world' as 'your own acquaintanceship', and 'nobody' as 'All the people in Great Britain except 1200'. In the late 18th century, Edmund Burke calculated that the people, i.e., those who might participate in politics, constituted about 400,000 souls in a total population of some 15,000,000. The 14,600,000 excluded from legitimate participation would still have their interests taken into account, he argued, because they were virtually represented by spokesmen in the House of Commons.[2] In mid-19th-century England, the right of the majority to participate in politics was finally asserted. The franchise was not granted to the majority of men until 1884, and universal suffrage was not achieved until 1918. The right of working-class men to hold high office in government was not realized until the first Labour government of 1923. Even today, the practice of local Labour parties in adopting candidates and, even more, the practice of Harold Wilson in appointing Cabinet ministers, suggests that there remain many who do not think that men who started life as manual workers are fit to hold high office in the state.[3]

In the United States, the Founding Fathers were far from flattering in their conception of the political capacities of the ordinary colonist. Madison, Hamilton and Jay in *The Federalist Papers* saw the American Constitution as a device to guard against the consequences of self-interest and short-sightedness among the mass of citizens. Initially, franchise laws in the new Republic placed property qualifications upon the right to vote; these did not wane in favour for half a century. By the end of the 19th century, Americans had become the most fervent advocates of a wide variety of institutions purporting to allow direct popular rule, such as the initiative, the referendum and the open primary for the choice of candidates for office.[4] Yet, notwithstanding the symbolic commitment to government *by* as well as *for* the people, American election laws even today disfranchise more people than any similar set of laws in the Western world. The traditional and now declining discrimination against Negroes is of less importance than the restrictive laws on voter registration, which effectively disfranchise up to one-quarter of the potential electorate at each election. Practices complained of in the report of President Kennedy's Commission on the subject in 1963 were abolished in Britain in the Representation of the People Act, 1918.[5]

Today, the conventional doctrine in both England and America is that most people ought to take an active part in politics, especially at election time, when popular participation is most clearly the norm. When an election is at hand, there are some people who buy seven or eight newspapers, talk to as many voters and candidates as possible, and regard attendance at a political rally as the only valid excuse for missing a radio or television programme about the campaign. One does not refer to these individuals as voters or good citizens but by that sometimes suspect label 'psephologist'. These election experts constitute less than a dozen members of the electorate in Britain; they are almost as scarce in America. The average citizen votes, but does little more than vote when an election is at hand. While each person now has only one vote, this does not count equally in influencing the conduct of government. In a great departure from precedent, the United States Supreme Court declared in 1962 that each person's vote should be made equal, by assigning voters to constituencies apportioned to contain equal numbers of voters. The doctrine that legislators should represent 'people, not trees or acres', has a good rhetorical sound. Nonetheless, if endorsed literally, it involves the repudiation of the United States Senate, the most unrepresentative directly-elected legislative chamber in the Western world. In Britain, disparities also exist in the value of votes, but their political importance is much less. The Scottish Highlands, for example, contain constituencies with less than half the number of people in the average English seat. This is a relatively small price to pay for maintaining the traditional community sentiment that elections in the Highlands may count rocks and rainfall, if not trees.[6]

The rise of totalitarian governments that attempt to compel people to do many things desired by party leaders has given a new twist to the study of popular participation in politics. When participation is not a voluntary act or individuals are mobilized to march in mass demonstrations by dictatorships it is less attractive to liberally minded people.[7] The ability of totalitarian governments to mobilize support is less great, however, than is often assumed. Anyone who has ever tried to organize a political group, or even an adult education class, has personal experience of the way in which ordinary individuals can easily resist exhortations to join organized activities. Studies of the first two decades of Communist rule in Russia have emphasized that there too popular resistance was important. The attractions of traditional peasant holidays and of vodka proved as great as party slogans in moving many people to action.[8] The difficulties of the Communists in finding incentives to spur production in postwar Russia suggests that people are not passively co-operative in response to totalitarian efforts.

Given the unattractive forms that popular participation sometimes take, it is hardly surprising to find serious social scientists writing 'In Defence of Apathy'.[9] Briefly stated, such authors hold that as long as a country is governed well, then the great majority of the adult population has no need or incentive to participate in politics. Political activity is not a means by which an individual achieves positive goals, but rather, a sanction to be invoked when things go wrong. Tacit consent becomes the best form of consent. The argument is most frequently advanced in discussions of British and American politics, where participation rates are lower than activists might wish. It is not clear, however, whether the argument starts from the assumption that low participation equals popular satisfaction with government, or that British and American government is satisfactory, and therefore anything associated with it must be desirable.

While empirical data cannot resolve disputes about the ultimate ethical question of who should participate in politics, few would wish to go as far as two English philosophers, Graeme Duncan and Steven Lukes, in arguing that 'the most basic features of much political theory' are those which 'often touch reality only at the edges and are only at that point open to empirical refutation'.[10] Looking at empirical data about motives and levels of political participation can indicate whether normative preferences tend toward Utopian or ultra-realist extremes. Fortunately, a large body of survey data is available concerning political participation in Britain and America. Moreover, findings show a high degree of consistency from study to study.[11]

The Civic Culture study found that the great majority of people in Britain and America participated in politics to the extent of feeling the effect of national government upon their day-to-day lives. In America, 85 per cent said they felt some effect and in Britain, 73 per cent. Only four per cent of people interviewed thought that they would be better off without government influencing or interfering with their lives; more than three-quarters said that governmental activities definitely improved their conditions of life.[12] In short, the ordinary person in these two countries does not resent his contacts with the various arms of government.

A favourable attitude toward being governed does not mean that people look to political action as the best way of coping with their personal problems. An English community study that I conducted in Stockport found that while the majority of people interviewed expressed personal concerns for which governmental action was relevant—e.g. job, housing, or pension worries—only 15 per cent said that they thought help could come from any political group.[13] A total of 71 per cent said that they would look to their family or their own resources for help. In short, when worried about a child's education, parents are more likely to change the child to another school than turn to political action to reorganize the school system years after their child has become an adult.

When asked about influence on government, the median Englishman and American claims some influence, but not a lot. American studies have found that only 11 per cent rank at the top in political efficacy, whereas 15 per cent put themselves at the bottom. In Stockport, 26 per cent claimed a lot or some influence on government, 37 per cent said they had a little influence and the remainder claimed no influence at all or uncertainty about what they could do.[14] The English study found that voters saw many different groups influencing government, a finding consistent with academic literature describing politics as a process of group conflict. Among the nine groups rated, only the Queen and the Church of England were ranked lower in influence than voters ranked themselves. Civil servants were also ranked low because the average person appears to think of a civil servant as a post office clerk rather than as a bright young graduate pushing his way up the career ladder in Whitehall, dreaming of a Permanent Under-Secretaryship and knighthood. Five groups—the Prime Minister, MPs, big businessmen, the press and trade unions—were reckoned politically important by a majority of respondents. In Robert Dahl's terms, voters see the system of which they are a part as pluralist, and one in which inequalities are dispersed. But to paraphrase Orwell, they also see that some are more unequal than others, and they themselves are among the least equal participants.[15]

Notwithstanding a sense of limited influence, most people continue to vote, though nowadays there are few polling stations where enthusiasts are allowed to vote more than once for the party of their choice. In postwar Britain 79 per cent of eligible electors have voted on average at each post-war election; in America the figure is about 59 per cent, reflecting the greater legal inhibitions to voting.[16]

One explanation for high rates of voting is that people get emotional pleasure from an election; it is a spectator sport like football. My impression is that sports enthusiasts take defeat more seriously than do political enthusiasts; certainly police court records indicate that soccer contests are more likely to be a cause of violence than contemporary elections. The Civic Culture study supports this view. Less than half the people interviewed in Britain and America reported feeling a sense of satisfaction when going to the polls. Similar sized groups reported feeling angry about the campaigns, or thinking them silly or ridiculous.[17]

The evidence of voting studies suggests that the majority of people go to the polls because they think it is their duty to vote, and not because they wish to make meaningful personal demands upon government. The importance of voting is stressed from childhood, and the majority of adults consistently endorse liberal doctrines about the value of elections. When asked to choose between liberal and disaffected statements about elections, for example, only one-eighth of Stockport respondents chose a disaffected alternative at least three out of four times. By contrast, 56 per cent usually affirmed liberal values.[18] During an election campaign, the importance of voting is reinforced by public and informal media of communication. On election day, an individual will feel that he ought to vote. For example, in Stockport 82 per cent of people interviewed said voting was a duty; only 18 per cent said that you didn't have to vote unless you felt like it. American surveys have shown that even among people who rank at the bottom of various measures of political involvement, a majority nonetheless feel impelled to vote.[19] Since the cost of voting is very low, a person can easily avoid feelings of guilt by dutifully casting a ballot.

In order to vote, an individual needs only the ability to mark an X on a piece of paper. Illiterates and infirm people can even get assistance in doing this. In order to vote meaningfully, an individual only needs a party or candidate preference. Party identifications can be developed gradually and with little conscious effort through a process of socialization begun in the home in childhood. Individuals would have to be remarkably obtuse not to have, by the time they are adult, some awareness of party characteristics relevant to themselves. Even in America, where party distinctiveness is relatively low and ballot forms help people to cross party lines in voting for candidates for different offices, 86 per cent of the population identifies with either the Republican or Democratic party. Another 10 per cent are sufficiently political to reject the labels of the two major parties and call themselves Independents. Only four per cent have neither a positive nor negative party identification.[20]

In the face of such knowledge, it is ill advised to speak of an election, as authors of voting studies sometimes do, in terms of the people's choice or a voter deciding. The language of decision theory or consumer economics is out of place in politics. It depicts an individual at election time like the heroine of that great drama of micro-economics, the housewife standing outside two High Street shops trying to calculate the optimal shopping strategy in the face of a variety of bargain offers and green stamps. Voters themselves reject the analogy of choice. In the Stockport study, people were asked pointblank whether there was anything that one of the other parties could do to make them change their allegiance; 69 per cent said there was nothing that could be done to the other products to make them want to switch. Voters also reject the idea that their ballot represents an effective demand for influence. The Civic Culture study found that when asked how government could best be influenced, only 7 per cent of Americans and 3 per cent British respondents said that they would change their vote at the next election.[21]

It seems to me more apt to think of party preferences in terms of the language of faith. At an election, people are asked to affirm or reaffirm an allegiance. Most people do not think afresh about their party preferences before an election, any more than they sit down on Friday to decide whether to go to a Jewish synagogue, a Seventh Day Adventist service or a Catholic mass at the weekend. Party identification, like religious identification, can more readily be predicted from knowledge of parental views than from knowledge of an individual's current views about the European Common Market. People may identify with an institution out of habit, and not for reasons of a deep and informed ideological conviction. Moreover, clergymen, like politicians, often seem unsure about the meaning and relevance of traditional ideological principles in a world where much is changing.[22]

Because popular political participation is much lower than liberals might hope, it does not follow that politics is less important to people than other organized social activities. Even though it makes more historical sense to call England a Christian country than to call it a democracy, churches face a similar problem of low participation. In spite of a considerable amount of religious activity in many parts of England for 1300 years, church involvement shows broadly the same pattern as party politics: the great majority profess institutional allegiances, a substantial number are occasionally involved, and a small fraction is actively engaged. In America, church attendance is higher, but it does not follow that religious belief is great. Interestingly, the chief exception, the Roman Catholic Church, is the one religious institution that resembles a 'movement' type party, with a total claim on an individual's life.[23] Trade unions provide a secular point of comparison with parties. Figures on union participation indicate that, if anything, it is even lower than in party politics.[24] All in all, the Civic Culture survey found that memberships reported for 'civic-political' organizations in Britain and America were neither among the highest nor the lowest of organizational ties. In Britain, 53 per cent said they did not belong to any kind of voluntary organization, and in the United States, 43 per cent of a nation of joiners reported that they were unconnected with any association.[25]

The majority of people in Britain and America spend most of their time in extra-political activities, though such acts as driving an automobile into the centre of a city have clear consequences for public transportation, taxation and planning policies. If people are not fascinated by politics and politicians, what do they do with their lives? The answer can best be apprehended by following the implications of the social psychological dictum: study situations from the point of view of those involved, and not just from the point of view of a social science discipline. This is very difficult to do, because no academic wants to write a book which does little more than tell how a housewife does her washing, the husband goes to work and returns home, and both sit down in the evening, the wife ironing and the husband with his evening paper, 'watching' television. The language of social science encourages us to write about people in terms of their roles in the political system. That familiar word 'voter' is, however, as much an abstraction as our old friend economic man. Most people spend an infinitesimal portion of their adult lives in voting, preparing to vote, or thinking about elections.

It would be much more accurate, albeit more cumbersome if, instead of writing about voting behaviour, we wrote about the behaviour of ordinary individuals in electoral situations.

In studying the political outlooks of the non-political, there is always the danger of expecting too much or drawing too little from the respondent. The standard method of study remains the survey interview. Occasionally, people whose lives are spent in an extra-political world are invited by interviewers to pause for an hour to talk about political issues that interest the sponsors of a survey. Confronted by questions of limited concern or meaning, many respondents give answers logically inconsistent or apparently random.[26] As an alternative, one might try to engage people in casual conversation to see how often political references are made. Life is short, however, and tape-recordings of conversations take a discouragingly long time to listen to or transcribe; hence, this strategy is hardly feasible. Robert Lane has tried a modified form of this tactic, conducting long semi-focused conversations about politics and about much else with 15 American men, until they had said all they had to say of conceivable relevance to the study of political ideology. The most laconic provided a transcript of 154 pages; the most talkative filled 322 pages. In this manner, Lane obtained substantial stimulus and illustrative evidence for a book on 'Why the American Man Believes What He Does', but as he himself admits, 'I can suggest but alas, I cannot prove'.[27]

The nub of the problem is the need to aggregate the particular and sometimes idiosyncratic patterns of individual attitudes in ways that retain as much as possible of the unsophisticated and sometimes nearly inarticulate character of respondents' responses. Without such a process of aggregation, we have no sense of number or proportion; we cannot say *how many* people are politically sophisticated or politically illiterate. With even the best of categories, there remains the danger that highly articulate and logical social scientists will read too much or read the wrong things into relatively abstract categoric labels. To my mind, the most significant effort to classify the ways in which people think about politics had been undertaken by the University of Michigan's Survey Research Centre. This involves careful analysis of a series of detailed answers to open-ended survey questions about parties and candidates. Voters are assigned to groups according to the kinds of replies they have given.

The authors call this a measure of levels of conceptualization. The hierarchical language has some unfortunate overtones, but it does emphasize the researchers' concern with measuring degrees of political sophistication. (*See* Table III:1.)

TABLE III:1 LEVELS OF CONCEPTUALIZATION IN AMERICAN POLITICS

	% *Total sample*		% *Voters*	
A. Ideology	11½		15½	
B. Group Benefits				
— Conflict perceived	14	42%	16	45%
— Single-group interest clearly articulated	17		18	
— 'Shallow' group benefit responses	11		11	
C. Nature of the times	24		23	
D. No issue content				
— only party orientation	4	22½%	3½	17½%
— only candidate comments	9		7	
— no content	5		3	
— unclassified	4½		4	

SOURCE: Angus Campbell *et. al.*, *The American Voter*, p. 249

The ideological group consists of persons whose responses showed consistent use of abstract political concepts or a consistent set of preferences which could be linked with more general political ideologies. The broad category of persons thinking of group benefits embraces a range of outlooks, from the sixth or so who see politics in terms of conflict between groups, to the 11 per cent who voice a vague but not intense awareness that politics can involve changes affecting people like themselves. Those who talk about politics in terms of the nature of the times have views about whether government is going well or badly, but do not link these general judgments with group interests or general principles. The bottom group in Table III.1 should be sub-divided to distinguish between persons whose views have some political content, even if only an awareness of party labels or candidates' personalities, from those whose views are meaningless or are idiosyncratically unclassifiable. In all, 90 per cent made some reference to issues, party labels or candidates. The small proportion (7 per cent) whose views were focused entirely on the candidate is specially noteworthy, given that the interviews were obtained during the 1956 presidential election, when the Republican candidate was Dwight Eisenhower, a man who combined the non-political virtues of Wyatt Earp with the familiarity of David Frost.

Evaluating these figures is difficult whether we approach them as social scientists, as citizens, or as educated people sitting in judgment upon our less educated fellows. For some reason that I cannot quite understand, rationality is often the criterion employed in judging how people vote. Unfortunately the term 'rationality' has many meanings, and emotional overtones for educated people. At the Scarborough Labour Party conference of 1960, I saw the late Hugh Gaitskell moved nearly to tears by the praise heaped on him for his love of rationality at a *Socialist Commentary* tea. In the social sciences, the concept may refer to a method of planning action, rather than to the substantive choice of goals. In *influencing voters*, rational campaigning is described as internally consistent, empirically plausible actions related to the stated goal of winning an election. In *an economic theory of democracy*, Anthony Downs assumes that men always weigh up costs against gains; he then concludes that few will have any rational reason to participate in politics. Because Downs has drawn out the full implication of assumptions about rationality in voting, his study has always seemed to me an elegant *reductio ad absurdum* of ideas frequently implicit in much that is written about voting.[28]

Elegant reasoning can be aesthetically satisfying, but it can also be misleading as a way of studying ordinary people in electoral situations. Concern with procedural rationality places emphasis upon logical thought processes. One cannot help wondering why a small number of abnormally educated people should expect the great mass of individuals to think as they themselves do. A study of voters in Britain by Blumler and McQuail has found that this is not the case. The least educated voters regard the substantive promises of politicians as the most important thing to notice in an election campaign; the most educated gave primary emphasis to general principles and politicians' personalities. Concern with promises is not a function of credibility, but rather, of scepticism. Promises are not evaluated in terms of attractiveness, but rather, compared with substantive achievements or failures of the parties in the past. In the words of one person interviewed:

> 'I think you should pay more attention to their record than their arguments. Arguments needn't be true. It's what they've done that counts. If you look back in the past, you'll see they promise all sorts of things, but they don't always do what they say.'[29]

In a sense, it is procedurally irrational for highly articulate social scientists to seek verbal explanations for political behaviour from people who are often politically inarticulate. In discussing this problem, John Plamenatz has tellingly noted: 'Can we say of a number of people about to get married that the ones who give the best reasons are likely to be most happy? And if we cannot, does it really follow that in marriage there are no wise choices, but only lucky ones?' Plamenatz goes on to suggest that the best criterion for evaluating individual participation in elections is that of *reasonableness*. 'A choice is reasonable, not because the chooser, when challenged, can give a satisfactory explanation of why he made it, but because, if he could give an explanation, it would be satisfactory.'[30] Plamenatz's criterion turns the social scientist into an attorney for the defendant, seeking explanations on behalf of the voter, rather than a prosecuting attorney, seeking to convict the voter of ignorance. Inasmuch as the first task of a social scientist is to understand people rather than to judge them, there is much to be said for this shift in emphasis.

Evaluating voters in terms of the reasonableness of their views raises the question: To whom should an explanation be reasonable? Plamenatz does not provide criteria. Do we say an explanation for voting is reasonable if the argument in its favour is internally consistent? Do we say it is reasonable if empirically plausible justifications can be advanced? Or do we say it is reasonable only if it leads to actions of benefit to the voter? Instead of pursuing the problem of definitions in the abstract, we might look again at the Michigan data on levels of conceptualization.[31] At each level, we can ask whether a reasonable account of voting could be given on behalf of persons in each category. Voters who think of politics in ideological terms by definition meet the requirement that they should be capable of giving an explanation of their position which is internally consistent. In recent years, however, some American writers have argued that the abstractions involved in creating a coherent ideology increasingly lead people to conclusions which are empirically implausible, in terms of means–ends relationships.[32] Social scientists, of all people, should be the last to criticize others for an excessive love of political abstractions. People who talk about politics in terms of group benefits can be called reasonable if one regards self-interest as capable of justification. For example, in the 1964 American election, a Negro did not need to be a genius or even a drop-out from the University of Arizona to reckon that Lyndon Johnson would help Negroes more than Barry Goldwater. It can be argued that people who think about politics in terms of the nature of the times are acting upon the constitutional assumption that governments are responsible bodies. If things go well, they vote for the party in power, and if things go badly, they vote against it. This simple calculation may lead to substantively better judgments than listening to special pleading by politicians anxious to explain why the party governing the country is not really responsible for such palpably dismaying events as war or unemployment, or why the opposition could do better than a government in office when times are good. Even some of the voters who do not mention issues can be said to be acting reasonably. If voters who view an election solely in terms of the competence of the two presidential candidates are acting unreasonably, then so are many journalists, and social scientists who write books to demonstrate that the electoral system can be reduced to competition between men, and justified on that basis.[33] People who can only reiterate party labels show a trust in parties, but then, so do MPs and Congressmen who trust the whips to see that they vote correctly when a division is called on a bill about which they know nothing. The woman whose political views are taken second-hand, casting a vote on her husband's instruction, is trying to maintain domestic harmony, hardly an unreasonable goal. Only the feeble-minded, the mentally ill, and other socially marginal persons might be said to vote for reasons which cannot be justified in some manner. What would happen, I wonder, if such an irrational person asked a researcher in a temporarily lucid moment: If you are so concerned with rationality, why do you come talk to me? Why do you give me a vote?

It is fair to assume that since three-quarters to nine-tenths of the American electorate has a 'reasonable' approach to politics, a similar proportion of Englishmen are politically reasonable, even though they do not go to the extreme of ultra-rationality. (It is worth noting that 'ultra' is a word imported into our political vocabulary from France, where ultras are much more prominent and destructive.) Perhaps 19th century proponents of universal suffrage were right in arguing that nearly everybody is sensible enough to vote in his own interest. Of course, by tightening up the criteria for a 'reasonable' justification of voting, it becomes possible to argue that a substantial part of the population, or even a majority, does not meet the standard of reasonableness. The key question is: Where does one draw the line? If forced to make their criteria of reasonableness or rationality explicit, many who take a dim view of voters might disqualify from the ballot booths everyone who was not elected by a university scholarship board. (At least, this liberalizes earlier criteria, which required a leader to be elected by God.) Would such a restriction satisfy everyone in an age of expanding higher education? Sometimes, it seems as if the critics of the ordinary voters would even begin to quarrel about the reasonableness of me and thee.

If it is reasonable for most people to pay little attention to politics, then on what grounds can we explain the behaviour of those few who are politically active? Understanding the motivations of this group is important because the character of politicians affects how a country is governed. It is also important because somehow sufficient numbers of people must be found to staff all the offices of state from Prime Minister to parish councillor, if government is to be carried on.

Delimiting this deviant group is not as easy as it seems. For a start, we can exclude the bulk of the population, on the ground that they only vote. A case could be made that people who belong to organizations such as trade unions which press demands on government in their name are participating in politics. Since most such organization members are uninterested in the political side of their group's affairs, it would seem wrong to describe as politicians people whose participation is virtual rather than real. We could take interest and knowledge about politics as our limiting criteria, since informed and interested people can constitute informed public opinion. Within their ranks, one can further discriminate people who are more or less full-time involved in politics, whether by virtue of holding an elective office, a position in a pressure group or a senior post in the civil service or a large local government authority. At a minimum, there are four levels of political activity—regular involvement, informed awareness, occasional involvement in elections, and parochial passivity.

The number of people who are regularly involved in politics, either as part of their job or as what is erroneously known as a leisure time activity, is of the order of about two per cent of the adult population. This figure is an estimate, for any meaningful definition must depart from a simple listing of elective offices, yet when it does so, it becomes extremely difficult to fit to available data.[34] The numbers of people who are interested and informed about public affairs may be indicated in a number of ways—by reading the serious press, holding organization offices, individual membership in political parties, etc., etc. What is noteworthy about these varied indicators is that each provides approximately the same estimate; the politically informed are something between 10 and 20 per cent of the adult population in Britain. In America too, figures are of a similar magnitude.[35] The number of people who confine their participation to voting, and do little else is of the order of 60 to 75 per cent of the adult population; 10 to 15 per cent constitute the parochials lacking even intermittent contact with democratic political activity. I am not sure whether one should say that the number of people regularly engaged in politics is as few as 750,000 adults in Britain and 3,000,000 adults in America, or whether one should say it is as large as the adult population of Glasgow or Los Angeles.

The difference in the character of political offices in Britain and America is much greater than is usually realized. Britain has the minimum number of elective offices consistent with the idea of a representative government. One representative is elected for each parliamentary constituency and several for each local authority constituency. No one in the executive branch of government is directly elected. A small proportion of the chief executives are chosen from among elected MPs or local councillors. The remaining chief positions are filled by senior civil servants and in the case of government committees, by people whose politicial skills and status have been acquired independently of running for elective office.[36]

6

By contrast, in the United States a large number of officeholders must seek direct election to executive and judicial offices as well as to the legislature. At the level of federal government, each elector casts four votes—one for a President, two for Senators and one for a member of the House of Representatives. In state and local elections, the ballot is much longer, with everyone from the Chief Justice of the State Supreme Court to the municipal dog-catcher liable to choice by election. The fact that lower level governmental authorities have more influence in American than in British politics enhances the importance of elected officials. In one mid-western state a few years ago, the ballot measured four by four feet, and contained the names of 246 candidates for office. It also carried a warning that each voter only had one minute in the polling booth to mark it.[37]

In general, public offices in America are filled by election or by formal or informal patronage, rather than by competitive examinations. In Britain, important political posts are filled by competitive examination, as in the civil service, or by patronage. The patronage now exercised in the United States, it should be emphasized, is not the award of plum jobs to party hacks or faithful financial backers. A few unimportant posts, such as Ambassador to the Court of St James, are saved for partisans with money, but key jobs in the White House and elsewhere in the executive tend to go to people who have earned their place by skilful or loyal service to the President in a fiercely competitive political system. By contrast, in Britain the patronage of the Prime Minister is exercised in a hot-house environment analogous to a boarding-school—the Palace of Westminster. Approximately one-third of the governing party's men must have jobs, if the Queen's government is to be carried on.[38] From the Prime Minister's point of view, however, it is never certain that he will be the man to carry it on, for his tenure of office is constitutionally uncertain; the envy of his nominal supporters in Cabinet is certain. In such circumstances, there is always a temptation to use patronage powers to appoint as ministers a few who, by their inferiority, will make the Prime Minister more secure, rather than men who, by their ability, will make the country better governed. Mr Harold Wilson has given an excellent example of the use of patronage powers as a means of playing off or submerging would-be rivals. For example, it was only after the devaluation of the pound in November 1967 that

Wilson appointed as Chancellor of the Exchequer a man who might be up to this very demanding job.

In both countries, there is a growing desire to recruit men for office because they have specially useful skills. Neither country has gone as far as Ethiopia, however, and established a statutory requirement that all candidates for Parliament must be literate. Given the complexity of the economic and social commitments of governments today, it is very understandable that men may be needed with something more to recommend them than a good debating style in the House of Commons, or the smile and a telegenic family so useful in American campaigning. Yet it is by no means clear what kind of skills are most useful for men in politics. Is a good politician a man with an appealing personality or a dominating personality, a man who readily acts as a conciliator among men, an inspiring orator, a super efficient bureaucrat, an entrepreneur or broker of ideas, or a man able to anticipate problems that his peers cannot yet see? There are uses for each of these characteristics in politics. It would be simplest to assume that good government requires a group of men with a mixture of skills, some of which are certain to be in conflict, hopefully, creatively so. The method of recruiting men to the federal government in Washington, does in fact provide a varied team of executives for a President's administration. Studies by the Brookings Institution have emphasized the extent to which functionally specific requirements are used in recruiting men to staff Cabinet and sub-Cabinet positions. For example, Robert McNamara's appointment to the Pentagon arose from the need to find a man skilled at sorting out administrative problems of a gigantic sort. McNamara had proved his skill at doing this in turning Ford from an old man's private empire into an organization as rationally organized as a mammoth firm might be. By contrast, Jim Callaghan was made Chancellor of the Exchequer in Britain in 1964 because he had to be given *something* important, not because he had ever demonstrated a firm grip upon economics or upon senior civil servants of Treasury calibre. Lest it be thought that the full-time politician has no skills, it should be emphasized that one of the important characteristics that many American recruits to important jobs in Washington share is previous experience in government work. Such men are, in Richard Neustadt's phrase, 'in and outers', alternately bringing extra-political experiences to government, and knowledge of government work to corporations, to professional practice and, not least, to the universities.[39]

Contemporary British discussions of the necessary qualities for government tend to be monomaniacal. Until very recently, it was customary to praise the virtues of the gifted amateur, the man whose skills were so general and so considerable that they could not be defined or measured, or alternatively, could simply be measured by family connections or skill in composing Pindaric odes. The ideal politician was once a man with both attributes. Nowadays, the fashion has swung full circle. In campaigning for office, Harold Wilson saw fit to refer to the fact that he had a house on a mortgage, rather than on a hereditary entail. Mr Heath tries to compensate for shedding what once must have been a lower middle-class accent by appearing in 'classless' photographs at weekends as if advertising a new cigarette. In Whitehall, the Fulton Committee, chaired by a man who was sufficiently new-fangled to have *earned* his peerage, has pronounced that henceforth it is more important for civil servants to be proficient in statistics and economics than in classics.[40] On balance, this is a reasonable corrective prescription, for the earlier bias towards classics and ancient history means that men with the attributes of mandarins will continue to occupy important posts in Whitehall until about the year 2000. Nonetheless, it would be a pity if they were superseded by a breed of senior policy makers who were so entranced by the abstractions of micro and macro-economics that they lacked what is colloquially called *nous*.[41] In view of the politically impracticable recommendations of some economists, it could even be a disaster.

Sociological enquiry suggests that the reason why many men become politicians has less to do with specific skills, and more to do with specific social characteristics. Huey Long's ideal of Every Man a King cannot be realized in America, for there is a constitutional prohibition against titles of nobility. But at least every man, whether or not he can stand the sight of blood or the sound of gunfire, can run for office as county coroner or county sheriff. If the salary seems inadequate, he can enrich himself, like a medieval monarch or ecclesiastic, by selling official favours. In Britain, one might suggest that the appropriate slogan is: Every Gentleman a Servant of the King. And, like good servants, many have been paid in honour rather than in cash. Until 1911, Members of Parliament received no salary and until 1964 the salary was calculated on the assumption that a Member had other sources of income—earned or unearned. The idea of paying members the appropriate trade union rate for the job was fought by some Conservative MPs with a ferocity that one might expect would only be shown toward a proposal to deprive them of their claim to a knighthood after years of safe, stolid party loyalty. In the Labour Party too, the idea of representation by social class lingers in the provision of safe seats for trade unionists with working-class backgrounds. As in the Democratic Party, there is a conscious desire to make the party leadership socially representative. The Labour Party equivalent of the Democratic Party's Negro, immigrant and Jew is the coal miner, the Scot and a woman.

Neither in Britain nor America do political leaders in any way begin to provide an approximate cross-section of the nation's adult population. The most obvious example of discrimination is one rarely cited: the under-representation of women in politics.[42] It is curious that men who inveigh so strongly against alleged class biases in public office never go so far as to advocate equal representation of men and women in the legislative and executive branches of government. One incidental advantage of electing a woman President is that her husband would almost certainly be sufficiently colourless to make an ideal Vice President.

Occupational and status considerations clearly influence political recruitment. In the United States, men with law degrees have traditionally been favoured for public office. Such a requirement is not an onerous one, for a law degree can be earned about as easily in America as a set of O or A level passes can be collected in a technical college in Britain. In Britain, recruitment of Conservative and Foreign Office officials have been biased in favour of people with middle or upper class social origins, usually signified by attendance at a public school. Labour leaders and senior home civil servants have come from a slightly lower social strata; they are men who entered Oxford, Cambridge (or occasionally another university) from less prestigious secondary schools.[43] Curiously, these generalizations do not apply to chief executives. In 20th-century America, only 5 out of 13 Presidents have had law degrees, and in Britain, only 8 of 15 Prime Ministers in this century had been born and bred in an upper-class manner. Nowadays, high-status politicians in Britain often identify themselves with plebians, probably because of misperception rather than calculated ambition. For example, the wife of Charles Morrison, an Etonian who took over his family estate in Wiltshire before succeeding to the family estate in Parliament, could assure a reporter in her stately home: 'We are just an ordinary family in an ordinary sort of house.'[44] In America, the new trend is for candidates to display their wealth.

While social characteristics affect the chances of an individual becoming active in politics, they do not determine his entry into political life. The most important feature of any social group with a disproportionate number of politicians in it is that the politicians constitute a very small fraction of all members of the category. For example, the 32 miners in the House of Commons are 9 per cent of all Labour MPs, but less than 1/100th of one per cent of the membership of the National Union of Mineworkers. Similarly, while Old Wykehamists were 9 per cent of the Labour Cabinet formed by Mr Wilson after the 1966 general election, Richard Crossman and Douglas Jay accounted for only 1/10th of one per cent of all Wykehamists born between 1900 and 1919.[45] It is entirely possible that more old Etonians are living dissolute lives on the Riviera in the style of the late Brian Howard than there are Etonians on the back benches of the Conservative party in the Commons. In order to explain why a minority, even a deviant minority of Etonians or miners go into politics, we must know about individual motivation, as well as about the cultural values and social characteristics that predispose them to political activity and predispose others to regard them as potential politicians.

In examining the influences that lead individuals into political participation, the family is the place to start. Parents have much influence upon the career aspirations of their children: a disproportionate number of doctors' sons become doctors, of miners' sons become miners and, it would seem, a disproportionate number of people in politics have first become interested because of family involvement. Few parents push their children to become anything as specific as the Prime Minister. For example, Harold Wilson's parents were apparently indifferent whether their son became a Cabinet minister, a professor of economics, or editor of the *Manchester Guardian*—as long as he made a name for himself.[46] Children raised by politically active parents tend to take public life for granted, hearing about public affairs at the dinner table, and tagging along with relatives to party meetings. Friendships are likely to form with others interested in politics and, sooner or later, the youth will be asked to do some political work, or conclude that he can do it as well as others. This pattern of increasing involvement fits the familiar hypothesis that participation is likely to stimulate increasing participation. The pattern works in ward politics and in Parliament. Among post-war Prime Ministers, Sir Winston Churchill, Sir Alec Douglas-Home and Harold Wilson were all raised in explicitly political families. In Harold Macmillan's case, a desire to gain freedom from the family publishing business may have pushed him toward politics, where his relatives by marriage were already active. Neither Clement Attlee nor Sir Anthony Eden had parents who were very active politically, but Attlee's father was a city solicitor and Eden's a landed baronet, both statuses close to public affairs. Even Anthony Wedgewood Benn's noble fight to permit an heir to a peerage to renounce membership in the House of Lords was also a fight to stay in the family business, the House of Commons. In America, three of the last six presidents—Franklin D. Roosevelt, John F. Kennedy and Lyndon Johnson—came from families with a history of political activity, and Harry Truman too was raised in a family with pronounced political views. Dwight D. Eisenhower and Richard Nixon are the only postwar Presidents to come from apolitical families.[47]

Because politicians form a small proportion of almost any social category, the most parsimonious way to account for their activities is to examine their personality characteristics. This approach can produce clinically interesting reactions. Students are often shocked when it is pointed out that Sir Winston Churchill was biologically a human being, and that psychological and biological points might be helpful in understanding his behaviour in his 20s as well as in his 80s.[48] In a complementary fashion, the desire of some authors to produce such shocks may lead them to draw implausible or illogical conclusions about individual motivations from inadequate data concerning a politician's life. In some cases, the desire to suppress analysis may be motivated by political calculations, as in the case of the Kennedy family's battles with William Manchester, author of *The Death of a President*. Yet the fact that the Kennedy family would commission the book from a man of no particular literary stature tells us something of the way in which people in politics wish to dramatize their affairs. There is the possibility that statesmen—well defined by Harry Truman as 'dead politicians'—will be abnormal in the psychological as well as the political sense. The lives of leading Presidents and Prime Ministers certainly give some grounds for believing this.[49] After reading about great wartime leaders, such as David Lloyd George, Woodrow Wilson, Franklin D. Roosevelt and Churchill, one would hesitate to give an affirmative answer to the age-old question: How would you like your daughter to marry one? Woodrow Wilson's personality probably imposed more strains on himself than on anyone else in his domestic establishment. The history of the Churchill and Roosevelt offspring, as judged by press reports from the divorce courts and other unfortunate places, suggests that the home lives of these famous men involved very severe strains upon those around them. Such observations are not scientific evidence, but they seem interesting in the clinical as well as the journalistic sense.

When I ask MPs informally what led them into the House of Commons, the answer most typically given is a smile and then a confession of uncertainty. In particular, I have a vivid memory of the way in which one MP calmly analysed his puzzlement—and a few years later died young from overwork. One important motive is non-political, a desire to improve social status by membership in what is often revealingly described by its members as the finest club in Europe. The symptoms are most clearly documented in the diaries of Henry Channon, a back-bench Conservative MP for more than 20 years. Channon was the son of a prosperous Chicago family sufficiently wealthy to send him to Oxford, but socially of such a status that he preferred to omit their name from his entry in *Who's Who*. His post-Oxford life was a continuing series of efforts to move up the social ladder. To Channon, membership in the House of Commons conferred status of itself and was also the ante-chamber to the House of Lords.[50] In fact, he died a 'mere' knight.

In view of the important part that senior civil servants play in government, it is perhaps more important to investigate the motivation of these politicians *in camera* than to examine those of men whose careers are, if anything, only too public. It could be argued that men who are the chief advisers at the Treasury or the Foreign

Office are not politicians. Yet this too raises questions: why should men want to get so near to politics yet remain somehow apart? Are their personalities such that they have no stomach for conflict, or only an abhorrence of public criticism? Do these guardians seek neutral roles because they have been deprived of political desires at an early age, as guardians of a harem might be neutralized in a Middle Eastern society?

The most reasonable assumption is that men enter the civil service as they enter elective politics, from a variety of motives.[51] Nowadays, job security is of little importance. Able recruits to the highest levels of government are very employable elsewhere. If anything, economic considerations militate against civil service work, for salaries are normally higher in industry than in government. Increasingly, senior civil servants are prepared to leave the civil service prior to retirement, though after they have reached a top job and a knighthood. A few young men must enter the civil service desiring to influence government policy. For instance, a bright young man might reasonably calculate that as a permanent Treasury official he could influence economic policy more than he could as a fleeting Chancellor. Some even quit the civil service when they realize than in order to reach positions of influence in their 40s, they must spend from ten to twenty years of their lives marking time as apprentices. The civil service can attract people who enjoy political activity but have a passion for anonymity.[52] Civil servants may advise in private, secure in the knowledge that their actions will be masked from attention and their persons safe from criticism. Civil servants are also ringside spectators of major political events. In David Riesman's terms, such men are 'inside dopesters', seeing all but caring little about the consequences of what they see.[53] The importance of the office as a means of maintaining the status of the wellborn seems to be declining, now that television, advertising, and even industry and commerce are regarded as acceptable career alternatives to the old and declining professions—the army, the church, the Civil Service and the Bar. Predictably, bright young men with lower social origins will rush in to fill the vacuum left by the default of their more socially confident contemporaries.[54]

It is noteworthy that one can write seriously and at length about the motivations of politicians without discussing political principles or policy goals. Conventionally, we expect politicians to state their motives in terms of public policy. For example, a questioner of John F. Kennedy might anticipate the answer: I am in politics to make America a better nation. One would certainly be surprised if Kennedy had said: I want to prove to myself and my father that I can do everything that he thought my older brother would do. We would be slightly less surprised by such an answer from Robert F. Kennedy. Tragically, such an answer would seem only too appropriate from the sole survivor of the four male Kennedys. Whether the motivation for entry into politics is to fight unemployment or the idleness of the rich, once in politics an individual is likely to develop new motives for continued political involvement, as initial policy goals are achieved or adolescent influences wane in significance. Studies of local politicians in Britain and America find that when they are asked what they would miss most if forced to leave politics, typically they refer to a loss of gratifications that arise from working with people.[55] In Congress and in the Commons, one can always see elderly men hanging on to office long after their chance of influencing policy has gone. Conservatives and Republicans seem readier to accept retirement than Labour politicians and Democrats. Perhaps, as one Labour Cabinet minister has said, 'They have so much more to live for outside politics.' To my mind, the ideal politician is a man whose private motives and public commitments reinforce each other, providing a strong personal drive to achieve general policy goals.

In a famous study of *Power and Personality*,[56] Harold Lasswell argued succinctly and extremely that a politician is a man who displaces his private needs upon public issues. Personality needs lead people to politics as a means of seeking gratification. The exigencies of politics compel the rationalization of these needs in terms of public policy statements. Yet one might as easily argue that insofar as individual personality difficulties are a consequence of larger social disorders, then political action is the most economical and efficient form of therapy. This is a reasonable gloss upon the position of many American Negroes. Insofar as Negro personality disturbances arise from growing up black in a white society, it makes sense to seek to change that society. Whether a Negro advocates black nationalism or integrationist policies is immaterial for when the source of his personal problem lies outside himself, the solution can be found there too. In many cases, the connection between an individual's personality and the policies that he advocates is uncertain. For example, James Forrestal, the first American Secretary of Defence, killed himself while under psychiatric treatment shortly after resigning from office in 1949. The fact that Forrestal was becoming mentally unbalanced toward the end of his public career does not necessarily vitiate the wisdom of the political policies he advanced while in office.[57]

Many people are confused in what they expect from politicians. On the one hand, politicians are expected to be people with good, wholesome personalities, as our society defines mental health. Yet we also wish politicians to have many qualities to excess. If we expect them to have virtues to excess, can we really complain if some also have undesirable traits in excess too? If we learn that a few politicians drink too much, that others chase women and occasionally a politician takes a decision while unbalanced, are we to conclude that politicians are therefore different from other men? The answer is almost certainly 'No'. Any sample of the population is likely to show that the virtues and vices of politicians are not different in kind, even if perhaps different in degree, from those of other men. Personally, I find it more reassuring to think that we are governed by human beings—libidos, warts, neuroses and all—rather than be told that our governors are made of some ethereal stuff. Men who can see their own warts should be better able to see the country's ills than those who see themselves and, by implication, the world, as they wish it were. Instead of revaluating politicians, perhaps what we really need to do is to re-evaluate our conception of normality.

While so close an examination of public leaders must inevitably de-mythologize them, it is not an attempt to argue that the political standards of the country are in decline. It is sobering to consider that political motives have always been mixed. Consider Sir Lewis Namier's catalogue of motives of men going into Parliament in 1760:

> 'The Inevitable Parliament Men; the country Gentlemen; The Politicians; the Social Climbers; Placemen and Purveyors of Favours; Professional Advancement: the Services and the Law; The Merchants and Bankers: Robbers, Muddlers, Bastards and Bankrupts.'[58]

The person chosen to illustrate the inevitable Parliament Men,

Philip Stanhope, also illustrates the category of bastards. Even in their idiosyncrasies, men who went into Parliament in the 1760s have something in common with men going into Parliament two centuries later. The point is important, for if the nature of politicians is in some ways stable, then by that token it is amenable to generalization.

NOTES—CHAPTER III

1. *The World We Have Lost* (London; Methuen, 1965) p. 194.
2. Cf. C. S. Emden, *The People and the Constitution* (Oxford: Clarendon Press, 1933) especially Appendix I. More generally, see Samuel H. Beer, *Modern British Politics* (London: Faber, 1965).
3. See Richard Rose, 'Class and Party Divisions: Britain as a Test Case', especially Tables 1, 2, 12 and 13.
4. Cf. Chilton Williamson, *American Suffrage From Property to Democracy* (Princeton: University Press, 1960) and A. Lawrence Lowell, *Public Opinion and Popular Government* (New York: Longmans, 1914).
5. Cf. *Report on Registration and Voting Participation* (Washington: Government Printing Office, 1963) and Neal Blewett, 'The Franchise in the United Kingdom', 1885–1918, *Past and Present* No. 34 (1965).
6. Cf. Vincent Starzinger, 'The British Pattern of Apportionment', *Virginia Quarterly Review* XLI:3 (1965).
7. Cf. J. P. Nettl, *Political Mobilization* (London: Faber, 1967).
8. See e.g. Merle Fainsod, *Smolensk under Soviet Rule* (London: Macmillan, 1959), and David Granick, *The Red Executive* (New York: Anchor, 1961), especially Chs. 15–16.
9. See especially W. H. Morris-Jones, 'In Defence of Apathy', *Political Studies* II:1 (1954).
10. 'The New Democracy', *Political Studies* XI:2 (1963).
11. The most convenient summaries are Robert Lane, *Political Life* (Glencoe, Illinois: Free Press, 1957) and Lester Milbrath, *Political Participation* (Chicago: Rand McNally, 1965).
12. G. A. Almond and S. Verba, *op. cit.*, pp. 80, 82.
13. Richard Rose and Harve Mossawir, 'Voting and Elections: a Functional Analysis', *Political Studies* XV:2 (1967) pp. 182ff.
14. Cf. *ibid.*, and A. Campbell *et al.*, *The American Voter*, p. 105.
15. Cf. *Who Governs?*, p. 228 and Richard Rose and Harve Mossawir *op. cit.*, pp. 185–86.

16. In Continental European countries, turnout is usually even higher than in Britain. Cf. Uwe Kitzinger, *Britain, Europe and Beyond* (Leiden: Sijthoff, 1964) pp. 186, 217.
17. G. A. Almond and S. Verba, *op. cit.*, p. 146, Percentages are calculated on the basis of all adult respondents. See also Jay Blumler and Denis McQuail, *Television in Politics* (London: Faber, 1968), pp. 81–82, 112.
18. Richard Rose and Harve Mossawir, *op. cit.*, p. 187.
19. *Ibid.*, and A. Campbell *et al.*, *The American Voter*, pp. 97ff. The one exception in Figure 5:3 involves only 10 per cent of the population.
20. A. Campbell *et al.*, *Elections and the Political Order*, p. 13.
21. G. A. Almond and S. Verba, *op. cit.*, p. 203.
22. See especially Bryan Wilson, *Religion in Secular Society* (London: Watts, 1966) and H. Richard Niebuhr, *The Social Sources of Denominationalism*, (New York: Holt, 1929).
23. Cf. Michael Argyle, *Religious Behaviour* (London: Routledge, 1958), Chs. 2–4, and Charles Glock and Rodney Stark, *Religion and Society in Tension* (Chicago: Rand McNally, 1965).
24. See e.g., Martin Harrison, *Trade Unions and the Labour Party Since 1945* (London: Allen & Unwin, 1960) and, more generally, Richard Rose, *Politics in England*, Table IV:2.
25. G. A. Almond and S. Verba, *op. cit.*, p. 302.
26. See especially, Philip E. Converse, 'New Dimensions of Meaning for Cross-Section Sample Surveys in Politics', *International Social Science Journal* XVI:1 (1964) and D. E. G. Plowman, 'Public Opinion and the Polls', *British Journal of Sociology* XIII:4 (1962).
27. *Political Ideology.*
28. Downs himself is explicit about the highly simplified nature of some of his assumptions, *op. cit.*, pp. 6ff.
29. Jay G. Blumler and Denis McQuail, *op. cit.*, p. 121. The whole of Ch. 6 is specially relevant here.
30. 'Electoral Studies and Democratic Theory: a British View', *Political Studies* VI:1 (1956) pp. 8–9.
31. For alternative approaches, see e.g. V. O. Key Jr., with Milton Cummings, *The Responsible Electorate* (Cambridge, Mass.: Harvard, 1966). Bernard R. Berelson *et al.*, *Voting* (Chicago: University Press, 1954) Ch. 14 and Philip Converse, 'The Nature of Belief Systems in Mass Publics', in David Apter, editor, *Ideology and Discontent* (New York: Free Press, 1964).
32. See Daniel Bell, *The End of Ideology* (New York: Collier Books, 1961 edition). Cf. *From Max Weber*, 'Politics as a Vocation'.
33. Cf. Joseph Schumpeter, *Capitalism, Socialism and Democracy*

(London: Allen & Unwin, 4th edition, 1952, Part IV and R. T. McKenzie, *British Political Parties* (London: Heinemann, 2nd edition, 1963) Ch. 11.

34. Cf. A. H. Birch, 'Citizen Participation in England and Wales', *International Social Science Journal*, XLL:1 (1960).
35. See Richard Rose, *Politics in England*, Tables IV.1, IV.2, and G. A. Almond and S. Verba, *op. cit.*
36. On criteria for recruiting politicians, see Richard Rose, editor, *Policy-Making in Britain* (London: Macmillan, 1969) Ch. 1, and sources listed in the bibliography there.
37. See *Report on Registration and Voting Participation*, p. 48.
38. Cf. Dean E. Mann with Jameson Doig, *The Assistant Secretaries* (Washington, D.C.: Brookings Institution, 1965) and Richard Rose, 'The Variability of Party Government'. *Political Studies* XVII:4 (1969).
39. See Richard E. Neustadt, 'White House and Whitehall', *The Public Interest* II (1966), pp. 55–69.
40. See *The Civil Service: Vol. 1 Report of the Fulton Committee 1966–68* (London: H.M.S.O. Cmnd. 3638, 1968) paragraph 76.
41. The description of this Greek philosophical term as a colloquialism by the *Oxford English Dictionary* may tell us more about the perspective of the dictionary's compilers than about the extent to which the word is widely used.
42. Cf. Pamela Brookes, *Women at Westminster* (London: Peter Davies, 1967), Lester Milbrath, *op. cit.* index references under Sex, and, for origins of sex differences, Fred I. Greenstein, *Children and Politics*, Ch. 6.
43. See e.g., Donald Matthews, *The Social Background of Political Decision-Makers* (New York: Random House, 1954); Andrew Hacker, 'The Elected and the Anointed', *American Political Science Review* LV:3 (1961) and W. L. Guttsman, *The British Political Elite* (London MacGibbon and Kee, 1963).
44. Quoted in *The Sunday Times*, May 1964.
45. See T. J. H. Bishop and Rupert Wilkinson, *op. cit.*
46. See Wilson's interview with Brian Blake, 'The Family Background of Harold Wilson', in Richard Rose, editor, *Studies in British Politics*.
47. On political families in America, see Stephen Hess, *America's Political Dynasties* (New York: Doubleday, 1966).
48. For a study of Churchill's distant relationship with his father and dependence upon his nanny and later substitutes, see R. W. Thompson, *The Yankee Marlborough* (London: Allen & Unwin, 1963). Cf. Victor Wolfenstein, 'Some Psychological Aspects of Crisis

Leaders', in Louis Edinger, editor *Political Leadership in Industrialized Societies* (New York: Wiley, 1967) pp. 167ff.

49. On the general problem of personality studies of leaders, see a special issue of the *Journal of Social Issues* XXIV:3 (1968). 'Personality and Politics: Theoretical and Methodological Issues', edited by Fred I. Greenstein, and Lewis Edinger, editor, *Political Leadership in Industrialized Societies.*
50. See *Chips: the Diaries of Sir Henry Channon*, edited by Robert Rhodes James (London: Weidenfeld and Nicolson, 1967).
51. Cf. the published versions of official inquiries into civil service recruitment in *The Civil Service* Vol. 3 (2) *Surveys and Investigations* (London: H.M.S.O.) 1968. For American data, cf. Franklin Kilpatrick, Milton Cummings and M. Kent Jennings, *The Image of the Federal Service* (Washington: Brookings Institution, 1964).
52. The title of the second part of the autobiography of Louis Brownlow, adviser to Presidents for three decades (Chicago: University Press, 1955–58).
53. *Op. cit.*, Ch. 8.
54. See particularly, Richard A. Chapman, 'Profile of a Profession', p. 10, in *The Civil Service*, Vol. 3 (2).
55. See e.g. S. J. Eldersveld, *Political Parties: a Behavioral Analysis* (Chicago: Rand, McNally, 1964) Ch. 11, John Bochel, *Activists in the Conservative and Labour Parties* (University of Manchester M.A. thesis, 1965), and Hugh Heclo, 'The Councillor's Job', *Public Administration* XLVII:2 (1969) p. 189.
56. (New York; W. W. Norton, 1948).
57. Cf. Arnold Rogow, *James Forrestal: a Study of Personality* (New York: Macmillan, 1963) and a review of it by Gene M. Lyons, *American Political Science Review* LVIII:3 (1964) pp. 711–12.
58. *The Structure of Politics at the Accession of George III*: (London: Macmillan, 1961 edition) Ch. 1. Cf. J. H. Plumb, *The Growth of Political Stability in England, 1675–1725* (London: Macmillan, 1967) pp. 188–89.

Four

Politicians' Roles

Tidiness is not the least of human virtues; anyone who has ever had to stumble through a badly organized book—as reader, editor or author—appreciates this point. Yet it can be a vice if the messy nature of political reality is tidied up to fit conceptual schema that have a place for everything, even if the wrong one. Tidiness is also a vice when the world is presented in simple dichotomies: a man must be either a political leader *or* a political follower, his motives must be explicable either in sociological terms such as class *or* in terms of vague psychological traits, and his actions must be evaluated as either wholly good *or* wholly bad. Some very liberally minded people can be surprisingly firm in maintaining the black-and-white segregation of ideas with all the fervour of a Southern legislature upholding an anti-miscegenation statute. Even so labile a thinker as Richard Crossman can see Bagehot's study of *The English Constitution* as simply a treatise on political institutions, ignoring that half of the argument that concerns the psychology of Englishmen.[1]

As usual, social scientists complicate problems, if only as an intermediate stage to new forms of abstraction and simplification. The attempt to see politicians in terms of both sociological and psychological concepts sometimes leaves the seams rough. Nonetheless, it promises to be twice as sophisticated as viewing politicians from only one perspective. (If political insights can be added, the view is even better.) Social psychology affords a binocular approach to politics, for it concerns the relations between individuals and social groups and institutions.[2] Although the subject is only infrequently professed by this name in Britain, it should have an intuitive appeal to educated young Englishmen, since so much of their education involves the incidental learning of ways to shape their behaviour in order to meet the expectations of those around them, whether hierarchical superiors in schools or inferiors of some sort. It fits American society well in principle, for it is the source of the concepts with which one can analyse such phenomena as *The Organization Man*.

The idea of 'roles' is one of the most useful concepts that students of politics can borrow from social psychology. Its academic definition is not very different from that of everyday language; a role is a socially recognized and expected form of behaviour in specified types of recurring relations between individuals. Political roles are therefore ideas about what people expect to do in different kinds of political situations, and what others expect of them.[3]

The concept is specially useful in providing a meaningful answer to that deceptively simple question: Who are the politicians? In Shakespeare's time, when language was perhaps used better than today, a politician was defined, according to the *Oxford English Dictionary*, as anyone 'practically engaged in conducting the business of the state'. Since the term had pejorative connotations even then, it is hardly surprising that practical men wished to disown the label, and appear in disguise as statesmen or civil servants, in order to practice more effectively the politician's craft. It is, of course, a *non sequitur* to claim that because men are appointed on 'non-political' grounds or strive to serve the public good that the roles they take will *ipso facto* be non-political. In practice, if a person expects and is expected to take a significant role in helping resolve conflicts concerning alternative public policy choices, then he is a politician, regardless of the formal status of the office he holds, or even if he holds no office at all. Senior civil servants are acting as politicians when they are advising on policy, but not when they are doing routine tasks. Men in extra-ministerial government offices, such as directors of the British National Coal Board, or American judges and law enforcement officers, are politicians insofar as they expect and are able to influence policies, whether by public or private advocacy. Officials of pressure groups usually take the role of a politician even though their *ex officio* commitment is to an organization outside government. An individual need not have any formal position in order to take a politician's role. The characteristic unofficial adviser is a personal friend of a politician from days of his anonymity. Such men may be given some formal title, such as executive assistant, but their political role is best described as a trusted and privileged *confidante* of a President or Prime Minister.

A role is a set of expectations about behaviour; it is not the activity itself. The distinction between what people think they ought to do and what in fact people do do is always important in theory. In practice, the distinction is sometimes a trivial one. We would not, for example, be very surprised if someone told us that 90 per cent of people who said that voting was the most important duty of a citizen actually turned up at the polls a fortnight later to cast a ballot. Moreover, failure to act consistently with one's intentions and perceived obligations is likely to be a source of stress or frustration. For example, a legislator who sees his role as that of a strong party supporter is likely to be upset in a situation in which obligations to party are in conflict with his role as an interest group spokesman for war veterans or Sunday Observance laws. The positive correlation between behaviour and an individual's definition of his political role is specially useful in generalizing about politicians. Instead of counting what legislators do week after week and month after month, one can ask a legislator to generalize about the main roles he sees himself taking.[4] The weakness of this strategy is obvious: there are always cases in which the gap is so wide between what a man thinks he is doing, what he does, and the consequence of what he does that it could not be filled by a year's bound volumes of *Hansard* or the *Congressional Record*. For instance, a public relations man with the ostensible role of influencing voters may in fact be trying to keep a party leader happy by publicizing his client, and, in the event, lose both the election and the client.[5]

Political roles exist prior to a single political event. A politician does not sit down each morning and decide whether he intends to act as a statesman, an administrator, or a vote-getter that day. Clear and well defined expectations already exist about how a legislator, a

Cabinet official or a judge should act; and these expectations do not change quickly or easily. When situations arise in which individuals have to consider whether or not to follow prevailing role expectations, then there can be a crisis for an individual, for his party, or his country. President Kennedy's Cuban policy illustrates what happens when people find themselves in situations where they are uncertain of the role they are to play. In the first Cuban crisis, the President and his immediate advisers defined their roles in relation to other government officials badly; they were trusting and willing to delegate responsibilities. In the second crisis, in part learning from their first experience, the White House staff were clear about how they wished to act. They kept more decisions in their own hands and were more successful in the event.[6] Normally, roles are well defined and can be learned by incipient politicians through a straightforward process of socialization into offices. For instance, after every election, a new group of men enter Parliament or Congress. The new recruits form perhaps one-tenth of the membership of the House. They are expected to watch how their elders behave, and to learn what roles are appropriate for a Member of Parliament or of Congress. This process of role-socialization is emotionally intense and highly compressed in time; it is the chief means by which people fit and are fitted into place in established institutions. In extreme cases, such as the introduction of a left-wing advocate of direct action into the legislature, socialization may involve learning to abandon habits appropriate to the agitator's role, and adopting those suited to the mutual give-and-take of a large club. The writings and, even more, the behaviour of such men as Aneurin Bevan demonstrate how a person entering politics to change the system can end up being changed himself.

In any study of roles, the most important and difficult point to remember is that a role involves reciprocal sets of expectations. In studying an MP's role in Parliament, we must look at what his parliamentary colleagues expect of him, as well as what he himself expects to do. As long as the two views are in harmony, that is, each reciprocates the expectations of the other, then relationships between MPs are easy. For instance, a bright young MP who tries to act as an informed and constructive defender of the party leadership will be taking a part that is expected and positively valued by his party's leaders. An MP who acts as a critic of the leadership may be unpopular with the whips because of his chosen role, but at least his actions will be understood. There are recognized sanctions to use against him. In time, such a person may come to be recognized as a typically deviant MP or Congressman, a character like Sir Gerald Nabarro or Senator Wayne Morse.[7] What most confuses and irritates party leaders is a man who swings volatilely between the roles of loyal supporter and awkward critic. As Aneurin Bevan once cautioned Richard Crossman in his days as an egregious backbencher: 'There are two ways to get ahead in the Commons—grovel or kick men where it hurts. The trouble with you, Dick, is that you do both.' As confidence in predictability falls, uncertainty and danger increase. The cost of making wrong calculations can be very high, as the Profumo affair illustrates. When charges of indiscretions were first placed against John Profumo in early 1963, his ministerial colleagues expected that he would take the role of a loyal colleague and tell them truthfully whether the accusations were well grounded. Profumo, however, failed to reciprocate the expectation that he would act as an honourable friend should do.

With good reason, Parliament and Congress have been wary of defining explicitly what their members should do with their eminence. For instance, Erskine May's authoritative volume, *The Law, Privileges, Proceedings and Usage of Parliament*, devotes two chapters to what MPs may *not* do or be; it also sets out details about permissible modes of action. Yet nowhere does it set out in a substantive fashion what MPs are expected to do or are likely to end up doing in the Palace of Westminster. Similarly, the United States Constitution confers broad aggregate powers upon Congress in Article I. It is very vague about the specific duties of Congressmen, beyond choosing a presiding officer and providing a quorum to do business. There has, however, been no shortage of descriptive and prescriptive literature about the roles of MPs and Congressmen. Bagehot's classic 19th-century analysis of the functions of the House of Commons is a good example of this *genre*. The functions that Bagehot attributes to the Commons as a whole imply correlative roles for MPs—judge of ministerial character, voice of public opinion, and law-maker.[8] Descriptions of Congressional functions and roles also stress the importance of conciliating interest group conflicts in the legislature. While descriptions of legislative norms are usually offered in a scientific sense, the fact that they also have normative implications makes them relevent too in debates on the reform of Parliament and Congress.[9]

Starting a study with the politician's definition of his roles lets a man speak for himself. The alternative is to put into the mouths of politicians ideas drawn from very general theories, or from the abstractions of the Constitution. The development of survey research techniques now makes it possible for students of political behaviour to go to the horse's mouth, as it were, and question politicians directly about what they think they are doing. This technique has been developed to high intellectual levels in American legislative studies, but the fact that political scientists outnumber Congressmen by more than 20 to 1 means that the field may become overdeveloped. For instance, I have myself witnessed a Congressman having lunch on Capitol Hill with three academics watching him in the name of research. (The Congressman in question, John Brademas, Democrat of Indiana, is admittedly himself an Oxford Doctor of Philosophy.) Soon American politicians may be able to save busy researchers' time by giving them sets of IBM cards, punched with ready-made answers to all the questions that a Congressman thinks an academic might wish to ask or, at least, with answers for all the questions that a Congressman thinks worth answering. To avoid a saturated arena, some Americans have taken to coming to the British House of Commons, as if it were a legislature like Congress. Those who cannot finance the air fare can still send out postal questionnaires.

As soon as one contemplates asking an MP the question—what do you think you are doing?—one realizes that the range of possible answers is vast. Yet much of the literature on Parliament—both descriptive and prescriptive—is based on the assumption that MPs are (or ought to be) a group of men in agreement about their roles. The one published study of MPs' attitudes toward their job, a survey conducted by Rudolf Klein of *The Observer*, found that they were divided in their views of parliamentary life.[10] The most striking disagreement arose when they were asked what they thought of the increasing tendency of MPs to be full-time politicians. Two-thirds of Labour MPs said it was inevitable or desirable, but more than three-quarters of Conservative MPs thought this change of role regrettable, presumably because it interferes with their other roles, such as barrister or Master of Fox Hounds. My own experience of parliamentary birdwatching suggests that while the number of recognizable roles there is limited, the disparity between them is great. Law-making is a role of little importance to MPs, for the task of drafting complex legislation is left to specialist barristers outside the House, and major policy decisions concerning legislation are confined to a small number of Cabinet ministers. MPs can take explicitly political roles, such as front-bench statesman or aspirant; spokesman for constituency interests; spokesman for pressure group interests; ideologue; party loyalist; party intriguer; advocate of cross-party ideas, e.g. homosexual law reform, or eccentric ideas, e.g. a revolving toothbrush. Many recognizable roles consistent with membership in the Commons have little direct bearing upon politics: barrister or aspiring High Court judge; company director; free-lance journalist; servant of the House, e.g., chairman of the kitchen committee; House jester; social climber; gentleman of leisure; trade union pensioner, or parliamentary bore. Even the parliamentary bore has his uses, for when he gets up to speak in an important debate, Members present can slip out to attend to business elsewhere or take tea. Inasmuch as the House attracts all sorts and conditions of men, it is perhaps fortunate that it offers roles suited to a wide range of aptitudes. If the House is to work easily, then some members must pursue non-political roles, while others give primacy to political ones. As Balfour long ago noted, an MP may further political ends by his eloquence; he may do so even more effectively by his silence.[11] The quiet stolid backbencher who rarely speaks, except to seek reassurance that he is voting correctly, contributes more to the predictability and stability of the House than the backbencher who every week announces a new revelation.

The roles of Congressmen more often bear upon law-making and policy-making, because Congress is a more independent and important institution than Parliament. Among the twelve Congressional roles that Lewis Dexter has identified, five have a direct bearing upon policy: representing constituency interests, planning legislation, criticizing legislation, helping to pass or defeat bills, and investigating problems and existing legislation with the intent of proposing new legislation.[12] At another extreme, one of his recognizable roles is that of shaking hands with visitors, whether of voting age or school children, from his home Congressional district.

A large survey of members of the House of Representatives found that the majority of Congressmen saw themselves in two policy-making roles. Four-fifths said that one of their tasks was representing the views of that conveniently intangible entity, 'The People'. Two-thirds saw themselves as necessary cogs in a lengthy process of drafting, vetting and enacting laws. In addition, about one-third said their job included producing new policy ideas, and one-sixth stressed their role as a broker, arranging compromise policies between groups with conflicting political demands.[13] Congressmen who take deviant roles can be much more influential than MPs in a similar position. A deviant MP is usually excluded from office and ostracized on the backbenches, even if or especially if his personality is as formidable as that of David Lloyd George or Winston Churchill. By contrast, a Congressman, thanks to the importance of seniority, can become a chairman of a powerful committee, whether his deviance arises from political principles or acute alcoholism.

A social scientist can calmly sort individual politicians into separate compartments according to their role or roles; a politician himself may find it difficult to sort and reconcile the sets of roles he is expected to take during the week: Member of Parliament, businessman, partisan, old school friend, husband, parent and so forth. In Britain, a conflict is most likely to arise between an MP's party role and his identification with an interest group, such as a trade union or the British Legion, or with a cause, such as the United Nations or Israel. The informal conventions of party government, for better or worse, give the individual MP clear guidance as to which role should receive priority.[14] In America, constituency pressures are more often likely to be the cause of role-conflict, although their actual strength is easily misunderstood by Congressmen, because of difficulties in obtaining accurate information about constituents' wishes.[15] There is usually agreement about how any role conflict should be resolved; if voting the party line risks defeat in a re-election campaign, then a Congressman is expected to put his constituency role first.

Many conflicts arise from the clash of political and non-political roles. A study by Philip W. Buck of the motives leading 82 MPs to leave the House of Commons voluntarily found that one-third of the resignations were compelled by the need to choose between continuing a business career or a parliamentary career. Another quarter resigned for reasons of health. The relatively low rate of resignations suggests that most MPs find little conflict between belonging to the House and their private roles.[16] In the majority of cases, politicians reduce conflict by adjusting their private roles. For instance, I once heard a Labour MP advocating comprehensive secondary schools interrupted by a heckler asking how the MP educated his children. He explained to the heckler that he sent his children to fee-paying boarding schools because his role as an MP left him little time to fulfil his role as a father. In some cases politicians try to have the best of both worlds by compartmentalizing their lives. This may mean pursuing a business career in the morning and politics later in the day, or women in the daytime, and politics in the evening. Charles Parnell and Sir Charles Dilke had political careers ruined by conflicts between private amours and public roles; David Lloyd George, however, survived and even left his long-time companion a Countess.[17] In America, an extreme example of role conflict arose during Nelson Rockefeller's campaign for the Republican nomination for the presidency in 1964. In this role, he spent much energy and money. Yet in his role as a man who had been a partner in an unhappy marriage, he was attracted to the wife of a former friend and neighbour. In the resulting conflict, his private role became paramount. Rockefeller was quickly divorced, remarried and became a father—at the expense of his chances for the Republican nomination.[18]

Since role-conflicts have numerous sources and a high probability of occurring, we should not expect a politician to be constant in his political behaviour. A successful politician is one who can usually combine the claims of disparate roles. An unsuccessful one will vacillate when put in a situation where role-conflict is inevitable. The ability to learn new roles and shed old ones, thus effectively changing modes of behaviour if not goals, is a prime requisite for a highly ambitious politician.[19] In England, the state now provides university scholarships so that youths like Harold Wilson and Edward Heath can learn to adapt to a world that upper class children know from birth. (Oxford, once known as the home of lost causes, might better be considered the home of lost regional accents; Non-U voice habits are disposed of there as easily as bodies are despatched in a crematorium.) Once in Parliament, an individual must first of all learn the roles appropriate to a backbencher, including the role of aspirant to the front bench. Once in office, a novice minister must learn the role of defending the traditional 'line' of his department against attack, even when this means a departure from his previous role of partisan critic of the departmental point of view. In America, the pressure on a politician to adapt new social mannerisms is much less than in Britain. In Washington, wives appear to carry the social burdens more than their husbands, whose roles emphasize substance more than style. The limited movement from Congress to the executive side of government means that much less re-learning is required than in Westminster, where a man with 15 years' experience in Parliamentary debating may suddenly have to learn from scratch how to administer a large department. Only 6 per cent of leading federal executives have previously been Congressmen, and about four-fifths have had some executive experience in government prior to appointment to a major federal office.[20]

Although the concept of political role is non-institutional in definition, analysis of the roles of politicians inevitably leads to a consideration of the powers of public offices and the institutions in which offices are embedded. The chief offices of a government not only convey formal legal powers but also involve their incumbents in sets of relatively specific role expectations. (A politician out of office has no formal authority and there are fewer informal expectations about how he should act.) In office, a politician must learn what is and what isn't expected of a man in his position. This is less easy to do than predicting what happens when he pushes buzzers on his desk or opens files in his inner office. If an individual seeks to act differently from his predecessors, then he must face the fact that many with whom he works will still be operating in terms of pre-existing expectations of what he ought to do. Usually when there is a discrepancy between individual preferences and institutional role expectations, it is the individual that changes. An excellent example of easy adaptation is provided by the British civil service. A bright recruit to the administrative class is expected to spend his early years learning how government departments work. In the first few years everything is new to him and, as a novice, he may be excused actions not normally expected of a civil servant. After this lengthy training period, the recruit then has an established position as a principal, where his job is to fit his behaviour to the expectations of those around him. After 15 or 20 years in modelling actions to fit the role-expectations of superiors who, in turn, had modelled their actions after their now-deceased predecessors, an individual is qualified for a senior post, that is, he is well socialized into prevailing Whitehall role-expectations.

The fact that roles are usually 'institutionalized', i.e., anchored in offices attached to powerfully persisting institutions, means that any explicitly normative discussion about how individual politicians ought to act immediately becomes entangled in a discussion of the merits or defects of the structure of government. This is true both in Washington and in Westminster. Those who advocate that MPs ought to take an independent line critical of the executive are not so much attacking individual politicians for lack of courage, but rather attacking the idea that Parliament should be a place where men talk harmlessly about policies that are made and unmade elsewhere.[21] Reciprocally, advocates of the doctrine that an MP's chief role is to sustain a government in office are not necessarily arguing that MPs should be as docile as lambs; instead, they are extolling the doctrine of Cabinet authority at the expense of liberal theories of the independence of the legislature from the executive. Similarly, in Washington believers in the doctrine of the pure separation of powers glorify a Congressman's role insofar as it permits action independent of executive influence. The debate is between those who would wish to alter the facilities and powers of a Congressman's office so he can be a more effective opponent of the executive, and those who wish to alter the office so a Congressman is more responsible to party and Presidential leadership. The similarity of controversy in both places is no accident, for the participants draw ideas from a common tradition of political theory and make frequent use of transatlantic references as a convenient stick with which to beat their domestic opponents. R. A. Butler, a master of the shattering innuendo, even managed a tri-cultural invidious comparison by describing the establishment of specialist committees in Parliament as an incautious move toward government '*a l'américaine*'.[22]

Institutional inertia is a great force for political continuity from day to day and from one administration to another, and a great obstacle to innovation. A politician who wants to change the way in which a country is governed must do far more than change his own behaviour. He must get others to act differently too, and act in keeping with his overall design. Typically, innovations in government involve proposals for institutional change. Such proposals face formidable difficulties: the problem diagnosed may even be insoluble, or at least impervious to institutional engineering. This seems to be the case of the management of the British economy, which for 50 years has had its ups and downs in spite of many different strategies used in managing it, ranging from centralized planning to a calculated policy of dismantling institutional machinery in favour of market mechanisms. In some cases reforms have been smothered as they are grabbed at by defenders of the *status quo*, embracing new ideas as a drowning man grips his would-be rescuer. This tactic has been very noticeable in discussions of the reform of the Treasury.[23] The usual panacea of the reformers is to create a new institution. The intention is logical, for it is easier to instil new patterns of action in a new organization than to change behaviour among people who have been socialized into roles in a well established agency, such as the Treasury or the Federal Bureau of Investigation. Yet setting up a new department involves its sponsors in a dilemma. If it is to be truly new, then it will take years to develop, and involve its sponsors in many running in difficulties. The initial difficulties of the American Office of Economic Opportunity in its efforts to innovate in welfare administration threatened the survival of the fledgling agency. Alternatively, a so-called new department can be built around the core of a large number of existing governmental bureaux. In the extreme case of the creation of the Department of Employment and Productivity in place of the old Ministry of Labour, one of the chief immediate changes was in the name plates outside its many offices.

Institutional inertia is most readily overcome in times of crisis. In America, the Depression and the leadership of President Franklin D. Roosevelt provided the impetus to alter radically the structure, the functions and the attitudes of the American federal executive. The process was hardly tidy, but under pressure of 15,000,000 unemployed, it was achieved. In Britain, the chief institutional innovations have occurred in war-time. During the First World War, for example, the government violated *laissez faire* norms on a scale previously unknown. Even the management of the Cabinet was put on a businesslike basis, with the creation of a small office of men to keep written accounts of what the Cabinet had decided.

In the Second World War, a civil service and government that had refused to expand its functions greatly in the face of depression suddenly became responsible for everything from the distribution of orange juice to children to the development of radar for home defence.[24]

While political institutions tend to be stable, the existence of persisting conflicts between institutions subjects individuals in high political office to strong cross-pressures. By the same token, it assures them some room for manœuvre and individual discretion in making policy decisions. For example, the institutionalized conflict between the Treasury and spending departments such as health and education, are constant, but the resolution of disputes is not fixed. Changes in the climate of the world economy can create situations in which spending departments must economize rigorously, just as changes in the domestic political situation, such as the advent of an election, create a climate in which spending departments can claim more money for popular benefits. In disputes which do not involve money, such as claims for priority in presenting legislation to the Commons or Congress, the resolution of conflicting claims is likely to have much to do with the stature of the individual heading a department. Insofar as a minister's personal success is judged by the number of victories he wins in inter-departmental battles, then the role of 'successful' minister is in conflict with his role as a Cabinet minister, looking at policies in terms of party principles and the inter-relationship of parts to a relatively co-ordinated whole. In the United States, there is less conflict between particularistic roles and broad commitments, because the sense of a single administrative programme is so weak. Even a president is inclined to think of his aims in terms of piecemeal achievements, rather than in terms of a co-ordinated set of policies. The loyalty shown to the goals of particular agencies, such as the Corps of Engineers or the Air Force, makes it possible for their officials to reduce institutionalized conflict between the executive and Congress by forming alliances with Congressmen. Men from both branches of government then take the role of advocates of particular programmes and interests.[25]

The endemic nature of conflict places a special premium upon the man who can play the role of a political broker, resolving conflicts between individuals and institutions. Brokers exist at many levels in politics, from that of the politician concerned with mediating between neighbours who quarrel on a small local council, to that of a man trying to maintain majority support for policies in Congress or Westminster. The theory of British government nominally denies the importance of brokerage roles. Government policy is determined by a consensus of Cabinet ministers, who are then collectively responsible. In newer and more glamorous versions of the Constitution, policy is unilaterally determined by a Prime Minister. Within a department, policy is meant to be laid down by the minister acting upon information and advice funnelled through a pyramid of officials, with the Permanent Under-Secretary particularly important in reducing conflicts in advice before problems reach him for decision. In practice, decisions of a Cabinet will not be endorsed equally by every member nominally responsible. One of the roles of a Prime Minister is to conciliate Cabinet ministers in disagreement, and to make sure that they continue to accept him as the Prime Minister. In the United States, the formal theory is the reverse: policy is meant to emerge out of a competition of conflicting demands from interest groups, from parties, from Congress and from the executive.[26] Of necessity, only a small number of politicians can take the role of broker at any one time, because there must be more people in conflict than there are reconcilers of conflict. These brokers are more than mere mechanical calculators of points of agreement between different men. In the process of defining a policy that might obtain the largest degree of acceptance from the largest numbers involved, they have considerable leeway in determining what is accepted. Their work is most important when the grounds of compromise or consensus are far from obvious.

The term 'broker' is not common in the vocabulary of English politics, and several of the usages listed for it in the *Oxford English Dictionary* are clearly derogatory. In England, politicians are expected to be leaders, not go-betweens. Leadership is usually described as if it were an intrinsic or even inherited trait, like blue eyes or a dimple. On this basis, British institutions build subtle—one might almost say, ineffable—criteria for divining leaders. With an un-English dash of Calvinism, children predestined to rule are sent to expensive boarding schools from the age of eight, to confirm inborn character.[27] Reciprocally, other institutions are created to foster attitudes appropriate to followers, or lieutenants and sergeants in the ranks. Aptitude for political leadership may be shown in seemingly esoteric ways, such as skill in Latin prose translation, in cricket or in sherry party conversation. Skill at these things has brought men to Downing Street in recent years, though latterly, ability to manipulate the cant words of economic theory has been more relevant than familiarity with the symbols of a humanistic culture.

The weakness of the trait definition of leadership is that it treats a characteristic of relations between people as something that can be identified by looking at only one side of a relationship. It fails to face such simple questions as: Who follows this man? Why do they follow him? Under what circumstances does he get other people to act or think as they would not otherwise do? Under what circumstances does he fail to change them? Does he simply 'lead' them where they are determined to go anyway? Such questions follow naturally from a social psychological approach. The crucial point of this approach is that leadership must be studied as a reciprocal set of relationships between so-called leaders and so-called followers. Empirical investigation usually reveals that leaders are often constrained by the expectations of their followers, and in some cases compelled to follow their followers or risk deposition as leader. The definition of what is expected of a leader is thus, in a literal sense, a delimitation of his influence.[28]

The primary source of a leader's authority is his office and not his personality. This is truer of Presidents and Prime Ministers than of any other group. The career of Lyndon Johnson illustrates the point dramatically. As Senate majority leader, he held an important office and exercised great influence in Congress. As Vice President, he was the presiding officer of the Senate, but, deprived of his former office, he could no longer exercise his influence there. As President, he again became a highly significant person with his influence there varying greatly. During this decade, Lyndon Johnson remained the same personality with the same philosophy of government, while his influence fluctuated wildly with his office.

To note the importance of office is not to argue that the office gives equal influence to each occupant. Men may define their roles in varying ways, and situational changes also affect what they can do. The important point is that as President or Prime Minister a man has substantial *ex officio* resources for influence. There is the expectation that he will use at least some of them. Woodrow Wilson commented that a President may try to be 'as big a man as he can'. Richard Neustadt adds, 'Nowadays he cannot be as small as he might like'.[29] Even Dwight D. Eisenhower, notwithstanding a conviction that the President's influence should be diminished, took major policy decisions in foreign affairs, defence, and in race relations, sending federal troops to Little Rock in 1957.

While office confers advantages upon leaders, it also imposes constraints in the form of relatively specific expectations of followers. A leader is not expected to lead just anywhere. A contemporary Prime Minister is expected to maintain the loyalty of his followers by meeting their expectations for continued electoral success, and to achieve already established policy aims. His obligations to Cabinet colleagues, backbench MPs, leaders in foreign nations, party supporters in the country, and the mass electorate will, from time to time, be in conflict.[30] An American President inherits an even more complex set of role expectations. He is expected to take the role of ceremonial head of state, party leader, chief diplomat, chief executive, and also be a propagandist for controversial policies.[31] The fact that there are many roles involved in the most important political offices gives a politician the discretion of deciding which to emphasize and which to ignore. He can, at the least, choose what he ignores. In seeking to keep his friends happy, much will depend upon the extent to which their expectations are loosely or precisely defined. A candidate returned to office in the expectation that a highly specific pledge will be carried out, e.g., steel nationalization, can ignore this pledge only at the risk of alienating followers. By contrast, a politician returned to office with a vague slogan, such as 'getting the country moving', can offer many symbolic or substantial achievements in the hope that at least some will meet the expectations of his followers.

Concentrating attention upon the small world of leader-follower relationships often obscures the importance of the environment constraining both. It is remarkable that so much press attention could be given to the reputed importance of Harold Wilson when his Premiership has served to demonstrate how much any British Prime Minister is at the mercy of economic forces outside the country. In the United States, Presidents can only achieve foreign policy goals if leaders of other nations take the role that the President wishes them to take in response to his initiative. For example, the Test Ban treaty negotiated by President Kennedy's staff was possible only on the condition that the agreement suited the expectations of other sovereign powers too. No constraint remains unchanging in its political significance. In 1940, the existence of the English Channel was a necessary condition of Churchill leading a government *not* in exile. In 1962, the decision of Mr Macmillan's government to seek entry to the European Common Market involved recognition that this geographical feature, so recently defined as an asset, was now a barrier to close involvement in Continental affairs. Short-term situational factors, representing transitory political phenomena or the concatenation of a series of events, create special and sometimes unpredictable opportunities for leadership. For instance, a new President or Prime Minister can expect greater support than a leader about to retire from office because of electoral defeat or internal party dissension. The assassination of Dr Martin Luther King created a situation in which civil rights legislation previously stalled in Congress suddenly became acceptable to a majority of Congressmen. In Britain, the November 1967 run on sterling created a situation in which Ministers who had previously insisted that devaluation of the pound was unthinkable now suddenly agreed that it was inevitable and immediately desirable. It would be going too far to say that crisis situations give a Prime Minister or President *carte blanche*. The maxim that any fool can govern in a crisis sometimes fails when tested. Crisis situations only create opportunities in which the latitude for action by a Prime Minister or President is enhanced.[32]

Given such complications, how is leadership to be judged? Office-holding is only proof of the ability to survive. It is not *ipso facto* proof of influence, since men who are pliable may survive stress best. Unfortunately, even so notable a scholar as R. T. McKenzie confuses office-holding and power.[33] Talking tough is no proof of leadership, for it begs the question: Who listens? Who acts? The only persons sure to follow such words are journalists. Just because a politician can impress his press corps, it does not follow that he can convince, say, his Treasury officials. Another alternative is observation of a politician's stated goals and comparison of his intentions with political outcomes. If one finds that a politician gets what he asks for, this *may* be proof of influence. The opposite inference is also possible: a politician may calibrate his requests so that they match what he thinks will happen anyway. In Britain, the existence of disciplined parliamentary parties means that a Prime Minister always enjoys the appearance, if not the reality of authority. By comparison, in the United States the autonomy of Congress means that the President usually receives less Congressional support than he asks for. Thus, it is possible to draw some inference about leadership from the proportion of Presidential requests approved by Congress, although they include a fair number of measures that will pass with little difficulty. In a provocative study of British and American foreign policy-making, Kenneth Waltz has argued that the very certainty of Parliamentary support makes a Prime Minister less ready to use influence in order to sustain morale among his followers; reciprocally, the uncertainty of support for presidential measures is a stimulus to a President to strive harder to influence others. The British cases that Waltz uses to illustrate his thesis, e.g., the protracted and confused negotiations about entering the Common Market and the recurring changes in British defence policy, show that there is something in this view.[34]

The most straightforward way to begin the evaluation of a political leader is to look at how he defines his own role. It is often forgotten that many men in high office define their role with great modesty. Some do so because they rightly sense the limits of their own abilities. For instance, Sir Alec Douglas-Home wisely ignored economic policy while Prime Minister; his slight knowledge of this important but intricate field left him much to be modest about. Others limit involvement on grounds of principle: Dwight D. Eisenhower was the most notable exponent of the philosophy that the less politicians do, the better a country is governed. The popular image of a Prime Minister or President nowadays is of a man who tries to get things done. This fits Harold Wilson, John F. Kennedy and Harry Truman. Their intention to influence events was, however, only indifferently matched by their achievements. For instance, in foreign affairs, Truman achieved more than he could have anticipated upon taking office, but in domestic policy, much less. Truman's successes and his failures reflected situational influences making Congressmen receptive to his diplomatic proposals, but not to his domestic policies. Even Mr Wilson's enemies cannot deny the fact that the circumstances confronting him were formidable. In Britain, sensitivity to situational factors was specially notable in

Harold Macmillan, who, like many of his Conservative predecessors, was ready to do as much or as little as he deemed possible. The extent to which a political leader in office lives up to his own expectations and those of others might be termed a test of competence. It is not a test of strength, for a man with a sense of his own limitations can be competent by limiting his influence.

In their haste to develop general categories of analysis, social scientists have been pitifully weak in developing measures of the extent to which different individuals in the same office vary in their competence. In fact, politicians like professors vary from the extremely impressive through the mediocre to those who are extremely depressing. Perhaps the best test of a politician's greatness is his ability to create new roles for an established office, or even, to create a new office. Situations such as a war or a major depression often help provide the opportunity for greatness, but it does not follow that great action will follow. For instance, the depression in America in the 1930s gave Herbert Hoover a great chance to innovate. Unfortunately, he defined the President's role in very narrow terms, and persisted in a refusal to act, just as Asquith, in the First World War in Britain, was hesitant to adapt the instruments of government to unprecedented problems. Franklin D. Roosevelt rejected Hoover's conception of the President's role, and established the expectation that any President could and should influence the economy and promote public welfare. Toward the end of his second term in office, the outbreak of war in Europe presented a second challenge to the traditional expectations of an American President's role. By devious means as well as by public pronouncements, Roosevelt responded in such a way that American Presidents since then have been expected to take a global role. A third innovation of Roosevelt influenced the character of the federal bureaucracy. He committed the federal government to action programmes and so greatly expanded the numbers of government employees that even years after his death, federal civil servants were inclined to think in terms of positive and expansive actions, rather than about saving candle ends, a goal exalted in Britain. It is doubtful whether any twentieth-century British Prime Minister has made so many changes in the office in Downing Street. Probably the greatest number were associated with Lloyd George's premiership. Notwithstanding long periods in office, Winston Churchill is better remembered for the way in which he performed and preserved traditional roles than for leaving greatly expanded powers to his successors.[35]

The ability of a leader to create new roles is one attribute of charismatic leadership. Unfortunately, this concept of Max Weber is now used so loosely that its original significance has been lost. Weber defined the term with explicit reference to the inter-action of leaders and led. Charismatic leadership is the capacity to evoke from others actions based upon the leader's presumed endowment with 'supernatural, superhuman or at least specifically exceptional powers or qualities'. Because of this, leaders with charismatic appeal can upset established political institutions. The appeal, Weber emphasizes, is intrinsic to situations, and not to an individual personality. The maintenance of a charismatic appeal requires the persistence of exceptional circumstances as well as exceptional skill. Weber's view echoes the lament of many politicians: 'If he is for long unsuccessful, above all, if his leadership fails to benefit his followers, it is likely that his charismatic authority will disappear.'[36] To paraphrase *Pal Joey*'s description of a banker as a man who is honest until he is caught, a charismatic leader is a politician who is all-powerful—until he is thrown out of office. The fate of so allegedly powerful a leader as Kwame Nkrumah illustrates the limits of personal power. The concept of charismatic leadership is much more appropriate to the Afro-Asian world than it is to Britain or America, for newly constituted governments are more easily upset or altered than are long established political institutions.[37] The ordinary Anglo-American politician, simply seeking office within an existing form of government, can be described as charismatic only by the most verbally intoxicated of publicists.

This is not to deny that great men may exist in politics, but rather to note that so-called great men are not all-powerful. After all such 'natural' leaders as Charles de Gaulle and Winston Churchill have had to sustain their sense of greatness through decades in the political wilderness. (Many have gone in the wilderness before and after them, claiming greatness where others could see only megalomania, or conceit.) Both Churchill and de Gaulle finally rose to high office in extreme situations arising from military defeat. Shortly after winning military victories, both men were repudiated by their electorates at the polls. Without office, awaiting the recurrence of an extreme situation of danger, these men remained notable personalities, but politically they were Samsons shorn of their locks.

The analysis of politicians in terms of roles and offices has something in common with the study of politics in terms of elites. It also, however, has important differences.[38] Both approaches concentrate upon a small and prominent number of people in society. Both reject the assumption that elective public officials are necessarily the only people who act as politicians. Moreover, there is accord that an individual's extra-governmental position may enable him to take a political role. The differences are sufficiently large that I think it desirable to avoid use of the term elite in *political* studies. At bottom, elite analysis cannot provide evidence about who is involved in political decisions or why they are involved because it is a deductive and static form of analysis. Certain *social* characteristics are treated axiomatically, as attributes of politically important people. Ergo, anyone with such characteristics must be politically influential. Yet, as we have seen, only a minority of people with any particular social characteristics actually enter political life. Insofar as the term is given a political definition—the political elite are the 'most important' people in politics—it is redundant or tautological. This definition cannot provide a starting point for research; it is a conclusion.[39]

The danger of attempting to infer current political behaviour from information about the social characteristics of politicians is emphasized in a careful study by Lewis Edinger and Donald Searing of politicians in France and Germany. They were testing hypotheses about the relationships of elite social characterististics to political attitudes, a connection which ought on *a priori* grounds, to be even stronger than connections with actions in office, since fewer constraints exist for attitudes. Using extensive interviews as well as biographical profiles of politicians, they found that social characteristics such as early education, proved of little value in predicting attitudes. The best predictors of attitudes were data drawn from recent adult experience, including political party involvement.[40] There is good reason to believe that current political roles are even more important than social background in influencing behaviour in Britain. Differences in attitudes have been much greater among politicians in Britain than have differences in social backgrounds. In America, a study of legislators found that even differences in means of entering politics had little effect upon current political roles.[41]

Whereas elite analysis tends to reduce the circle of politicians to a relatively few Etonians or Harvard men, role analysis tends to expand the universe. Many people who are not full-time politicians intermittently take political roles, whether in business, education or as shop stewards in plants where strikes affect the national economy. As public policy continues to influence wider and wider areas of life, many activities once considered outside the ambit of politics acquire political implications. In England, the importance government policy-makers have given to increasing industrial production politicizes the activities of manual workers. A man taking an extra 10 minutes on his tea break or working harder to meet an export order is now in a political role. In America, the pervasive importance of race relations has suddenly made significant political actors out of Negroes who had previously been regarded as among the most downtrodden members of a community. The poorest he that is in Harlem or the poorest field hand that is in Mississippi can find himself in a political role by taking to the streets or highways in protest. I remember a decade ago meeting Mrs Rosa Parks, the Negro seamstress who started it all in Montgomery, Alabama, in December 1955, by refusing to move to the back of a Jim Crow bus because she had had enough of segregation, and both her feet and her heart were sore.[42] The striking thing about Mrs Parks was not any resemblance to Martin Luther King, to Malcolm X, or to any other leaders of her race, or a resemblance to Eleanor Roosevelt, to Barbara Castle, or to any other political leader of her sex. The most striking single thing about this spark of a great movement is that she looked exactly like millions of other people.

NOTES—CHAPTER IV

1. Cf. his preface to the introduction of the Fontana edition of the book (London: 1963) and my review, 'Bagehot Today and Tomorrow', *New Society*, May 2, 1963.
2. For a useful introduction, see W. J. H. Sprott, *Human Groups* (Harmondsworth: Pelican, 1958) and Sidney Verba, *Small Groups and Political Behavior* (Princeton: University Press, 1961).
3. The best short discussion of role analysis in politics is in Heinz Eulau,

The Behavioral Persuasion in Politics (New York: Random House, 1963) Ch. 2.

4. The leading study using this technique is John Wahlke, Heinz Eulau, William Buchanan and LeRoy Ferguson, *The Legislative System* (New York: Wiley, 1962).
5. Cf. Richard Rose, *Influencing Voters*, especially Ch. 9.
6. See e.g., Arthur Schlesinger, *A Thousand Days* (London: Deutsch, 1965) Ch. 10 and 30, and Robert F. Kennedy *13 Days: The Cuban Missile Crisis* (London: Macmillan, 1969).
7. Cf. Ralph Huitt, 'The Outsider in the Senate—An Alternative Role', *American Political Science Review* LV:3 (1961).
8. *Op. cit.*, Ch. 4.
9. For ideas about reform, see e.g., *Parliamentary Reform* (London: Cassell, 1967); Bernard Crick, *The Reform of Parliament* (London: Weidenfeld & Nicolson, 1964), Roger Davidson, D. Kovenock and M. O'Leary, *Congress in Crisis: Politics and Congressional Reform* (New York: Wadsworth, 1966) and, by contrast, Charles L. Clapp, *The Congressman: His Work as He Sees It* (Washington: Brookings Institution, 1963).
10. See Rudolf Klein, 'What MPs think of their Jobs', reprinted as Appendix B of Bernard Crick, *op. cit.*
11. Earl Balfour, *Chapters of Autobiography* (London: Cassell, 1930) p. 134.
12. See his contribution to R. A. Bauer, Ithiel Pool and L. A. Dexter, *American Business and Public Policy* (New York: Atherton, 1963) pp. 406–432.
13. See Roger Davidson *et al.*, *op. cit.*, pp. 74–75. See also the various role analyses contained in Robert L. Peabody and Nelson Polsby, editors, *New Perspectives on the House of Representatives* (Chicago: Rand, McNally, 1963).
14. See e.g., John Millett, 'The Role of an Interest Group Leader in the House of Commons', *Western Political Quarterly* IX:4 (1956), Leon Epstein, *British Politics and the Suez Crisis* (London: Pall Mall, 1964), Jorgen Rasmussen, *The Relations of the Profumo Rebels with their Local Parties* (Tucson: University of Arizona Press, 1966), and Nigel Nicolson, *People and Parliament* (London: Weidenfeld & Nicolson, 1958).
15. See particularly, Warren E. Miller and Donald Stokes, *op. cit.* and L. A. Dexter, 'The Representative and his District', in R. Peabody and N. Polsby, editors, *op. cit.*
16. See *Amateurs and Professionals in British Politics, 1918–59* (Chicago: University Press, 1963) Ch. 7.

17. Cf. Frances, Countess Lloyd George, *The Years that Are Past* (London: Hutchinson, 1967). In Lloyd George's case, his private affairs did no more than reinforce the animus of opponents who were already attacking him for alleged political sharp dealing.
18. While the impact of his private affairs on voters was possibly limited, as Rockefeller lost the crucial California primary by a margin of only 70,000 votes in more than 2,000,000 even a small defection was enough to be fatal. Cf. Theodore White, *The Making of the President – 1964* (New York: Atheneum, 1965) Chs. 3–4.
19. See Richard Rose, 'The Emergence of Leaders', *New Society*, October 17, 1963.
20. See David T. Stanley, Dean E. Mann and Jameson Doig, *Men Who Govern* (Washington: Brookings Institution, 1967) pp. 137, 145.
21. See A. H. Birch, *Representative and Responsible Government* (London: Allen & Unwin, 1964) Ch. 13.
22. Quoted in Bernard Crick, *op. cit.*, p. 168.
23. For a sympathetic account of attempts at institutional reform, see Hans Daalder, *Cabinet Reform in Britain, 1914–1963* (London: Oxford University Press, 1964). For an unsympathetic account, see Brian Chapman, *British Government Observed* (London: Allen & Unwin, 1963). For a systematic description of changes, see F. M. G. Willson, *The Organization of British Central Government, 1914–1964* (London: Allen & Unwin, 1968).
24. See E. M. H. Lloyd, *Experiments in State Control* (Oxford: Clarendon Press, 1924) and R. M. Titmuss, *Problems of Social Policy* (London: H.M.S.O. and Longmans, 1950).
25. See e.g., Richard F. Fenno Jr., *The Power of the Purse* (Boston: Little, Brown, 1966) Chs. 6, 7 and 11.
26. David B. Truman, *The Governmental Process* (New York: Knopf, 1951).
27. See e.g., Rupert Wilkinson, *op. cit.*
28. For a general discussion see Sidney Verba, *Small Groups and Political Behavior*, and for illustrations, Eleanor Maccoby, Theodore Newcomb and Eugene Hartley, editors, *Readings in Social Psychology* (New York: Holt, Rinehart, 3rd edition, 1958) Chs. 5 and 11.
29. *Presidential Power*, p. 5.
30. See Richard Rose, 'Complexities of Party Leadership', *Parliamentary Affairs* XVI:3 (1963).
31. See Clinton Rossiter, *The American Presidency* (London: Hamish Hamilton, 1957).
32. Thus, any attempt to generalize from crisis powers to non-crisis powers, as C. Wright Mills does in his *The Power Elite* (New York: Oxford University Press, 1956) is ill founded.

33. See the critique of McKenzie in Richard Rose, 'Complexities of Party Leadership', pp. 259ff.
34. *Foreign Policy and Democratic Politics* (Boston: Little, Brown, 1967) Chs. 5–7, 9.
35. For a discussion of the comparative constriction of the growth of the Prime Ministership, see Richard Neustadt, in conversation with Henry Brandon, '10 Downing Street, Is it Out of Date?' *Sunday Times*, November 8, 1964.
36. Max Weber, *The Theory of Social and Economic Organization* (Glencoe, Illinois: Free Press, 1947) pp. 358, 360.
37. Cf. David E. Apter's early study of Nkrumah, re-issued as *Ghana in Transition* (New York: Atheneum, 1963), and Aristide Zolberg, *Creating Political Order* (Chicago: Rand McNally, 1966).
38. For standard discussions, see e.g., C. Wright Mills, *op. cit.*, Daniel Bell, *op. cit.*, William Kornhauser, ' "Power Elite" or Veto Groups?', in S. M. Lipset and Leo Lowenthal, editors, *op. cit.*, and Nelson Polsby, *Community Power and Political Theory* (New Haven: Yale, 1963).
39. My own view is that analysis of the social origins of politicians tells us more about the expressive value of those who support them than about the actions taken by those in receipt of such support. See 'Class and Party Divisions: Britain as a Test Case'.
40. Lewis Edinger and Donald Searing, *op. cit.*
41. See Kenneth Prewitt, Heinz Eulau and Betty Zisk, *op. cit.*
42. For Dr Martin Luther King's description of Mrs Parks, see *Stride Toward Freedom* (New York: Ballantine, 1958) pp. 34ff.

Five

The Imperfect Market for Information

The most effective form of political communication is that which requires the least amount of talk, but the greatest amount of understanding. When members of a group understand each other's roles clearly, then little talk is necessary. Because they have to tell them little, Presidents and Prime Ministers find it useful as well as congenial to be surrounded by people they have worked with for years. For example, President Kennedy did not need to brief his brother Bobby all the time about the President's views, for they were formed by experiences often shared together. Similarly, a good senior civil servant in Whitehall, working for a Cabinet Minister with clearly defined policy preference, does not need to talk to his superior about every matter that comes up. He can anticipate what the minister would say to him. When political roles and values are clearly defined much communication is implicit rather than explicit; it is part of the silent working of government.

If everyone knew what everyone else wanted and agreed about what they should get, then there would be no politics. Politics arises from the expression of conflicting opinions. They are communicated in many ways—through the press, in the pseudo-face-to-face relationship of television, by pamphlets and books, and by word of mouth, whether proclaimed publicly and proudly or privately, with a mixture of prudence and guilt. Unfortunately, the currency of political communication is much less tangible than the currency of commerce, whether that be gold, shiny beads, or even worthless cheques. This is true if the subject of talk is a familiar object, like the national interest, for such a phrase is a symbol without specific meaning. It is also true if the subject of talk is something material, like the nation's standard of living, for this can be measured in ways greatly varying in reliability and validity. There is nothing remarkable in the fact that politicians talk to each other and to people who make demands upon government. The important point, as the title of the chapter emphasizes, is that in any society as large as Britain or America (and conceivably on small desert islands) political communication involves a degree of imperfection. We should not judge politicians by absolute standards, but by their relative knowledge or ignorance of that which is relevant to their work.

Because communication is basic in politics, its study is sometimes presented as if it were tantamount to the study of power itself. Faced with Lasswell's demand to describe politics in terms of 'who gets what, when, how',[1] one might, before answering the question rephrase it to describe politics as 'who talks to whom, when, about what?' This altered phrasing is not quite so pointed as the original, but it is relevant and it is far easier to answer by observation than questions about that curious chemical or alchemical substance, power. (Cf. Chapter VI.) In treating communication as necessary in the exercise of power, one must avoid assuming that because X talks to Y about something and Y later acts as X would wish, he does it because of X. After all, a jockey who rides a horse to victory is not *ipso facto* the cause of victory; it may be that the jockey was the handicap that the horse was carrying.

It may be that the distinction between communication and power is dissolving both in life and in the social sciences. In a very imaginative study entitled *The Nerves of Government*, Karl Deutsch has argued that we should look upon government 'somewhat less as a problem of power and somewhat more as a problem of steering'. He adds, 'Steering is decisively a matter of communication.' In Deutsch's analysis, the goals of politicians do not exist unchanging and independent of their environment. The public policies of government are continually subject to modification by feedback, 'the results of its own action (in the form of new information), by which it modifies its subsequent behaviour'.[2] Through the feedback of information, politicians can adjust the activities of government to obtain a good fit between public preferences, governmental intentions and what it is possible to achieve in an ever changing environment. The concept is drawn from the engineering sciences and, needless to say, works best there. It is easier to hit a moving target such as the moon with a space rocket than it is to hit a target such as a five per cent rate of economic growth. In the engineering sciences, all the major components of information are known or can be estimated with considerable exactness. In politics, the basic causal links between action and reaction are often unclear, and few things can be calculated with exactness. Chancellors of the Exchequer, seeking to combine full employment, steady prices, a favourable balance of payments and economic growth, must envy physicists and astronauts the easy course that they have to steer.

While there is nothing mechanical about political communication, outlining a simple model of communication helps clarify what it is that makes communication a pervasive but slippery concept. Communication involves a *sender* transmitting a *message* through one or more *channels* to an *audience* simultaneously subjected to many other *environmental* influences. The sender may be a prominent politician, seeking to address a nation, or a humble elector, posting a letter of complaint to his Congressman or Member of Parliament. The message may be a military ultimatum or it may be a seemingly small request that bureaucratic regulations be waived so that a welfare grant can be paid. The channels of communication include the private media—telephones, letters and conversations in shadowy corners of the corridors of power—as well as such public media as the press and television. Audiences vary greatly in their size and composition. In general, the larger the audience, the less the political influence of individual members. Only at election time does the mass electorate clearly determine what happens in politics. Small audiences are not, *ipso facto*, powerful, but those who make decisions about any single public matter are sufficiently few in number so that they could, if necessary, fill the audience of a small theatre or even, if their passion for anonymity were less, simply fill a stage. Typically, the few dozen or few hundred opinion leaders on an issue are addressed through the quality press. Most readers of *The Times* or *The New York Times* are not politically powerful, but most politically powerful people sooner or later learn about news that appears there. Environmental influences may contradict the messages that politicians direct to national audiences. People hearing that their leaders are working for peace or prosperity may be sceptical, if the message reaches them when they are surrounded by unemployed workers, or falling bombs.

The term 'political communication' is often used to refer to one part of this outline. For example, a description of a politician appearing on television or a description of political propaganda leaflets is considered a study of communication. In fact, it omits a very important element, the intended audience and its reactions. A politician without an audience or a politician whose audience does not understand his message is an example of a *failure* of communication. Communication is a process in which audiences and enunciators of views relate to each other. As repeated studies of audiences, especially political audiences have shown, they are not mercurial or easily swayed by old or new forms of communication. The leading review of the literature by Joseph Klapper emphasizes the significance of selective perception, that is, the tendency of consumers of the mass media to expose themselves to information that is congenial.[3] Most political communication transmits information that can be interpreted in very different ways. For instance, in 1964, supporters of all British parties agreed, after seeing all the party leaders on television, that Harold Wilson had special assets. One asset was described as 'malevolent dynamism', i.e., strength plus cunning. These attitudes toward party leaders did not lead viewers to switch votes. Instead, Conservatives whose opinion of Sir Alec Douglas-Home had worsened downgraded the importance of the leader.[4] The main influence of the media in politics is that it reinforces pre-existing attitudes and loyalties; it seems to be no more a medium of conversion than a three-quarters empty church on Sunday.

As a process, communication can take many forms, ranging from non-communication—a politician simply talking to himself—to elaborate networks of multi-lateral communication. There is nothing necessarily unidirectional in the communications process. Even a viewer in front of a television set can tell a politician what he thinks of him by turning the set off. If his set is one of the few thousand used to estimate the viewing habits of millions, his reaction is magnified greatly in significance. Often, two-way communication is imperfectly realized. A speaker may wrongly interpret crowd applause as intended for himself, when it may be meant for the party he represents, or as an expression of solidarity against an opponent. In a political debate, each side is physically able to hear what the other side says, but psychologically unable to accept what is directed at them. For communication to result in a full exchange of information, everyone concerned must be attentive and perceptive. This happens at times. For example, pressure group representatives and public officials can bargain together for so long a time that they can know each other's minds quite well. Yet even small groups of political partisans, such as Cabinets, often include in their ranks members who do not hear or are not told what is happening politically.

The classical liberal model of government by public opinion emphasizes the importance of information flowing in one direction—from voters to their elected representatives. In a small New England community governed by a town meeting, or in a parish council where all the residents are equal (say, retired Colonels), then this type of communication is technically possible. In big cities or even in not-so-big towns, it is impossible. In such an environment, there must be a time lag between the initial voicing of public concerns, their articulation to representatives, and the reaction of the representatives, even when representative government is working well.

Studies of public opinion in Britain and America have found that the fundamental obstacle to government by public opinion does not rest in the communication process, but rather in the character of public opinion. The mass of the British and American people have a limited range of things that they wish to communicate to their governors; on many everyday concerns of government, the majority opinion is 'Don't Know'. This is ironic, for many of the early sponsors of public opinion research were great believers in government by the people, and the rhetoric is still found in discussions of their work. Discovering that most people do not want to govern is hardly surprising, given our knowledge of popular attitudes toward politics. This is not to say that people have no views about what the government should do, or about the competence or sincerity of men in government. At election times, members of the general public can express their preference about *who* should govern. Between elections, the measures that most concern them are simple but basic

—peace and prosperity. The complex economic and diplomatic means to these ends are hardly appropriate for solution by referendum. If voters were offered the choice of three alternatives—policy A, policy B, or leaving the formulation of policy to the government of the day—one suspects that the third alternative would often prove the most popular, for the details and mechanics of policies are not easy to grasp. The government is supposed to be responsible for this. It is unrealistic to expect that the general public should have detailed knowledge or interest in decisions made, say, by the Department of the Interior in America or by the old Commonwealth Relations Office in Britain, just as it would be out of character for a politician to say that he was a 'Don't Know' when confronted with a problem.

Even when many members of the public do have views about an issue, it is no easy matter to make these views add up in a way that is agreeable to everyone, or even in a way that provides a clearcut guide to a decision. In weighing public opinion, how much extra should be allowed for knowledge? Alternatively, how heavily should views be discounted if they are based on ignorance, and who should decide who are the ignorant people? In assessing public opinion about whether Britain should join the Common Market, an act that would affect the majority of British people in many ways, should everyone's views be allowed to count, or only the views of those who can tell the Common Market from its competitor, the European Free Trade Area? When the debate started, the Gallup Poll found only 31 per cent of all respondents knew that Britain was a member of the latter but not of the former. Yet 68 per cent of those interviewed had views on the issue.[5] How much weight should be given to the strength of opinions on an issue? Should intensely held opinions count more than lukewarm views? The issue is particularly important in such emotionally charged areas as capital punishment and race relations. What allowance should be made for the possibility that the views of individuals are changeable? In an American series of three surveys over several years, Philip Converse found that 60 per cent at least once expressed an opinion on the relations of government and private enterprise. These people could be divided into three almost equal groups—those whose views were consistent on this issue in all three interviews, those who gave contradictory answers, and those who sometimes had an opinion and sometimes didn't. The group with stable attitudes consisted of one-fifth of the electorate.[6] When politicians look at an opinion poll, normally they have the results of only a single survey. How much change can be induced in these opinions by the actions of politicians? How much should be induced? Politicians are free to overestimate the extent to which their own actions might reasonably be reckoned to change the views to their followers. The Suez War provided a striking example of this phenomenon. As the Conservative government moved toward military action against Egypt, the proportion of Conservatives favouring action rose, as did the proportion of Labour voters disapproving it. In both cases, the party leaders in the Commons were providing the cues for their supporters' attitudes.[7]

The greater the number of alternative policies, the less the probability that any one will receive an endorsement from a majority of people with opinions. The nearest that government comes to 'direct' democracy is in a referendum, a device used in America, but no longer popular. In such instances, voters are asked to vote for or against a specific piece of legislation, or a tax assessment.[8] In such circumstances, the cards can still be stacked in favour of influence by the few. As General de Gaulle has shown, it is possible to frame referendum questions which make one alternative far more attractive than another—vote for a constitution or for anarchy or military rule—or to time them at moments propitious for success. Even when views are vastly simplified, four answers are always possible. Some individuals are likely to be in favour of the proposed law and others against it. A third group is likely to give it only conditional approval or be partly for and partly against. The fourth group will be Don't Knows. For example, during the long, hot summer of 1964, Americans were asked their views about race relations. A total of 31 per cent favoured desegregation, 23 per cent favoured segregation, 2 per cent were Don't Knows, and 44 per cent said they favoured something in between, a group aggregating a variety of dispositions.[9]

Ironically, the media—press, radio and television—are most influential politically when they most belie their name. When a channel of communication is doing no more than transmitting views of the general public accurately, then, like the Post Office, it is performing a necessary service but hardly an important one. When the media are distorting or inventing policy preferences, which are then directed at political leaders in the name of the general public, their claim to an independent influence is greater. The media are hardly automatic reflectors of public opinion, for the canons of journalism place a high premium on novelty. The most journalistically interesting opinions of men in the street are not the most representative; unfortunately, the most representative are hardly news because they are common. In the one section of a paper devoted to readers' views, the Letters to the Editor column, the voice of readers is not properly presented. An American study found that political letter writers constitute about three per cent of the electorate. In 1964 this group was so atypical that it was the only one in America that favoured Barry Goldwater for President.[10]

In television as in the press, technical considerations are important as constraints upon the presentation of political news. A first-hand study by Jay Blumler of how British television producers handled the 1966 British general election campaign illustrates the importance of professional considerations.[11] The broadcasters had to shape their programmes in form and in content to conform to laws requiring a fair balance of political news. This requirement is specially important in television, in view of the government's power over station licences. When politicians tried to pressure broadcasters to emphasize a party angle, the men concerned tended to react against them, because of a trained scepticism about sources. The BBC programme directors were, however, divided about the attitude they should take toward the election. Some adopted what Blumler calls a 'sacerdotal' approach; programmes were seen as information for those predisposed to participate in this great occasion—or mystery. The viewpoint is probably peculiar to the BBC. Others tended to regard the election as an event competing for public attention with many other items of news. In newspaper offices, a different set of technical and professional considerations affects editorial policy. The result is the same. Organizational pressures tend to be against conscious efforts to manipulate voters. Moreover, many things that affect the news output of the media are determined in circumstances in which the audience is not considered at all.[12]

Politicians too limit what the general public can communicate. Some politicians conceive their primary role as that of giving voice to public opinion. The job is simplified by the fact that public opinion is usually defined as what they think other people are or ought to be thinking. Their multitude of roles establishes many claimants upon politicians' attention besides members of the general public. Most are immediate and more claimant than people back in the constituencies. Because of their unsystematic and sporadic contacts with the public it is reasonable to suggest that the things that a politician hears and hears clearly are the things that he already knows himself.[13] For example, it is a fact that the upbringing, style of life and public and private activities of John F. Kennedy rarely brought him into personal contact with ordinary Americans. Note, for example, Theodore White's revealing remark that Kennedy, when first confronted in 1960 with the unappetizing rations doled out to unemployed workers in West Virginia, 'gaped and said, "Do you mean people really eat this?" '[14]

The difficulty of politicians in receiving communications from the people 'out there' is illustrated by an account of what happened to a Conservative Cabinet Minister of good intentions, Bill Deedes, when he tried to do something to bridge the gap.[15] In 1962, Deedes, a journalist by trade, was a Minister without Portfolio, concerned with public relations for Harold Macmillan's government. He was so much impressed by reading a chapter on social change in America in Theodore White's *The Making of the President* that he thought it would be a good idea to have similar information available about the British electorate. After giving some thought to the things they ought to know, Deedes commissioned the Central Statistical Office to get up facts in the form of figures. When the figures were presented to him, he found they did not make easy reading; after all, no set of statistics is self-interpreting. Judging that his Cabinet colleagues would have the same difficulty, Deedes commissioned a journalist friend to write the material up in a prose form suitable for circulation as a background paper for members of the Cabinet. It evoked sufficient favourable comment so that Deedes then gave the document to the press, although it had been written as a paper for private circulation only. The view it communicates is such that British students to whom I assign it treat the document as if it had been written as election propaganda. They cannot believe that men in high office would give serious attention to a report which contained so many highly questionable statements. This in itself is an interesting comment on communication between politicians and novice students of politics.

Deedes' survey begins with the assumption that changes in

popular attitudes in recent decades can easily be inferred from census-type statistics about material circumstances. While it is possible to infer attitudes from non-attitudinal data, what is inferred may turn out to be the attitude of the author, rather than that of the population nominally being discussed. The weaknesses of the survey are worth noting, because they are not confined to politicians of one party or one country, or only to politicians. The chief difficulty is that basic concepts are undefined. We are never told what changes in living conditions most affect attitudes, and what attitudes are most important for political decision-makers. Coupled with a wooliness about subject-matter is a vagueness about how changes might be measured. The things that most interested Bill Deedes, a public relations minded politician, would have been more appropriately measured by opinion surveys. Reliance upon census statistics did not, however, mean that the author had what infant school teachers call 'a sense of number'. For example, an increase from 0·2 per cent to 1·4 per cent in the number of people using private medical insurance in a decade is regarded as a noteworthy phenomenon. Yet such a rate of growth could require about 420 years before a majority of the population became independent of the National Health Service. At times, the author's obvious fluency leads him to rhetorical statements of dubious accuracy. For instance, at one point Stoke-on-Trent, perhaps the grimiest and dullest town of a quarter million people in Britain, is referred to as 'a great city in the United Kingdom'.

The sloppy thinking evidenced in the Social Change study is not characteristic of all government reports on the conditions of the British people. The average Government white paper has a significant factual base, and the amount of information given in the text and in proliferating appendices is growing perceptibly. Major Royal Commission studies, such as the Robbins report on Higher Education, may include significant quantities of empirical research. It does not follow from this that the politicians and very senior civil servants to whom such reports are presented have the time or the inclination to read such materials, and to read them critically. It is just as plausible to believe that much of government-sponsored research is undertaken to support already arrived at decisions, or, if it contradicts the value preferences of those to whom it is offered, it is ignored. In America, the complaint is sometimes heard that there is too much information available and too little done about it. The sheer volume of factual material at hand from the Government Printing Office, from private resources and from semi-public university research, is very great. A study of the reaction of politically informed people to the controversial Moynihan report about the condition of the Negro family is a reminder that the central problem—the ability of politicians to exercise selective perception in the interpretation of information—exists on both sides of the Atlantic.[16]

In an important sense, governors and governed communicate best when the distribution of opinions among those in government is similar to the distribution of opinions among those being governed. In such circumstances, politicians talking to each other could obtain the same views they would get from talking with a cross-section of the nation. Whether such a congruence in attitudes exists can be investigated by asking the same questions of politicians and of a cross-section of the national population. Several American studies have done this, and found considerable congruence in the profiles of attitudes.[17] This does not, however, mean that a consensus exists, because if governors reflect deep division on an issue among the general public, then conflict is only accentuated. Similarities in attitudes do not automatically translate into political decisions, for opinions may be relatively non-directive.

To my mind, public opinion research indicates that political leaders enjoy very considerable leeway in what they do while in government. As the late V. O. Key noted, in concluding his comprehensive study:

> 'Politicians often make of the public a scapegoat for their own shortcomings; their actions, they say, are a necessity for survival given the state of public opinion. Even if mass opinion assumes forms incompatible with the national interest, the articulation between government and mass opinion is so loose that politicians enjoy a considerable range of discretion within which to exercise prudence and good sense.'[18]

In other words, the opinions that count most are those of men in government. The channels of communication that are most important are horizontal links between men in different parts of central government. Unfortunately, here too there are many obstacles to perfect information.

What a politician hears is primarily determined by the characteristic role expectations of his particular office. People in major government offices expect to read files and to hear the informal talk that collectively constitutes that curious metaphysical substance, the mind of the government. When they speak, they will expect others to listen, for their office assures them that many things cannot happen until they have had a chance to state their views. This is especially true when Cabinet government acts consistent with its theory, which gives ministers the right to be consulted in advance of major decisions, as the price of their collective responsibility. In American government, leading officials in the executive departments may not be told everything they would like to know. Richard Neustadt has gone so far as to recommend that Presidents should maintain channels of communication direct to middle-rank executive officials, in order to find out things that Cabinet secretaries may not wish the President to know, or may not know themselves.[19]

Middle echelon politicians and office-holders enjoy communications advantages because of their position in the middle.[20] They receive information directly from people on the periphery of politics, as well as from men at the top. This accessibility to communication from two directions increases their insight into the connections and disjunctions between government policy and what happens to the subjects of government. It is an unusual political leader, however, who makes a practice of consulting regularly with middle-echelon men, aware of things that men at the top do not know about or do not care to see. An economist with experience in Whitehall, Samuel Brittan, has half seriously suggested that from time to time secret ballots should be taken on government policies. In this way civil servants whose duty it is to reinforce their minister's faith in the rightness of his policies could tell him what they really think.[21]

The distance that a message must travel within government is a second major determinant of who hears what. Distance is not measured in land or nautical miles, but rather, in hierarchical layers in an organization chart, or in the inter-continental gaps between one department of government and another. The politician at the top, if he is imaginative, must often wonder what people a few floors underneath him are doing—drinking tea? shuffling papers whose meaning is no longer known? working overtime in unhealthy and cramped conditions? actively figuring out ways to ignore his latest regulations or passively frustrating directives by ignorance of their existence? All of these activities are possible alternatives to that of providing an attentive audience for the minister's commands. The extent to which political distance is a liability or an asset varies with the discretion granted officials at the bottom. In the Post Office, a politician's ignorance of what goes on in a small rural station may make him culpable of many minor irritations, but not for a major error, since post office officials tend to work by a rule book. In the Home Office, a politician may be responsible for much graver matters, because he does not know what is happening beneath him. For example, much discretionary authority is given to the policeman on the beat. Information derogatory to the police is, quite reasonably, usually suspect because of the motives of informants. In consequence, Cabinet Ministers have been embarrassed not only by police incidents in the far-off Scottish Highlands, but also by practices in the Central London police district, within walking distance of the Home Office.[22]

In America, distances are greater not only because of the size of the country, but also because of the federal structure of government. The problem is specially great in race relations, where local authorities in the South can systematically resist attempts by federal officials to find out what is happening to the civil rights of Negroes within their jurisdiction. In foreign affairs, too, distance is not strictly a function of geography. The fiasco of the Bay of Pigs invasion of Cuba in 1961 showed the President misinformed about a country very close to American shores. It was, however, made 'distant' by the intelligence services.

Ease of communication is also influenced by the size and tasks of government departments. In both Britain and America, such departments as the Foreign Office and the Treasury have a relatively small number of high-powered civilian employees concentrated in national capitols. There are relatively few low level jobs, by comparison, to the Post Office or Agriculture. In such circumstances, problems that arise will be handled at high level and by small numbers of people, who, because they are few, can more easily maintain contact. In the case of diplomats, the problem is not that of communicating with each other, but rather, of maintaining communications with the millions of non-diplomats who live in the country they are supposed to represent. By contrast, in the Post Office and social service departments, lines of communication from regional and branch offices to the centre are very long, and the ratio of high level policy-makers to low level officials is much less. Problems are usually dealt with at low level because they are limited in their national impact. Incidentally, this indicates that the departments whose officials are most frequently in direct personal contact with the population are also those considered unimportant by leaders of the central government.

Within government as outside it, the effects of distance can most easily be minimized when reciprocal role relationships are so good that little or no overt communication is necessary. This type of communication is particularly important between ministers and civil servants. In a government department, many routine problems are handled by civil servants in the name of the minister, with little or no reference to him. It is the job of a Minister to establish an awareness of his views in the minds of many civil servants beneath him. In this way, they will be able to give a correct answer to the question —what would the minister wish?—when taking decisions about questions which the minister lacks the time, inclination or knowledge to consider. Civil servants must try to be adept in reading cues from their political superiors, for ministers usually have a limited amount of time in one department to make their mind known. They may even put more emphasis upon a casual remark or a transitory whim of a minister than he himself wishes. In America, the practice of bringing a large number of partisan appointees into a department and appointing more men with subject-matter expertise makes it easier for a governing party to communicate its views to middle-echelon officials in government.[23] On the other hand, the resistance of individuals to influence is so great, because of the system of checks and balances, that politicians often have to shout very hard to make themselves heard even a little.

The growth in the scale of government since the outbreak of the Second World War has made it impossible for politicians in different spheres of government to know each other well enough to anticipate each other's moves. The demands of the job at hand further constrict personal relationships to the politician's home base. Outside his department, he is dependent upon a formidable apparatus of committees to keep him informed of what is happening. In Britain, the

Cabinet still provides the formal mechanism for keeping members of the government informed of what is being done in their name. The amount of time available to discuss matters at Cabinet committees has not expanded proportionate to the pressure of work. The dilemma is neatly stated in the debate about the appropriate size of a Cabinet. If it is small, a dozen men or less, all of whom are 'co-ordinating' ministers, then communication within the group will be good, but communication between the group and those responsible for administering specific departments will suffer. Reciprocally, if communication between ministers and operational executives is good, the time available for co-ordination is constricted.[24] Within a department, the man responsible for representing the department on inter-departmental co-ordinating committees is likely to find himself faced with a similar dilemma. The greater the understanding he develops of those outside his own office, the greater his remoteness is likely to become from his official colleagues. In a sense, office insulates a politician: he can choose whether to be insulated from the outside world, or to be out in the cold *vis-à-vis* his overly insulated departmental colleagues.

The theory and practice of American government regards the insulation of the executive, the legislature and the judiciary from each other as a good thing *per se*. Even in the early 19th century, when the number of politicians in Washington were few, non-communication between people in different branches of government was the rule. The plan for government offices in the city—with Congress and the White House at opposite ends of Pennsylvania Avenue—gave physical embodiment to this value.[25] Today, with thousands of important people dispersed across both sides of the Potomac River, nominally linked by traffic bottlenecks and large green malls, some degree of non-communication is a necessity if anyone is to get any work done. The contingency of annual appropriations guarantees that executive departments maintain contact with Congress, though their relations can be cautious.[26]

In crisis situations, when a problem such as war or peace overrides all others, communications can improve greatly. The number of people involved in a key decision, such as the invasion of Suez in 1956, or the Cuban missile crisis of 1962, is relatively small. Leading politicians, civil servants and military men can communicate on a face-to-face basis, and may choose to do so to guarantee secrecy.

All the individuals concerned for the short period of the crisis work fulltime together. The gravity of the crisis ensures that messages are not lost in the pipeline, and concentrates the flow of information. In the case of the 1962 Cuban missile crisis, American government policy was made with considerable skill, because President Kennedy and his colleagues were communicating on the basis of assumptions congruent with the outside world. In the case of the Suez crisis, however, the small group of people with whom Sir Anthony Eden communicated were in touch with each other, but out of touch with the Middle East.[27]

Typically, political decisions are made in non-crisis circumstances; then information is likely to be very imperfectly co-ordinated. The Profumo affair provides a classic illustration of communication difficulties, since all relevant information was known by people living within a five shilling taxi ride of each other in Central London. The Security Services, the Metropolitan Police, the Prime Minister's Office, the Leader of the Opposition's office and dozens of journalists each knew some pieces of the story concerning the relationships between John Profumo, Christine Keeler, Captain Eugene Ivanov and Stephen Ward. People in each of these groups were working, eating and sleeping in close proximity to each other. Moreover, the Prime Minister's Office, the police and the security services, were all supposed to be working for the same government. Yet institutional barriers, plus problems of access, plus the values of many concerned, including Sir Norman Brook, Secretary to the Cabinet, and Harold Macmillan, meant that the Prime Minister was the last person to hear the full story of what was happening.[28] When communication is so imperfect on a simple issue which might be an interesting and stimulating conversation in a group of masculine politicians, one hesitates to contemplate the failure of communication likely on issues as complex and decentralized as housing or local government.

Institutional problems of communication in government are compounded by the scarcity of time. Time is the most inelastic of all resources of a politican. A group of men preparing the annual budget of Britain or America has the same amount of time in which to complete their task as the honorary treasurer of a local Rotary club. No sooner has one budget been enacted in law than unanticipated difficulties begin to arise. Fortunately, this often occurs when the job of writing the next year's budget is about to begin. At the level of the individual politician, deciding how he will allocate his time is probably the most important decision he makes. The demands of many roles—as administrator, partisan speaker, public relations man, careerist, and even husband and parent—mean that he cannot do all his tasks well. Contemplating a full 'In' tray while sundry people parade through his office on deputations, he may feel that there is not time to do even one thing well. The pressures upon time are aptly illustrated by an account of how Ernest Marples, an unconventional Conservative Cabinet minister, set about trying to find time enough to do first things first.[29] Marples reckoned that if he did departmental paper work at home from 5 a.m. to 8.30 a.m. he would keep up with his work, and could suffer the multitude of interruptions that mark a politician's day and evening, subject only to the overriding priority of naps after lunch and dinner. The position of important civil servants is no better than that of Ministers. Lord Strang, while Permanent Under-Secretary at the Foreign Office, calculated that the job could be done by working twelve to fourteen hours a day for seven days a week, taking one weekend off in three.[30] Even at that, he often felt he was hard pressed to keep up with his responsibilities.

In America, the demands upon the time of men in the White House are at least as great as those upon their British counterparts.[31] The President, unlike British ministers, is not required to hang around the legislature regularly, listening to dull debates. However, the time saved in this task may be consumed by meetings with Congressional leaders, keeping his influence alive in that branch of federal government. As ceremonial head of state, the President is expected to devote a substantial amount of time each week to tasks that the Queen undertakes in Britain, such as greeting Girl Scout leaders or foreign potentates.[32] The President is not alone in his ceremonial burden. What is most impressive in any weekly diary of a politician is the amount of time spent in activities which communicate symbolic interest or concern rather than practical information or guidance. Invitations to many public luncheons and dinners must be accepted, because attendance confers prestige, and a refusal to attend could be taken as an affront. When a major jail break or a plane disaster occurs, a responsible political official is expected to be 'on the scene' to show his concern. He may be photographed viewing the wreck with dismay, or watching the prison cell being locked after the felon has flown.

Time is also a constraint in a second sense: many things that decision makers want to know cannot be known precisely because they concern events in the future. This limitation is particularly relevant in attempts to plan the economy and the provision of welfare services.[33] A bunch of 16-year-olds can make an august Secretary of State for Education look foolish by staying on at school in greater numbers than can comfortably be accommodated. Teenage girls can make the Minister of Health look foolish if they leave school to have babies younger and more often than plans for maternity services predict. In trying to make allowance for the future, the simplest thing that a politician can do is to ignore its existence. He can strike a bargain that is good for the day it is issued, even if the result may be chaos or renewed controversy tomorrow. Mr Neville Chamberlain's foreign policy in the late 1930s is a 'good' bad example of hand-to-mouth policy-making. A more justifiable approach is to extrapolate the future from events in the present and recent past. If a trend of some sort has recently been manifest, assume it will continue; if there is no trend, then assume everything will remain the same. In some fields, such as pension demands or housing needs, it is possible to make relatively sophisticated actuarial estimates. It is not, however, an easy matter to forecast accurately what effects the government's actions are likely to have upon a situation. Politicians can make confident forecasts about the advantages of their initiatives; analysis after the event suggests that policies have disadvantages too, and that some of both are unanticipated by those who promote changes. The most difficult of all things to forecast are major shifts in governmental priorities. For instance, the American government committed itself to vast domestic expenditures to combat poverty in the 1960s, yet the emergence of the Viet Nam war imposed new priorities on federal budgets and on the time of national leaders. In Britain, shifts in priorities most often involve a familiar cycle between government-induced inflation and government-induced deflation.

Eppure, si muove. And yet government moves. Both British and American governments administer policies which sometimes approximate desired policy goals and are usually 'not irrelevant' to gross social problems. To accept this fact does not compel endorsement of every imperfect piece of information used to justify the mistakes made by governments acting in the name of the Queen. (Obviously, the Queen is no economist.) In America, the glorifiers of all that is done in the name of the people praise the wonderful energy put into the conflicts that produce government policies as a byproduct, rather than the thoughtfulness and information upon which these policies are based. What is needed is an understanding of the ways that the leaders of central government become aware that something is going wrong with government policy when it is actually applied 'out there'.

At any given moment, the great majority of things that a government does are considered matters of routine administration, not worthy of close attention by political leaders, though they are ultimately responsible for what is done in their name. Only by treating the printing of postage stamps as a routine operation can politicians concentrate their attention upon the relatively small number of controversial problems requiring non-routine handling. Typically, a policy is regarded as routine a few years after it has been in operation. By this time, administrative difficulties have been overcome and the programme is no longer a novelty. For example, the introduction of a national pension scheme is far more interesting than the tenth or fiftieth annual report of its operation. Implicit in routinization is the assumption so favoured of economists: 'all other conditions remaining constant'. Yet the environment in which routine policies are administered is not unchanging, even though changes may occur slowly. Information about a *de facto* change in a government policy is likely to appear first in data about market conditions. As long as the supply of a government policy remains a constant, then variations in the demand for government services will effectively alter its character. For instance, when old people live longer than anticipated, the total pensions bill rises. When the cost of living rises and a pension remains paid in a fixed cash sum, then the real value of the pension falls. Politicians and their advisers, subject to the tyrannical rule of first things first, are unlikely to notice such changes. The convenient view is that a routine policy works well. In fact, this means that it was working well *as far as they knew when last they asked*. Often their judgment is based on information dating from the time the last major controversy arose in the policy area.

Awareness of a change in policy will be communicated first to people affected by a failure of routine policy to fit their changing circumstances. For instance, young people having difficulties in gaining admission to university, because birth rates and secondary education have risen faster than new university buildings, will immediately be aware that something is not quite right.[34] At this point, affected persons are likely to articulate their grievances by standard pressure group tactics. In the case of major grievances, this involves a swing against the governing party in opinion polls and in by-elections.

Once a matter of administrative routine has been returned to the realm of political controversy, the government of the day will begin to seek information about the issue at stake. There is nothing automatic about the speed or the perceptiveness with which new information will be sought and evaluated. If one believes in the power of inertia in human affairs, then politicians and administrators would be expected to be slow to admit that something had gone wrong with 'their' programme. The usual political tactic is to deny that any difficulty exists, or to stall those who are lobbying for change. Governments have a panoply of devices for stalling aggrieved groups of citizens. In the United States, one might argue that separating the legislature from the executive institutionalizes delay. It certainly provides a justification for slow action. In Britain, the fact that the Cabinet of the day can be sure that its legislation goes through Parliament does not mean that problems are promptly dealt with.[35] The slowness with which governments respond to such non-party measures as a Channel Tunnel or decimal currency, each of which was broached nearly two decades ago, suggests that the habit of institutional inertia and the desire to conciliate political opponents is at least as strong in Britain as in America. Sooner *or* later, changing market conditions will be recognized as sufficient to justify a change in policy, either through the invocation of a new principle or the invocation of a traditional symbol. In both types of situation, the resulting changes in government intentions are likely to involve an element of continuity with past administrative practices, as well as some action intended to prevent the problem from occurring again.

Once a new bill is passed and changes made in administrative arrangements, then politicians once again regard the problem as solved and able to be forgotten. It is just at this point, however, that the consequences of the government's new decisions are being communicated to an affected public. By the time these are fully understood and those affected have reacted, policy-makers are likely to have lost interest in the face of competing claims for attention. A new cycle of policy-making has begun. In Britain, a single cycle can last 20 to 25 years, judging by the frequency of major innovations in educational policy in the past century. In America, the de-centralization of decision-making inherent in the Constitution makes it more difficult to hazard opinions. Certainly, Congress can change its readiness to support legislation as rapidly as biennial elections occur. In general domestic policy, large bundles of innovations have been passed about once a generation—in the Progressive period before America's entry in the First World War, in the New Deal of the 1930s, and again in the Kennedy-Johnson Administrations.

Communication in the form described above is sufficient to permit British and American governments to adapt to changes in the societies they govern. Judged by comparative historical standards, one might even say that both governments are relatively good at keeping informed about the world around them. After all, the last major war that Britain lost was the American Revolution, and American governments have yet to be humbled by defeat.[36] Yet it is Panglossian to argue that we live under the best of all possible governments, for survival is not the only criterion for judging a regime, particularly one where threats to survival are usually remote. It is noteworthy that both British and American governments in recent years have become aware that the information used in governing could be improved. In the United States, this has brought about an interest in social indicators comparable to economic indicators of unemployment and gross national product, giving a simple, clear and regular indication of how well social policies are working. In Britain, government publications now record with shame the fact that senior administrators normally receive only three hours of training in statistics, and are not necessarily versed in anything else immediately relevant to government.[37]

'Does it really matter, old boy?' one can almost hear the veteran Whitehall official say. 'Do we really need all those figures, and all the chaps that come with them?' In Washington, a White House staff man might comment more equivocally, 'Don't you worry. Our job is to see that the President gets the statistics that he wants.' The answer to such questions is capable of some quantification. In the case of a five-year delay in raising pensions to meet rising living costs or a five-year delay in raising the national minimum wage, one can estimate with some precision how many hundred millions have been lost by the affected low-income groups. It is more difficult to estimate the cost of depriving thousands of Englishmen in the 1940s, 1950s and early 1960s of a university education because government higher education policy was not then as generous as it became in the 1960s. Measuring the loss simply in terms of reduced earnings would be crass, for higher education, if it has any value at all, involves more than pounds, shillings and pence. In America, it is similarly difficult to estimate the cost of depriving millions of Negroes of justice before the law and equality in public policy, *after* the climactic Supreme Court decision of 1954. It is a matter of political controversy whether the cost of imperfect government information—often, to be sure, reinforcing imperfect wills—is 'too high' or 'about right' in these instances. One thing is certain: as the actions of government affect the lives of more people in more ways, the cost of government ignorance and misinformation is sure to rise.

NOTES—CHAPTER V

1. Harold Lasswell, *Politics: Who Gets What, When, How* (New York: Meridian Books, 1958 edition).
2. Karl W. Deutsch, *The Nerves of Government* (New York: Free Press, 1966 edition) pp. xxvii, 88.
3. Joseph T. Klapper, *The Effects of Mass Communication* (Glencoe, Illinois: Free Press, 1960). Cf. David Sears and Jonathan Freedman, 'Selective Exposure to Information: a Critical Review', *Public Opinion Quarterly* XXXI:2 (1967).
4. Jay Blumler and Denis McQuail, *op. cit.*, Ch. 12.
5. *Britain and the ECM* (London: Gallup Poll Report, 1961), p. 17.
6. 'New Dimensions of Meaning for Cross-Section Sample Surveys in Politics', *International Social Science Journal* XVI:1 (1964), p. 28. On more general problems of summing preferences, see Robert Dahl, *A Preface to Democratic Theory* (Chicago: University Press, 1956).
7. See Leon Epstein, *British Politics in the Suez Crisis* (London: Pall Mall, 1964) pp. 139ff.

8. The chief study of referenda remains A. L. Lowell, *Public Opinion and Popular Government* (New York: Longmans, 1914) especially Chs. 11–15.
9. Figures from the 1964 nationwide opinion study of the Survey Research Centre, University of Michigan, Deck 5, column 43.
10. Philip Converse, Aage Clausen and Warren E. Miller, 'Electoral Myth and Reality: the 1964 Election', *American Political Science Review* LIX:2 (1965).
11. See Jay Blumler, 'Producers' Attitudes Towards Television Coverage of an Election Campaign: A Case Study', *Sociological Review Monograph* No. 13 (1969).
12. For discussions of the working press in politics, see e.g., Ch. 3 of Richard Rose, *Studies in British Politics*; Douglass Cater, *The Fourth Branch of Government* (Boston: Houghton Mifflin, 1959) and Dan Nimmo, *Newsgathering in Washington* (New York: Atheron, 1964). More generally, see Fred Siebert, Theodore Peterson and Wilbur Schramm, *Four Theories of the Press* (Urbana: University of Illinois Press, 1956).
13. Cf. Richard Rose, *Influencing Voters*, Chs. 8–9.
14. *The Making of the President—1964* (New York: Atheneum, 1965), p. 14.
15. The report is printed as 'Social Changes in Britain', *New Society*, December 27, 1962. For background see House of Commons, *Debates*, Vol. 671, Cols. 406–16 (February 5, 1963). For another reaction, see Ronald Fletcher, 'Social Changes in Britain: a Paper for Tired Ministers', *Political Quarterly* XXXIV:4 (1963).
16. Cf. Lee Rainwater and William Yancey, *The Moynihan Report and the Politics of Controversy* (London: MIT Press, 1967).
17. See e.g., Herbert McClosky, *op. cit.*, 'Issue Conflict and Consensus among Party Leaders and Followers', *American Political Science Review* LIV:2 (1960); Robert Dahl, *Who Governs?*, and the introduction and articles contained in Norman Luttbeg, editor, *Public Opinion and Public Policy: Models of Political Linkage* (Homewood, Illinois: Dorsey, 1968).
18. V. O. Key Jr., *Public Opinion and American Democracy* (New York: Knopf 1961) pp. 557–58.
19. *Presidential Power*, passim.
20. Cf. Karl Deutsch, *The Nerves of Government*, pp. 154ff.
21. See 'The Irregulars', in Richard Rose, editor, *Policy-Making in Britain* (London: Macmillan, 1969) pp. 235–36.
22. See e.g. the case of Det.-Sgt. Harold Challenor, found insane after an active period in Central London police work. *The Times*, June 5, 1964.

23. See the argument in Richard Rose, 'The Variability of Party Government', and sources cited therein.
24. Cf. Hans Daalder, *Cabinet Reform in Britain 1914–1963*, especially Part III.
25. See the very perceptive study by James S. Young, *The Washington Community, 1800–1828* (New York: Columbia University Press, 1966.)
26. For a case study of relations between Congressmen on the House Appropriations Committee and executive department officials, see Richard Fenno, *op. cit.*, Chs. 6, 11.
27. Cf. Arthur Schlesinger, *op. cit.*, Chs. 10, 30. Robert F. Kennedy, *op. cit.*, and Anthony Nutting, *No End of a Lesson* (London: Constable, 1967).
28. See Clive Irving, Ron Hall and Jeremy Wallington, *Scandal '63* (London: Heinemann, 1963) especially pp. 130–31 and Lord Denning's *Report* (London: H.M.S.O., Cmnd. 2152, 1963).
29. See 'A Dog's Life in the Ministry', *Sunday Telegraph*, November 22, 1964, reprinted in Richard Rose, editor, *Policy-Making in Britain.*
30. Cf. Lord Strang, *Home and Abroad* (London: Deutsch, 1956) p. 274, also reprinted in Richard Rose, editor, *Policy-Making in Britain.*
31. Cf. the detailed diary of a President's week, reported in 'President Kennedy Minute by Minute', *The Times*, May 10, 1963.
32. For an interesting account of how a ceremonial head of state allocates time, see Dermot Morrah, *The Work of the Queen* (London: Kimber, 1958) pp. 51ff.
33. For a recent review of British planning machinery, see e.g., Samual Brittan, *Inquest on Planning in Britain* (London: PEP Planning Broadsheet, XXXIII: 499, 1967). For a retrospective consideration of the experience of the Attlee Government, see D. N. Chester, 'The Machinery of Government Planning' in G. D. N. Worswick and P. H. Ady, *The British Economy, 1945–50* (Oxford: Clarendon Press, 1952).
34. Cf. Richard Layard, 'The Anatomy of Student Expansion', *Financial Times*, March 11, 1968.
35. Cf. Kenneth Waltz., *op. cit.*, and A. P. Herbert, *Anything But Action?* (London: Institute of Economic Affairs, Hobart Papers No. 5, 1960).
36. For an interesting comparative analysis of Britain's ability to organize its domestic war effort better than its opponents, see Mancur Olson, Jr., *The Economics of the Wartime Shortage* (Durham, N.C.: Duke University Press, 1963). As studies of America's involvement in the Viet Nam war come out, undoubtedly they will show the importance of imperfect information.

37. See *Fourth Report from the Estimates Committee, Session 1966–67* (Government Statistical Services (London: HMSO, 1966)) p. 12. Cf. the volumes of the Fulton Report, especially *The Civil Service: Vol. 1*, and, for American examples, Mancur Olson Jr., 'The Plan and Purpose of a Social Report', *The Public Interest* No. 15 (1969), and Raymond A. Bauer, editor, *Social Indicators* (Cambridge, Mass.: MIT Press, 1966).

Six

The Pursuit of Power

No doubt the earliest approach to the study of political power was based on the most primitive form of political communication: the gossip of inside dopesters at the Palace of the Pharaohs or in the pleasure domes of Babylon. The gossip of the King's servants may have been trivial or self-serving but at least it meets the first criterion of scholarship: it was often based on first-hand knowledge. If the gossip was written down, it meets a second criterion: it has the form of unpublished papers or papyruses of long dead people. The study of power has altered somewhat since the period that most interests Egyptologists. For example, Kremlinologists, almost as remote from their subjects as the students of King Tut, are willing to invoke the aid of computers or of clinical psychologists in efforts to find out who rules Russia today.

With the growth of writing, philosophers began to apply their minds to less transitory aspects of political power, and to record their observations in the more durable form of books. In many instances, philosophers discussed questions of ethics: how can one man's power over another be justified? how ought a just governor to exercise the authority he enjoys? Their answers have varied enormously but still retain relevance, as illustrated by the latterday apostles of the doctrines of Plato, Locke, Rousseau and others. In a few instances, philosophers such as Machiavelli considered empirical questions in a relatively amoral vein: how can power be maximized? how can power be maintained? Occasionally, as in the case of Lenin, concern with practical action and an apocalyptic morality has been fused.

Among contemporary social scientists, some continue to study political power solely by means of reasoning and arranging ideas into aesthetically pleasing, logically satisfying theories. In such theories, the sources of power are specified. Locating powerful people in a given situation thus requires little more than a few quick deductions. Power may be attributed to *ex officio* rulers; to economic notables; to an Establishment based on age or Oxford or Ivy League colleges, or to a demon, such as Communists, Jews, the Pope or any other reputed agent of the Anti-Christ. Power may even be attributed to that democratic reification, The People. The clarity and logic of theories are useful in understanding the manifold ways in which power *might be* exercised. In one respect, however, relying exclusively upon reason is itself unreasonable: there is no way of telling whether any theory, for all its internal coherence, is also consistent with any form of government known to man.

Power, like sex, can be talked about in the abstract but it cannot be understood simply by solitary meditation. In order to pursue—if not to capture—the nature of political power, one must join something of the first-hand knowledge of the inside dopester or the participant, with the linguistic clarity and logic that should mark the builder of theories. It is also useful to have the skills of a lot of other social scientists in between. Moreover power must be pursued in some sort of empirical context, whether it be a city council chambers, a lobbyist's hotel suite, the President's airplane, or some network of institutions or problems that brings together these and other probable or improbable groups.

Power can be studied in many contexts that are non-political, or at least usually thought of as outside the realm of politics, e.g. a children's play group, a secondary school, a church women's league, a tennis club, or the kind of nagging husband-wife relationship that makes good theatre or disturbing divorce court hearings. Harry Eckstein has gone so far as to argue that the patterns of authority in such seemingly non-political contexts have important consequences for the way in which governments exercise power. For instance, people learn about power first inside the home, as children trying to get favours from their parents or trying to avoid parental sanctions. An adult is more immediately affected by patterns of authority at work, in domestic matters, and in relations with friends and neighbours than he is by remote judges or quasi-judicial administrative authorities. Eckstein does not go so far as to argue that the exercise of power must be the same in all these social spheres. He suggests that governments will be stable if there is 'a high degree of resemblance' between authority as exercised in government and that exercised in such para-governmental organizations as political parties and pressure groups. Governmental stability will also be encouraged if even those areas relatively remote from government, such as bowling leagues or sewing circles, imitate the forms of authority that government employ in some of their business practices or rituals.[1] This theory is used to account for the relative stability of government in Britain, where authority patterns tend toward congruence, albeit one in which deference is usually the norm. It is also used to account for the instability of government in Weimar Germany, where a democratic constitution was imposed upon a society in which authoritarian relationships were then the rule. While Eckstein's scheme is an ingenious and interesting attempt to explain more remote social influences reinforcing or undermining the authority of government, it cannot provide any direct evidence about the way in which power is actually exercised in government or about the most immediate determinants of such power.

One practical and parsimonious way to study power in government is to fix attention upon a major political institution. The choice might fall upon Congress or Parliament, upon the political parties that choose the men who formally govern, or upon the civil service that forms the permanent state. All of these institutions are considered significant, and each is sufficiently complex so that it is difficult to do justice to it without concentrating more or less exclusively upon its operations. Intensive concentration can give insights into generic features of power, but the sense of the whole may be lost in the analysis of the part. In Britain, this error is most often seen in studies of Parliament. Nearly all of these books are concerned with the internal structure of Parliament, implicitly assuming that Members of Parliament are powerful legislators. If the authors had started instead, with the question—who has power to make laws in Britain?—less might be learned about the Parliament and MPs, but more about the influences determining the things that MPs can and cannot do. It is unusual to come across an author such as Bernard Crick, who starts a book on Parliament with the frank and cheerful admission that it is potentially powerful only as a check upon those who govern, and not as a positive source of political initiative.[2] In America, the Presidency is the institution most typically wrenched out of context by students of politics. The personalization of the Presidency makes this dangerously easy to do. Some authors can even manage to write about Presidents independently of the hundreds of agencies nominally under their authority. Such studies, at best, can be good biographies; at worst, they are conventional hagiography. Not the least virtue of Richard Neustadt's *Presidential Power* is that the author emphasizes the problem of maximizing presidential power *vis-à-vis* other power holders in government. The President is not studied in isolation, but rather, as a man in a central position in a complex and often disjointed network, where influence is changeable and sometimes reciprocal.

Case studies avoid fixations about institutions. A particular problem is studied wherever its ramifications lead. The good case study of politics answers at least four basic questions of reportage—Who? What? When? and Where? In a world where theories are getting cheaper and descriptive facts more expensive or harder to discern, one should not scorn such down-to-earth knowledge. The literature of pressure group politics in Britain and America has been specially enriched by such case studies. When the case at hand is the story of the Suez crisis or American involvement in the Viet Nam war, then the intrinsic interest and importance of the case is sufficient to justify a narrative account for its own sake. Yet even the best of cases is embellished when the author tries to say *why* things happened as they did, as well as to describe what happened. Some assumptions about power are inevitably implicit in the way in which the teller of a story arranges his information, unless it is a case study in the style of *Finnegans Wake*, with the motto H.C.E. standing for 'Hopelessly Confused Evidence'. Making assumptions explicit is necessary to clarify the general significance, if any, of the case at hand. Hugh Wilson's study of the lobby that introduced commercial television to Britain illustrates the strengths and weaknesses of case studies.[3] Wilson dug hard and shrewdly to come up with much information about backstairs political intrigue inside and outside Parliament. His account of the role of business and Conservative Central Office officials was sufficiently pointed to bring threats of libel actions, as well as a House of Lords debate. Few would begrudge the time it takes to read this short, fast-paced narrative. Yet the book is ultimately frustrating, for notwithstanding its generic title—*Pressure Group*—nowhere does the author state whether he thinks the story is to be regarded as typical of the way in which power is exercised in Britain, or as a deviant case. It seems to me that the case is not typical, since neither civil servants nor Cabinet ministers took much interest in the issue. If my interpretation is wrong, the author could have set me right by publishing his own.

As many authors have shown, it is feasible to write up a case study of pressure group activities in such a way that the general significance of the case is made clear. This might happen more often if case studies were written about dull matters, such as the establishment of conditions regulating the transportation of passengers from Britain to North America in the early 19th century. Landed with a subject unlikely to attract the attention of many readers, an author might then be impelled to draw from his materials something of general significance. From just this unlikely topic Oliver MacDonagh produced an ingenious argument about the importance of power-seeking civil servants as agents expanding the scope of government regulation of society in *laissez faire* Britain.[4] If an author cannot produce a general thesis from his materials, then he might at least try to produce a readable narrative. A study of the difficult passage of emigrants in sailing ships to America might be turned into a best-seller with a title such as *Twenty Days to Boston*. High-level social science theories could be dramatised with Beckett-type titles, such as *Waiting for Inter-Action*. If an author can make his story neither instructive nor delightful, then perhaps he might abandon writing to more apt followers of that well-known Elizabethan communications theorist, Sir Philip Sidney.

Studying political power within a single community provides a practical opportunity to combine several virtues of the foregoing approaches. The labourers in the field of community power studies have none of the muckraker's contempt for theory; instead, they share with the deductive theorists a passion for constructing formal models of influence and the influential. Hypotheses are deduced to be tested by reference to a series of case studies. This avoids the fallacy of assuming that generalizations elucidated from a single case are 'proven' by reference to the situation that led to their formulation. Focusing upon a community, rather than upon a particular political institution, avoids constricting attention to a single branch of government. Instead, all the institutions of local government are brought into view and can be seen in relation to each other. Since every social scientist, no matter how anti-social he is, lives in a community of some sort, studies can be enriched by participant-observation. Studying one's own community greatly reduces research costs though it means that the college towns of America have been better studied than the large cities, which contain much of the population and most of the country's urban problems. In Britain, fortunately, the study of community politics has started in the red-brick universities, and thus produced studies of ageing industrial towns. Immersion in such places as Glossop and Newcastle-under-Lyme may not be an attractive experience for authors, but at least it gives them something in common with a large portion of the British people.[5]

The most obvious limitation of community power studies is that it is no easy matter to define a community. In a sociological sense, a community exists among a group of people who feel that they 'belong together'.[6] This feeling is unlikely to run parallel with local authority boundaries. In a large city, individuals may identify with one part, e.g. the South Side or the West End. In the case of Negroes, Jews, the Irish or other distinctive ethnic groups, people may feel a sense of community with their own kind, wherever they live. Suburban residents may have loyalties divided between the particular suburb where they live and the central city of the metropolis of which they are a part. Legal boundaries of local government units cannot always be concurrent with community feeling. For example, when the legal definition of London was changed from that of the London County Council, with a population of about 3,200,000 to that of the Greater London Council, with about 8,000,000 people, the numbers thinking of themselves as 'Londoners' did not automatically increase by 145 per cent when the act went into effect. The rigidity of local authority boundaries contrasts with the mobility of population in both Britain and America. While gaps between legal and social psychological definitions of community are substantive and likely to be increasing, political scientists have usually chosen to study a community defined by local government boundaries. These are significant for purposes of taxation, education and many important personal services. Moreover, since it can take 10 man years or more to study one local government area properly, this seemingly simple choice makes strenuous and time-consuming demands upon even a well financed research team.

While a local government area constitutes a *de jure* political system, it is not a self-contained system. Every level of government is part of a large set. In America, politics in a given place reflects the influence of municipal government, county government, and state government as well as that of the federal government. In England, there are usually only two or three tiers of authority, with large county boroughs directly under the central government and smaller authorities under county councils subject to central authority. In large metropolitan centres, such as New York and London, relationships are complicated by the fact that there are several large cities, several counties and, in the Greater New York area, three states with some influence upon decisions affecting the metropolitan community.[7] An ideal community for a social scientist (and perhaps for others too) would be a South Sea island, inhabited by a few thousand people whose only contact with the mainland came from an occasional boat bringing supplies and a few carefully vetted outsiders. Then, the boundaries of the community studied and the boundaries of the subjects' action would tend to be the same.

In America, the study of the impact of different levels of government normally is described as the study of federalism. Morton Grodzins' research has illustrated how officials at different levels of government need to bargain and co-operate with each other, if political power is to be maximized. He describes the process as one of 'co-operative' federalism. Similarly, he has shown how the existence of federal institutions gives citizens a 'multiple crack' at influence.[8] Negroes without influence in their local community may appeal to the Federal Supreme Court for redress of grievances, just as whites defeated there may appeal to state and local officials to interpose themselves between the white community and the Court.

In Britain, little has been written of a sophisticated kind about the tugging and pulling that goes on between local authorities and central government; scholars tend to treat central government as one thing and local government as another.[9] All local authorities are formally subordinate to central government. Yet judging the difficulty that central government has in altering county boundaries, many of which go back to medieval times, one might wonder whether local authorities are as subordinate as the Constitution makes them appear.

Local communities differ greatly in the power that they have over their own affairs. At one extreme of a continuum is a company town, in which everyone's livelihood is dependent upon a single factory owned by an absentee corporation. Such a community has limited control over its own affairs, and cannot guarantee the means of its own survival. A study appropriately named *Small Town in Mass Society*[10] portrays an upstate New York township of 3000 in a way that suggests the politics of the township have much less effect upon the community than decisions taken by larger neighbours and by state and federal agencies. At the other extreme are large cities such as London and New York, with resources sufficient to provide a vast range of goods and services for their residents. Yet the attraction of the big cities to the poor and under-privileged as well as to the rich means that these communities have great burdens as well as great resources. The influence of large cities seems to be growing in America, as evidenced by the creation of a Cabinet department on Housing and Urban Affairs to channel federal aid there. It is ironic, however, to attribute power to institutions that can force other levels of government to give assistance, so that they, the 'powerful', do not suffer bankruptcy, squalor and civil disorder.

Enormous social differences exist between communities. In Britain, an elaborate statistical analysis of census data by Claus Moser and Wolf Scott discriminated 14 different types of towns, primarily on the grounds of the social class of their inhabitants, population changes since 1931, and bad housing.[11] The 14 groups could be further reduced to three types: resorts and professional centres such as Brighton, Bath and Oxford; industrial and commercial towns ranging from Bristol and Southampton to the grimmest Welsh mining towns and Wigan; and suburbs, some exclusive and some for manual workers. One's picture of local politics, as well as of

English urban life, would clearly differ if one chose as a community for study Bournemouth, Salford, or Slough. If politics were studied in terms of very general models, then the difficulties arising from social contrasts would be overcome. It would still leave the question: who or what had the power to make these communities so different?

The causes as well as the nature of community differences can more clearly be discerned in the United States. Many influences are of the past: the date of initial settlement, the ethnic and religious character of the first settlers and the fate of the community in the waves of the late 19th-century westward movement from Europe to America, and again, from the East Coast towards the Pacific. Within a large American metropolitan area, one can see how economic and social influences create and sustain divisions, typically entrenched in state constitutions.[12] There are separately incorporated one-industry towns with industries so dirty that few would want to live there and taxes so low that many corporations like to invest there. Anyone who has seen some of the approaches to New York City through New Jersey or read Dante's *Inferno* will have some idea of what such communities look like. At the other extreme are communities that are almost entirely residential; the only people working there are servants to residents of the big houses. In between are more and less prosperous suburbs or sections of the central city, where religion and ethnic origins, as well as income and life style, help impart a distinctive character to an area of a few square miles. Negroes are the most important of all the clusters of peoples within a metropolis. In the North, urban ghettoes have been developed primarily in response to social and economic pressures. Suburbs have proliferated as central city land is all built upon, with separate suburbs catering to whites of varying income groups and prestige levels. They attract people for many reasons. One is the fact that informal arrangements usually make it relatively easy to exclude Negroes. It can be argued by black militants as well as by whites that Negro concentration in the central city of a metropolis is desirable. A ghetto makes it easier for a group to maintain its own customs, to enjoy some limited sense of security, and it provides an electoral base for politicians. As long as councillors in local government are elected by wards, then residential segregation guarantees some representation, just as coal miners concentrated in a relatively few British constituences are informally guaranteed representation in the House of Commons. Moreover, the proximity of Negroes to the heart of most major cities means that they are strategically located to call attention to grievances by such extra-legal but hardly non-political measures as demonstrations and riots.

The foregoing remarks emphasize the limits of what can be proven by the study of power in one community. Rather than linger upon these, it is more constructive to turn to the best of the studies of community power to see what has been learned within the limits set forth above. In a large and growing literature, Robert Dahl's study of New Haven, Connecticut, still stands pre-eminent in influence, although the climate of opinion in which it was conceived in the 1950s is now passing. Dahl's *Who Governs?* is based on the argument that statements about power in local politics can only be tested by observing what happens in the resolution of particular political issues. So stated, the approach hardly sounds controversial; but it is. It conflicts with another equally 'common-sense' approach, studying power by asking well placed local people: Who runs this town? Dahl marshals his case studies, supplemented by survey and recruitment data, to show that there is no integrated power elite in New Haven. Instead, influence is dispersed among a variety of individuals in many positions. The elected Mayor, formally the chief authority, is also the most important among the influentials. From this, Dahl concludes that while inequalities exist, they are *dispersed*; almost everyone has some form of influence. This conclusion is not so much used to rebut egalitarian myths, but rather to refute the argument, advanced by C. Wright Mills, Floyd Hunter and others, that politics in America is dominated by a single power elite. The evidence of the New Haven study is interpreted as justifying the characterization of America as a pluralist democracy: 'Instead of a single center of sovereign power there must be multiple centers of power.'[13]

The basic model on which Dahl's analysis builds is straightforward. Power is not defined as an attribute of a single individual or office. The author is too sceptical to assume that one can infer actions from personality traits or legal claims to authority. Power is defined as a relationship between people. The one that he has most clearly elaborated is simple in the extreme: it is a dyad, that is, a relation between two actors,[14] A and B. Intuitively, Dahl defines power as a relationship in which A has power over B to the extent that he can get B to do something that B would not otherwise do. Different aspects of the relationship can be analysed: the base of power, the means employed to exert power, the amount of power, and the range or scope of power. The exposition of this model of micro-politics is clear and logical. Yet upon re-reading the study, slightly to my surprise I found it much less convincing than I had recalled, because many problems are set aside.

While Dahl gains great clarity by concentrating his discussion upon the power-relationship of two individuals, he also loses relevance.[15] In any country larger than Lichtenstein (and perhaps even there), government takes place on such a large scale that the number of potential paired relationships is virtually infinite. Many of the most interesting problems in politics arise precisely from the fact that summing up the power or preferences of many individuals is not an easy, mechanical task. Dahl's paradigm reminds me of Sir Isaiah Berlin's discussion of the problem of 'the beastly scramble for the biscuit'. It arises if two men are stranded on a desert island with only a single biscuit, sufficient to keep one of them alive until help arrives. The problem is as difficult as it is unappetizing. Yet it is simplified because it is at the levels of micro-politics. By the appropriately American device of thinking big, the problem can be made complex. Imagine 1000 men or 500 men and 500 women abandoned with 500 biscuits distributed randomly on an island 500 miles square. The only happy solution would be if half the persons were game theorists and sat down to calculate the most rational strategy for building a winning coalition to seize all the biscuits, while the less mathematically gifted half ate up all the food.

Taking Dahl's paradigm on its own terms, one might first note that it implies that B will have little difficulty in doing anything that A asks of him. In the illustrations Dahl uses, such as voting in the Senate, it is fair to reckon that B will be capable of nodding his head Aye or Nay. But what if A pulls a gun on B and says, 'Jump out the window and fly to the moon'? In such circumstances A has the power to punish B for refusing to obey his command. If B stands still he is shot, and if he jumps he breaks his neck. Yet B's death also signifies the failure of A to realize his intention. Many of the most important problems in politics are now less easy to solve than that of flying to the moon. For example, the President of the United States may order his general in the field to eliminate Viet Cong resistance in South Viet Nam, or the Prime Minister may order the Chancellor of the Exchequer to make sterling safe from foreign speculation. In both instances, failure for the subordinate is also failure for the man who gives the order. A politician who gives impossible orders is not necessarily impotent; he is, however, incompetent.

In Dahl's paradigm, A and B, like a pair of lovers in a remote trysting place, have only each other to worry about. But one can ask in the cold light of day: Who has power over A? Whom does B have power over? An answer to this question would quickly run through the Roman, Greek, Cyrillic and Hebrew alphabets, in search of characters to symbolize the numerous people involved. Politics is essentially a multi-lateral activity. In the Viet Nam example, the President has power over the general, but the President is subject to regulation by the sum of people whose votes are sufficient to remove him from the White House, as well as subject to more immediate pressures in Washington. The general has power over his troops, but he would seem to have little power over his nominal allies, the South Viet Nam government, and even less over his opponents in the field. In the British example, the Prime Minister might feel superior to his Chancellor, but not to bankers in Zurich, officials of the International Monetary Fund and, perhaps, to a few of his colleagues whom he suspects of trying to depose him. A further complication is that in some contexts A may have power over B, but in others B may have power over A. For example, a Prime Minister has power over the membership of his Cabinet—until the day he loses the confidence of that Cabinet. Dahl's paradigm applies most readily to a situation in which the question of power is capable of a clearcut once-for-all resolution: e.g., the relationship between a prisoner and his executioner.

A shorthand way to refer to all the personal and impersonal constraints upon A and B is to describe them as products of the environment and of the particular situation under review. The general's inability to win a war may partly reflect the difficulty of securing total victory against a guerilla army fighting in a jungle, and partly a situational weakness of the South Viet Nam regime. A Chancellor's difficulty in defending the £ is determined by the degree of confidence in the international money market and other factors 'external' to Britain's nominal sovereignty. In America, where the cultural norm is—'the difficult is done at once; the impossible takes a little longer'—it is hard to draw the line between environmental and situational constraints. A person commanded to fly to the moon may express willingness to do so—as soon as the National Aeronautics and Space Administration opens up a travel agency there. In terms of practical politics, situational changes made the passage of civil rights legislation possible in 1964 after the intensification of Negro protests; previously, no President had been able to obtain such measures. In Britain, the government's intermittent involvement in the affairs of business and labour reflects situational fluctuations in the resistance of businessmen and union leaders to being managed.

A parsimonious way to limit the range of people relevant to a conflict situation between A and B is to ask: Whom should we expect to be involved in this situation? This question can be answered in many different ways, most of which have clear-cut ideological overtones. A statement that only A and B should participate is elitist. A statement that everybody should participate in all decisions all the time is a prescription for Utopia or Chaos. Perhaps to some fuzzy-minded revolutionaries, Chaos is Utopia. A reasonable compromise would be to suggest that one need only examine the activities of persons likely to be affected by a particular government action. This proposition has some less than obvious implications. For example, it implies that in the field of law enforcement, one would expect criminals to participate in and influence the decisions that police and public prosecutors take in efforts notionally directed to put criminals in jail. Anyone familiar with law enforcement at the level where green symbolizes the colour of money as well as grass roots may think there is something in this imputation. A second implication of the dictum is that one should expect the recipients of public welfare measures to participate in the framing of policies that directly affect them. Such an expectation is clearly unrealistic when one thinks of treating the insane or young children. Their interests will be stated and formulated for them by persons recognized by authorities as spokesmen on their behalf. Is it equally unrealistic to expect slum dwellers, or coloured people, or immigrants to be consulted and to speak for themselves when decisions are taken that effect them? In a sociological sense, there is much evidence suggesting that it is improbable that a large proportion of poorly educated people of low status would feel able or attempt to speak for themselves. For instance, Dahl reports that about three-quarters of New Haven residents with below average incomes are 'highly inactive' politically.[16]

In *Who Governs?* Dahl presents what is, in effect, a theory of 'virtual' participation. People may participate indirectly, at least, in local political decisions, by voting in local elections. Politicians are asserted to take anticipated future elections into account when making policies. Since the proportion of people who actually vote at local elections is often less than a majority of the adult population in England and America, Dahl extends the idea of vicarious participation by arguing that the right to vote is enough to ensure that the views of non-voters will be more or less taken into account. A vote is a slack resource. If politicians go 'too far' in ignoring the views of those whom they are supposed to represent, then they can be censured or ejected from office by disapproving voters pulling taut the loose reins they usually allow their leaders.[17] While not impossible, the argument is difficult to prove or disprove empirically. Dahl's study of New Haven does not provide conclusive evidence on the point.

Many problems that arise from abstract formulations of power can be put in perspective, though hardly solved, by asking the hard question: What are people trying to use their power for? An obvious answer is: to make decisions. Such an answer leaves up in the air the issue: Which decisions? As Dahl notes, any test of power must involve decisions that 'either constitute the universe or a fair sample from the universe of key political decisions taken in the political system'.[18] The use of the language of survey research is highly appropriate. Once a basis for identifying the universe of key political decisions is stated, it is a relatively straight-forward matter to draw a representative cross section sample of different types. In practice, students of community power are surprisingly vague about the selection of the decisions they study. Nelson Polsby, one of Dahl's associates, suggests that key decisions can be identified 'by preselecting issues generally agreed to be significant'.[19] It is ironic that Polsby proposes that the reputation of an issue is a sign of its importance, for elsewhere he attacks those who argue that people with a reputation for political power must be powerful. In *Who Governs?* only one paragraph is devoted to the choice of cases for intensive study.[20] Studies of cases in public education and urban redevelopment are presented as investigations of the formal power of local government officials. Party nominations are studied as an example of informal mechanisms for the exercise of power. Each of the three issues discussed at length is important in at least one respect, and of a type likely to occur in many communities. Yet the same could be said of other issues too, such as welfare services for the poor, law enforcement and white-Negro relations. The struggle to provide a bare subsistence for the poorest members of the community has different overtones than a study of a fight for good schools. A study of the definition of crime, inducements to crime, and the extent to which law enforcement officials are drawn into a symbiotic relationship with those whom they pursue raises other issues. Case studies of race relations indicate that even when a plurality of groups exist, they can stand in the relationship of superior and subordinate. On *prima facie* grounds, these issues are as important as the 'liberal/progressive' issues chosen by Dahl, though not necessarily more important. Certainly the study of such issues would produce an analysis with very different overtones—both emotional and political—than the New Haven study. For example, Edward Banfield has done community power studies in Chicago that concentrate attention upon such things as Negro housing, welfare regulations, and multi-million dollar real estate operations that redevelop the city and relocate slum dwellers.[21] Somehow, his studies leave a reader with the feeling that Mayor Daley's Chicago isn't such a nice place as New Haven. It is also a much tougher town in which to try to exercise power—especially if you are a Democrat in disagreement with the Mayor.

Whatever decisions are studied, it is by no means easy to decide at what point analysis should begin. At one extreme, a decision-making study might concentrate upon the events of a few days, e.g., the British decision to devalue the pound in late November, 1967. Here, attention would focus upon Harold Wilson, James Callaghan and a few Whitehall officials.[22] Yet if one asked these men to account for their power, they would probably disown responsibility, and claim that the decisions were pre-determined and forced upon them by a whole range of earlier decisions scattered across two continents. The chain of causation would certainly be extended back to include 13 years of Conservative government from

1951 to 1964, and it could further extend to the last previous devaluation in 1949. Dahl recognizes this problem very well. In analysing a decision in the mid-1950s concerning public education in New Haven, he begins with the decision to establish free schools taken in 1641. Quite sensibly, the discussion concentrates upon events of the past half a dozen years. Such a choice is practical and leaves few questions unanswered. Even if a very immediate problem, such as a race riot, was the subject of study, the analysis might need to be extended back to the time of the emancipation of slaves, or to the condition of Negroes in slavery. While the general outlines of the situation are clear in a riot situation, it is rarely certain when *or* whether any group made a specific decision which led to the riot. A decision-making study focusing on a well defined event or public agreement might unintentionally give more weight to the role of individuals in causing a long-term trend of events than historical analysis would justify.

It is also difficult to know where a decision-making study should end. Most studies conclude after a piece of legislation has been passed or an appropriation confirmed. Such activities are easy to isolate as conclusions of a particular phase of politics, and attractive to study for just that reason. It can also be argued that many politicians look no further than the end of a legislative session when making up their minds—and that they are well advised to take a short-term view. Yet, unless we assume that decisions have no further implications, or that the implications of actions are meaningless to those engaged in them, it is fair to suggest that the study of the consequences of decisions might tell us something about the exercise of power. For instance, if we studied the election campaign of reformers pledged to clean up the local police force and rid a city of crime, initially, the reformers might appear powerful. Yet, if we followed out the story of what happens to reformers in office, we might end up more impressed by the power of criminals to resist or recuperate from the attacks of reformers. In the case of Dahl's study, an interesting test of generalizations would be to look at New Haven again today, to see what has happened in consequence of decisions made a decade ago about redeveloping the city centre, increasing expenditure on public education, and nominating a particular slate of politicians.[23]

The course of race relations legislation in Britain neatly illustrates the disjunction between politicians' intentions and the consequences of their acts. In 1965, the Labour Government introduced and passed a hastily written Race Relations Act, intended as a symbolic commitment against discrimination, yet lacking practical means to combat it. The men placed in charge of administering the legislation, led by Mark Bonham-Carter, took it upon themselves to make their first priority lobbying the government to strengthen the Act, rather than administer it in accord with the intention of the Cabinet. The result was the introduction of another act, less than three years later. Hence, a measure that had initially appeared as a defeat for British liberals became in retrospect a milestone in the campaign for anti-discrimination legislation. In America, the reverse has usually been the case. Decisions to attack discrimination have usually been followed by less action in the direction intended.[24]

Concentrating attention upon the consequences of government policies sidesteps the problems that arise in considering attitudes toward the performance of government. In the latter approach, the key question is often whether there is a 'consensus'. Unfortunately, consensus is a vague word. It can be used to describe an identity of opinion, or, in a much weaker fashion, agreement about a particular matter, even if agreement is a compromise reconciling views that are far from identical. In the weaker sense of the word, a consensus can almost always be said to exist, except in the midst of civil war. For example, there is a consensus that the federal government cannot legislate on behalf of civil rights for Negroes—until there is a consensus that it must legislate on behalf of civil rights for Negroes! In Britain, there is normally a consensus of official opinion that what the Treasury does today about the economy is right, and that what it did yesterday was not quite right.

When a consensus of opinion is complete, i.e., agreement is unanimous and perpetual, there is, as Dahl notes, 'no conceivable way of determining who is ruler and who is ruled'. One interpretation that can be put on such harmony is benign. It can be said to represent an important invariant characteristic of the culture, or of the ability of office-holders to make decisions consonant with popular demands and preferences. But this harmony could also be interpreted as evidence of the ability of the governors to manipulate the views of the governed, so that they approve everything done in their name. Critics of Dahl have been quick to allege that a 'false' or 'manufactured' consensus is the best explanation of harmony. Occasionally, it is possible to test the validity of such assertions empirically. For instance, in New Haven, Mayor Lee and the city's business leaders were in agreement about plans to rebuild the city centre. This could be interpreted as evidence of political leadership, or of business manipulation of the Mayor. According to a first-hand observer, the chronology of events indicates that it was the Mayor who took the initiative in deciding what public policy should be, selling his idea to business leaders.[25]

One way to determine whether a particular point of community consensus requires any explanation is to see whether it is common across a range of cultures. If it is prevalent in different cultures, then it does not need an explanation particular to a single community or society. For instance, it would not be appropriate to explain the laws of a particular community about incest or murder in terms of events specific to a single place, for these acts are publicly condemned and prohibited in many different kinds of societies. When a consensus exists that is not common to a number of societies, then there is something to explain. For instance, Nelson Polsby states that in New Haven it is 'inconceivable' that the privately owned water company would be turned into a municipally owned utility company.[26] In Britain, it is equally inconceivable that central government authorities would seek to denationalize the supply of water, gas or electricity. Any group that sought to challenge either position would be involved in much more than the usual give-and-take of group conflict. The challengers would be trying to change a cultural norm, a conflict in which the odds are always very much against the challenger. From the perspective of a single culture, there is nothing to study in either attitude because no decisions or conflicts arise. From a comparative perspective, there is a very obvious question to answer: Why is there agreement about the virtues of privately owned utilities in one community, and about the virtues of publicly owned utilities in the other? Given the variations in patterns of utility ownership within the United States, one could even compare wide variations in attitudes within America. One might also ask who are the beneficiaries of the consensus, and who is relatively disadvantaged.

In many respects, agreement about the ways to resolve political disputes, i.e., the rules of the political game, is more important than agreement about goals or interests. If political leaders and followers agree about how political conflict should be conducted, then there is every reason to believe that disputes will be settled peacefully by methods accepted as binding by all concerned, even though some procedures, e.g. logrolling votes in Congress or party discipline in the Commons, may be disliked in principle. Among full-time politicians, the incentives to agree on rules for settling disputes are great. Agreement is needed to keep government stable; leaders must trust each other to alternate in office. Since people in office are successful in terms of existing rules, they have little reason to desire change. For example, civil rights agitation in American cities is rarely started by Negroes already established in public office, and it is often abandoned by agitators who become office-holders with a stake in the system. In Britain, similar changes can be noted among left-wing propagandists in the government of Harold Wilson; their numbers include men strongest in holding onto office as the Labour government moves right.

Among the mass of the electorate, the reasons for accepting the rules of the game are also clear. Indifference and ignorance protect many people from feeling resentment against whatever a government does. Even if people feel that things ought to be changed, the cost of challenging the *status quo* is great, economically and emotionally. A determined majority, by threatening the freedom or security of protesters, can effectively induce many who do not support their regulations to comply with laws—whatever they are. People are most likely to challenge the rules of the game when the cards are greatly stacked against them, or the outcome is something that they cannot live with. The problem most obviously arises in a nation occupied by a foreign army. Yet even here the striking thing is that usually only a minority of the subjugated people will carry their private opposition to the point of running the risks of publicly challenging their alien regime. In America, it is arguable that the group that has most to gain by challenging the rules of the game is not prosperous college students, but rather, poor Negroes. It is certainly clear that the civil disorders promoted by Negroes in recent years have produced more government action on their behalf than did years of acceptance of the local, legal *status quo*. In Northern Ireland, the civil rights demonstrations of Catholics in 1968, similar in many respects to those of American Negroes, similarly produced more evidence of change from a Protestant government than did almost 50 years of voting in elections where Catholic candidates were always foredoomed to opposition.

The rules of any political game inevitably discriminate in favour of some groups and against others. In Schattechneider's pithy phrase, '*Organization is the mobilization of bias*'.[27] For instance, if schools supported by public tax money are organized and run by professional educators intent upon bringing out the maximum of a youngster's skill in reading, writing and arithmetic—no more and no less—then this biases the educational system in favour of those who, because of family background and other outside-of-school advantages, are quickest and most predisposed to learn their three Rs. Simultaneously, it biases the schools against children from broken or culturally deprived homes, where the attributes of a conventional education are either not understood or positively scorned. In Britain, the Labour Government's efforts have been directed to making more in-school provisions for youngsters less ready to take to learning. In American cities, the challenge to reorganize education has taken a much more radical form, for black militants have argued that nothing less than a pro-black bias in city schools and colleges will compensate for years of bias in the opposite direction. Confronted with such dilemmas, a sensitive liberal can only take solace in the fact that he is offered a choice of horns on which to impale himself.

Professional politicians can organize the agenda of debate so that the ordinary voter is even denied a choice. For instance, in Britain, leaders of both parties have tried at various time to take religion out of party politics. This means that neither party provides a distinctive alternative on the issue. In the American Presidential election of 1968, Republican and Democratic leaders sought to organize things so that neither anti-Negro voters nor pro-peace in Vietnam voters would have candidates with these views. Those who rallied around Senator Eugene McCarthy failed in their efforts to provide such a choice. Those on the right were luckier, for Governor Wallace stood as a candidate in their cause. The 9,000,000 votes cast for the former Alabama governor, running without a party behind him, suggest the number of people who can be left out when, as Schattschneider notes, 'Some issues are organized into politics while others are organized out'.[28] Such events as these add unanticipated weight to

Dahl's offhand comment, 'The professionals, of course, have access to extensive political resources which they employ at a high rate with superior efficiency. Consequently, a challenge to the existing norms is bound to be costly to the challenger.'[29]

So much smoke has been generated by the controversies about community power that one might conclude that where there is so much smoke, there can be little clarity of vision. To my mind this would be unfair. Disagreements about the way to study power have clarified issues and have been very relevant to substantive problems of American and of British society. From the controversy, I conclude that in order to pursue the study of power, one must face at least four basic questions. The first is: Where should power be studied? A community is a fair place to start. However, one cannot draw very general conclusions from studying a single community. Generalizations can only emerge from the comparative study of communities, testing for similarities and differences in central cities, in suburbs, in small towns and in rural counties.[30] Comparisons between communities should involve some awareness of differences across political cultures. This provides a means of noting empirically the sorts of things that do *not* happen in a country. For instance, a comparison of an American community with one in Britain or Italy would lead even a mediocre researcher to conclude that there was a need to explain the absence of Socialist policies, or of clerical and Communist problems. In parts of Italy and America, he might find similarities too, as in problems of criminal gangs. Comparative studies also highlight differences in the institutions of government. American local authorities are among the most powerful in the Western world. In Britain, local authorities only enjoy such powers as are delegated to them by central government. In France, Italy and elsewhere, prefects, acting as agents of the central government, keep a close watch upon local officials to guard against localized political disaffection.[31] Studies making comparisons across time also give perspective to studies of local communities in crisis. Such studies can portray the normal pattern from which 'crisis' government deviates, as well as avoid the danger of drawing optimistic or inappropriate conclusions about the consequences of decisions not yet implemented when an author completes his book.

Unfortunately, community studies do not directly confront the question: What do we make of central government? It is all very well for hard-pressed academic researchers to explain that the proper study of one or a few medium-sized communities exhausts their research funds, or the models that they wish to test. But this is not even the beginning of an intellectually respectable discussion of the similarities and differences between local politics and national politics. A study of relations between local government agencies and the central government gives one kind of insight into the workings of Washington and Westminster. It is an insight that will, by definition, emphasize pluralism, for the existence of legally distinctive political jurisdictions is a very likely sign of dispersed power. In many fields, however, such as foreign policy, defence and economic policy, the politicians at the centre cannot share their responsibilities with local authorities; they alone are responsible for decisions taken. While all kinds of influences come to bear upon the small nucleus of men responsible for deciding a particular policy, most of the attempts will cancel each other out. There is also far more information overloading the centre than can be digested in a short period by individuals who have no more hours in the week than the inspector of weights and measures in a town of 20,000 people. It is just conceivable that what is labelled 'national' politics in some ways resembles small town politics. Only a limited number of people are involved, most knowing each other, and many oblivious to the world outside their immediate ken. It seems more sensible politically as well as geographically to think of Washington as a community whose 'local' politics are national in impact than it does to think of it as the centre of a continent. In Britain, central government is not located in a large city, but rather confined to a small part of London. Central government has now outgrown the area literally within sight of Westminster Abbey, but it is still largely confined within one of London's 32 boroughs.

Who should be studied? Most social scientists would agree that it is necessary to observe who does and who does not participate in politics. But sociologists have disagreed about the need for first-hand observation. For instance, C. Wright Mills based his influential study, *The Power Elite*, upon the analysis of the social backgrounds of decision-makers, supplementing these 'observations' by reference to a few accounts of high level politics, especially foreign affairs. Even when first-hand observation is involved, the techniques available are various. For instance, a social scientist may become a participant in community politics. This gives him greater awareness of the viewpoint of political activists, but the increased sympathy he gains for some protagonists may be offset by a loss in sympathy and perspective elsewhere. Some social scientists, such as Floyd Hunter, have emulated journalists, like John Gunter, systematically interviewing local notables in search of answers to the question: Who runs this town? A third alternative, exemplified by Dahl's New Haven study, is the use of precise social survey techniques to measure agreements and disagreements between political leaders and the general public, combined with first-hand study of specific political decisions.[32]

The fourth and final question is: Power over what decisions? Conclusions can only be general if they are based upon case studies that represent a cross-section of the problems requiring resolution in community politics. This does not mean that every decision need be studied, let alone every instance of decision-avoidance or 'non-decisions'. Rather than dispute about the exercise of power in conventionally observed instances, one should have a typology of decisions, extending from occasional crisis decisions of wide scope to frequent and routinized decisions affecting single individuals. Since Dahl and others attach considerable importance to the general public's potential for influence, it would seem appropriate to consider their potential interests too.[33]

At this juncture, the ideological implications of the study of power become very clear. The potential interests of a citizen need not be the same as the interests recorded in public opinion surveys or inferred by politicians or political scientists from evidence of popular apathy. Disputes about the 'potential' interests of citizens cannot be settled empirically, for the debate turns on conjectures and future events, as well as on values. Proponents of change are not only arguing that alternative arrangements of society are possible, but also, that such changes *would be* popular. The only way to find this out for sure is to try to make the changes, by one means or another. The bigger the changes, the greater the amount of revolutionary confidence necessary before an individual is likely to believe that the conjectured future is better and brighter than the familiar 'devil you know'. Some people will, of course, believe that any future is better than the present, just as they will believe any description of a power elite so cleverly elusive that its influence can only be known by repute or inference. Perhaps such faith tells us more about believers than about the world it means to describe. As David Riesman wrote, in a telling commentary upon the intellectual response to his argument that power in America is 'situational and mercurial':

> 'People are afraid of this indeterminacy and amorphousness in the cosmology of power. Even those intellectuals, for instance, who feel themselves very much out of power and who are frightened of those whom they think have the power, prefer to be scared by the power structure they conjure up than to face the possibility that the power structure they believe exists has largely evaporated. Most people prefer to suffer with interpretations that give their world meaning than to relax in the cave without an Ariadne's thread.'[34]

The proponents of the pluralist theory of democracy are equally attached to ideological belief, albeit of a very different sort. The great social scientific strength of the pluralists is that they are willing to test the accuracy of their hypotheses by reference to empirical data. On formal as well as on common sense materialistic grounds, there is much to be said in favour of examining carefully issues that do in fact arise. There is a diminishing law of returns in concentrating attention indefinitely upon the problem of what kinds of conflicts would exist in an ideal community. (Obviously, from the point of view of many power elite theorists, the ideal community would not be ideal unless it had *lots* of conflicts.) In their concern for studying whatever is, the pluralists at times seem dangerously near the point of arguing 'Whatever is, is right'. For instance, Nelson Polsby casually asserted in a book published in 1963, that 'most of the American communities studied in any detail seem to be relatively healthy political organisms'.[35] In the writings of Dahl, satisfaction with what he finds in America today shows up in his movement away from an initial theoretical interest in polyarchy, i.e. situations in which leaders are directly responsive to popular views through electoral pressures and other mechanisms. Empirical investigations demonstrated that usually the many are peripheral or passive rather than actively ruling. The few who rule are, however, observed to be divided and in competition. These important empirical findings have led to a change in emphasis from democracy or polyarchy *per se* to pluralism. A plurality of groups provides an immediate guarantee of choice and their competitive activities appear to compensate, or provide virtual representation for, the passive many. Whether American government is primarily polyarchical or pluralistic, in one aspect it remains constant: it is always a good thing.

The great strength of the pluralist analysis of political power is its flexibility. One only has to demonstrate a negative—a small group does not enjoy a monopoly of influence upon decision-making—to claim that the power elite theory is false. Dahl and many others have done this very thoroughly. Once the power elite theory is refuted, however, the doctrine of pluralism is a platitude. All kinds of communities, from the ideal democratic *polis* through those divided into petty sovereignties to those where a strong boss fights gangsters, bankers or disorganized opponents can be said to be pluralistic. National governments in countries as different as America, Britain, Italy and Japan are pluralistic, because each has competition among leaders. Even seemingly monolithic Communist societies are marked by intrinsic internal divisions, as party *apparatchiks* and technocrats compete among themselves to decide who governs.[36] In effect, pluralism is a vague generic term capable of fitting every government of a society more complex than that of a desert island.

No large society is perfectly monolithic or perfectly pluralistic. These ideas are ideal-types, polar opposites in a long continuum. Most communities and most nations fall somewhere in between the two extremes. As Dahl is at great pains to emphasize, even a 'good' community such as New Haven has many inequalities. After accepting emotionally the probability that inequalities exist in human societies, the most constructive thing to do is to measure them to see the extent to which a city more nearly approximates either of the two idealized models. Clearly, one would expect to find variations within a single country. The size of a community, the state of party competition, or any one of a number of other things might make a difference in the dispersion of power. The distance of central government from ordinary individuals might also affect the responsiveness of leaders, especially when they are protected by the duopolistic two-party system, in which one man must always win, even if he is only the lesser of two evils. In comparisons across nations, one might ask whether the political inequalities are greater or less, for example, in societies where working-class Labour or

Socialist parties contest elections, or where the chief industries are owned by the state.

To argue that the truth about power lies in between the two extremes of egalitarian pluralism and monistic elitism is not to argue that all societies can be equated as pluralistic power elites. Not only are there great variations in the location of societies on the power continuum, but also there are differences in the direction in which societies move. From the viewpoint of the ordinary citizen of a community, the question of how his country stands in comparison with Norway, Nigeria, Yugoslavia or Bulgaria, is not very important. The immediate question is: in which direction is the system changing, and how fast are changes taking place? The rising importance of such groups as the military and black power advocates in America, and of students and external financial powers in Britain, indicates that the answer is as important as it is 'non-obvious'.

NOTES—CHAPTER VI

1. Harry Eckstein, *Division and Cohesion in Democracy* (Princeton: University Press, 1966), Appendix B, 'A Theory of Stable Democracy', especially pp. 239ff.
2. Bernard Crick, *op. cit.*
3. Cf. H. H. Wilson, *Pressure Group* (London: Secker & Warburg, 1961).
4. Oliver McDonagh, *A Pattern of Government Growth* (London: MacGibbon & Kee, 1961). Cf. Henry Parris, 'The Nineteenth-Century Revolution in Government: a Reappraisal Reappraised', *The Historical Journal* III:1 (1961).
5. An up-to-date guide to studies of community power in America is best obtained from the footnotes of the most recent polemical discussions in the academic journals. In Britain, no such bibliography or polemics yet exists. Several excellent studies have been conducted. See e.g., A. H. Birch, *Small-Town Politics* (London: Oxford University Press, 1959), Margaret Stacey, *Tradition and Change* (London: Oxford University Press, 1960), and J. M. Lee, *Social Leaders and Public Persons* (Oxford: Clarendon Press, 1963).
6. *From Max Weber*, p. 183. The diffuse use of the term is indicated by the fact that the new *International Encyclopedia of the Social Sciences* contains four different articles on community studies.

7. See e.g., Robert C. Wood, *1400 Governments* (New York: Anchor, 1964) and Frank Smallwood, *Greater London* (Indianapolis: Bobbs-Merrill, 1965). For a general discussion, cf. Norton Long, 'The Local Community as an Ecology of Games', *American Journal of Sociology* LXIV:6 (1958).
8. Morton Grodzins, *The American System* (Chicago: Rand, McNally, 1966).
9. Two exceptions are D. N. Chester, *Central and Local Government* (London: Macmillan, 1951) and J. A. C. Griffith, *Central Departments and Local Authorities* (London: Allen & Unwin, 1966).
10. Arthur J. Vidich and Joseph Bensman, *Small Town in Mass Society* (New York: Anchor, 1960).
11. *British Towns* (Edinburgh: Oliver & Boyd, 1961).
12. For a more theoretical discussion, see Terry N. Clark, 'Power and Community Structure: Who Governs, Where and When?' *Sociological Quarterly* VIII:3 (1967).
13. Cf. Floyd Hunter, *Community Power Structure* (Chapel Hill: North Carolina Press, 1953) and C. Wright Mills, *op. cit.*, with this judgement, quoted from Robert A. Dahl, *Pluralist Democracy in the United States* (Chicago: Rand McNally, 1967), p. 24.
14. Dahl states, *ibid.*, p. 203, that A and B symbolize actors, which 'may be individuals, groups, roles, offices, governments, nation-states or other human aggregates'. His illustrations in the article are drawn from relations of individuals. Moreover, it would be difficult to analyse the problems discussed here in his language, for A and B, whether they stand for individuals or larger entities, cannot be disaggregated for purpose of further analysis.
15. For an illustration of the complexities that arise when one goes from a single-unit or a dyadic analysis of power to a system approach, see Terry N. Clark, *Community Structure and Decision-Making: Comparative Analyses* (San Francisco: Chandler, 1968) pp. 45ff.
16. See, among other sources, Dahl, *Who Governs?* p. 283.
17. *Ibid.*, Books IV–V.
18. 'A Critique of the Ruling Elite Model', *American Political Science Review* LII:2 (1958) p. 466.
19. *Op. cit.*, pp. 114–15.
20. *Who Governs?* p. 96.
21. *Political Influence* (New York: Free Press, 1961) and Martin Meyerson and Edward C. Banfield, *Politics, Planning and the Public Interest* (Glencoe, Illinois: Free Press, 1955).
22. Cf. 'The Eight Day Countdown to Devaluation', Insight report, *Sunday Times*, November 26, 1967.

23. There have been, for example, race riots large enough to receive national press attention.
24. Cf. Keith Hindell, 'The Genesis of the Race Relations Bill', *Political Quarterly* XXXVI:4 (1965). More generally, see a forthcoming study by E. J. B. Rose with Nicholas Deakin *et. al.*, *Colour and Citizenship* (London: Oxford, 1969).
25. I am indebted to Professor Raymond Wolfinger, one of Dahl's colleagues in the study, for first-hand information on this point. More generally, on the role of businessmen in politics, see Robert Dahl, 'Business and Politics—A Critical Appraisal of Political Science,' *American Political Science Review* LIII:1 (1959) and Richard Rose, *Influencing Voters*, Chs. 5–7, especially 7.
26. *Op. cit.*, p. 133.
27. E. E. Schattschneider, *The Semi-Sovereign People* (New York: Holt, 1960) p. 71. Italics in the original.
28. *Ibid.*
29. *Who Governs?* p. 320.
30. A sophisticated study that meets many of these criteria is the comparative study of two Northern and two Southern communities in America over more than a decade, Robert Agger, Daniel Goldrich, and Bert Swanson, *The Rulers and the Ruled* (New York: Wiley, 1964). Cf. also Donald Matthews and James W. Prothro, *Negroes and the New Southern Politics* (New York: Harcourt, Brace, 1966).
31. Cf. Brian Chapman, *The Prefects and Provincial France* (London: Allen & Unwin, 1955), and Robert Fried, *The Italian Prefects* (New Haven: Yale, 1963).
32. Cf. Floyd Hunter, *op. cit.*, and, e.g., Raymond Wolfinger, 'Reputation and Reality in the Study of "Community Power"', *American Sociological Review* XXV:5 (1960).
33. The comparison of what does not happen in one place with what did happen elsewhere seems to me much superior to its comparison with what might have happened in the first place. Cf. Peter Bachrach and Morton Baratz, 'Two Faces of Power', *American Political Science Review* LVI:4 (1962).
34. *Op. cit.*, pp. 257–58. Robert Lane's study, *Political Ideology*, suggests that fears of a power elite are not widespread among ordinary people. It is entirely possible that such fears (or hopes) are greater among aspirants to power and students of power.
35. *Op. cit.*, p. 134.
36. See Ghita Ionescu, *The Politics of the European Communist States* (London: Weidenfeld & Nicolson, 1967).

Seven

What Do Governments Do?

If one asks the man in the street what he does, the question is an easy one for him to understand. Whether he is a computer programmer or a coal miner, his answer should be straightforward. People rarely ask politicians what they do, and politicians lead such active lives that they rarely have time to ask themselves: what am I doing? If one were to put this question to the President or the Prime Minister, no matter how glib the leader, he might only be able to give a vague or semi-coherent answer. There are more obvious difficulties in asking a man what his organization is doing. A worker or businessman can give a textbook answer: the company produces goods and services to sell, hopefully at a profit. In America, the fact of making a profit might also be cited as a service that the company is performing for society. In Britain, a miner for the nationalized coal board might claim that the fact that the Coal Board was losing money meant that it was a social service, providing cheap fuel and uneconomic jobs. Balance sheet standards do not apply in government, notwithstanding the adventures of Chancellors of the Exchequer and Secretaries of the Treasury; they only metaphorically go toward the brinks of bankruptcy. If one cornered a spokesman for Her Majesty's Government or the American government and asked—What does government do?—it is not clear what the reply would be. Perhaps the American would modestly say: 'Our government provides the greatest number of benefits for the greatest good of the greatest number of people in the history of the world. And under the new Administration, it is doing this job even better.' An Englishman might disarmingly reply, with a stutter that sometimes seems pathetic, and sometimes a cunning tactical weapon: 'Wh-wh-wh-wh-why, it g-g-g-governs!'

The author of a book on British or American government might find it as difficult as a politician or a coal miner to explain what he was doing. If asked to write a book about government, where would you begin? The practical man's answer, still reflected in many textbooks, is: begin on page 1. Almost certainly, by the time he reached the end of his manuscript, the author would once again have demonstrated the truth of Keynes's dictum that every practical man is in fact in thrall to the concepts of some long dead and long discredited social theorist. There is need for a definition of government which abstracts its primary characteristics. This would help a person organize his thoughts not only in the familiar world of Anglo-American government, but also in other lands. It is not a bad armchair exercise to contemplate what one would need to know to write a book about government in Mozambique or Afghanistan. In all countries, the problem is the same: What to leave in? What to leave out?[1]

If one stops to think about it, the word 'government' is really a very high order abstraction. While as familiar as the University of London or the University of California, like those two institutions it is sprawling and disjointed, with its parts sometimes unruly or in conflict. Even a conglomerate corporation must, by its articles of incorporation, have a specific registered address. In their own country, governments do not need even this: only abroad do they confine themselves to a single building, an Embassy. If one stepped into a taxi in Washington or London and asked to be driven to 'the government', what would the cabby do? (In an ideal world, he might offer to read you some Wittgenstein while the cab sat still, and then ask if you wanted to repeat your request.) In Washington, the cab driver might give you a tour of the White House, the Capitol Building and the Supreme Court, with detours to the Pentagon and the State Department optional. The more legalistic driver, or the one more aware of the importance of symbols, might drive straight to the National Archives Building on Constitution Avenue, where the curious and the believing venerate the Constitution, the Bill of Rights and the Declaration of Independence, preserved with the dignity worthy of a relic of the Holy Grail or of Lenin. In London, even a reductionist-minded cab-driver might be uncertain whether to take his fare to Parliament, 10 Downing Street, or perhaps to the Treasury Buildings in Great George Street, which lies athwart the two. The man with an outlook more appropriate to the days of horse-drawn cabs would almost certainly go down the Mall to Buckingham Palace. The most up-to-date driver might speed for London Airport, and suggest his enquirer pursue his search further by taking the next Swissair flight to Zurich or Pan-American flight to Washington.

Academically speaking, the term 'government' usually describes a constitutionally sovereign set of institutions. In Britain, the government is the Crown-in-Parliament, a set of institutions carrying out the wishes of the Queen, as expressed by her ministers on behalf of her subjects. Concretely, this is taken to refer to Members of Parliament, the Cabinet and Prime Minister and, more uncertainly, senior civil servants. The judiciary is probably best omitted since the use of courts to restrain the executive is a very 'un-English' practice, and is specially difficult in the absence of a written Constitution. Until recently, authors of British textbooks confined their attention to the formal parts of the Crown-in-Parliament, with no significant recognition of such things as parties and pressure groups.[2] In America, it is even more dubious whether there is a single sovereign government.[3] The theory of federalism implies that the states as well as the central government have some inalienable powers. At both the state and federal level, three sets of institutions —an executive, a legislature and a judiciary—are separate and nominally equal branches of government. Either the courts or the legislature are meant to be most nearly analogous to 'separate but equal' Negroes.

Carried to its extreme, concern with constitutional forms can be very misleading. The fault is amusing when one reads a report of the Inter-Parliamentary Union that declares, deadpan: 'In Bulgaria, the National Assembly lays down the "essential lines" of Bulgarian foreign policy.' The failing is less than funny when one reads in the same document: 'The present Constitution of Czechoslovakia has in the main taken over the provisions in force before the war. There are two procedures, one set in motion by the Government, the other by Parliament, and these alone can bring about the fall of the Government.'[4]

Another common practice is to describe the government as that group of party politicians who occupy the highest formal offices in the land. In Britain, one speaks of Mr Wilson's government, or, less certainly, of the government of Sir Alec Douglas-Home. In America, the term 'Administration' is often preferred, e.g., the Nixon Administration or the Johnson Administration. This distinguishes the persisting institutions of a regime from the transitory groups of men who occupy major offices in the regime. Its chief limitation is that it confuses the partisan part with the whole of central decision-making. According to this formula, no recognition can be given to the role of F.B.I. men such as J. Edgar Hoover, or of senior civil servants at the Treasury.

To my mind, it is at least as meaningful to use the term 'government' to refer to all the multitudinous agencies which operate with the formal authority of the state behind them. I do not wish to argue that every social activity is somehow under the jurisdiction of government, whether it be acts between man and wife in a society where birth control is illegal, or the operation of a poultry store or a hamburger stand in a society in which the government claims the right to prevent pollution of the stream of commerce.[5] What this definition points to is a group of offices rather smaller than the Washington or London telephone directory, but larger than the number conventionally found on an organization chart.

In the United States, a convenient proximate description of the government—at least, at the national level—is contained in the nearly 900 pages of the *Congressional Directory*, a Government Printing Office publication useful to people who need to find their way around the federal capitol.[6] The Guide is divided into the three conventional headings—legislature, executive and judiciary—but the contents are sometimes surprising. The 400 pages or so referring to Congress contain much ritual padding, such as the incantation of Masonic affiliations in Congressmen's biographies. More than one-quarter, however, refers to men who are not themselves Congressmen, but important as staff assistants in places ranging from private offices of the Senate to the Library of Congress. The section on the executive starts, appropriately with the President and his Office. Even more appropriately, it omits any mention of an office of Vice President. In a burst of cosmopolitanism, international organizations with offices in Washington are listed before the Department of State. Nearly 200 pages record the government's official concern with Indians, intelligence and rural electrification, as well as with the Gorgas Memorial Institute of Tropical and Preventive Medicine, the Railway Retirement Board, and the Freer Gallery of Art. The listing of courts is short and reasonably straightforward. Interestingly, the Directory concludes with a catalogue of newspapermen accredited for admission to the Congressional press gallery. Undoubtedly, these men would repudiate the notion that they were employees of the federal government. But they could not refute the argument that their work was 'affected with the public interest'.[7]

In Britain, *Whitaker's Almanack* provides a more or less comparable listing of the range of public offices operating with the formal authority of the state behind them. Appropriately enough, Whitaker's is, as the Bank of England may still be,[8] under private management, but in the edition from which I quote, it chooses to dress itself up in royal associations.[9] The catalogue of agencies runs from the Ministry of Agriculture, Fisheries and Food to the White Fish Authority. In the course of 90 pages, it not only includes all government departments and nationalized industries, but also such things as the Tate Gallery, the Church Commissioners, the Registry of Friendly Societies, the Prices and Incomes Board, Trinity House, who have guided British voyagers along the coast since at least 1514, and the Ministry of Technology, now charting a course for Britain into the 21st century. Appropriately, this is followed by 101 pages listing bodies that are at least partially public, under such headings as 'Commissions, etc.', 'Banks and Banking', 'Law Courts and Offices', 'The Armed Forces', 'The Church of England', and 'The Universities', until a clear break is established by a chronology of the events of the year and a picture of the Queen and Duke of Edinburgh. Truly, one can say of this catalogue, even more than of the *News of the World*: 'All human life is there.'

The fascination and the difficulty with the *Whitaker's Almanack* definition of government is that it converts the concept from a dichotomous stipulation of things that are or are not governmental into a continuum, reaching from such central institutions as the Cabinet Office and the Treasury to the periphery of the Horserace Totalisator Board, the Court of the Lord Lyon and Amgueddfa Werin Cymru (The Welsh Folk Museum at St. Fagans). In America, the continuum extends to the International Pacific Halibut Commission. The universities are an obvious instance of how difficult it is to divide the continuum into governmental and non-governmental sections. On the one hand, it is conventional to say that British universities are not state universities, as is often the case in America. Yet it is also becoming common for Cabinet ministers to expound on the duty of the universities to meet national, i.e., governmentally defined, needs. Through the almost complete dependence of universities upon public finance, the views of the Cabinet can directly affect policies of universities. The blurring of lines can also be seen in the fact that Oxford and Cambridge, anticipating the possibility of a Labour Cabinet enquiring into their workings, drew upon two established Whitehall men—Lord Franks and Lord Bridges—to prepare reports on their behalf, independently of Whitehall and to forestall Whitehall. When Oxford University issued the Franks Report, if a person had gone along to Her Majesty's Stationery Office to buy a copy, would he have been exceptionally ill informed or exceptionally shrewd? I would say the latter. In the United States, 'private' universities increasingly find that funds for pupils, for buildings and for research come from the federal government. As state universities are able to draw upon private resources for funds to an extent unknown in Britain, the mixture of public and private sponsorship in education is intensified.[10] Any attempt to draw boundary lines involves an element of arbitrariness. It is easier nowadays to speak of things being more or less governmental than to draw a line between public and private things. My own preference is to define government in more inclusive, but not all-inclusive terms. This also seems to be the preference of men who run government.

The taste of social scientists today is to define governments (or political systems)[11] in terms of functions, instead of by reference to the kind of concrete institutions that can be listed in telephone directories. Functions of government may be identified in many different ways. One might start by trying to list the ostensible purposes of a government. In countries with written Constitutions, these are often stated there. The preamble of the American Constitution states as functions of government: establishing justice and domestic tranquillity, defence against external attack, promoting the general welfare, and securing liberty. At the other side of the world, the founders of the Republic of India showed a most unBritish fondness for abstractions in stating as their aims: 'Justice, Liberty, Equality and Fraternity'.[12] In Robert K. Merton's terms, we might speak of these as the manifest functions of government. The latent functions of government are those results that are not consciously and publicly defended, but which are nonetheless verifiable.[13] For example, a latent function of government in America is to deprive Negroes in Harlem and Texans in Texas of their own nation-state, just as a latent function of British government has been to maintain aristocratic privileges. The greater the burden of inference involved in describing latent functions, the more it might be appropriate to describe such things as *imputed* functions. This would make it clear that the activity in question may mean one thing to the social scientist studying it and very different things to the men being studied. Theories of government popular today often emphasize imputed functions, justified by intellectual theories developed to describe the 'basic' functions that all governments have to perform.

Talcott Parsons has provided the most widely read and best regarded contemporary framework for analysing the necessary functions of all systems of inter-action, including government. In Parsons' world, all social systems, whether small groups or large societies, can be studied in terms of the performance of four activities. The first of these is maintaining patterns of behaviour and values. The second is adapting group activities to cope with changes in their environment. Goal-attainment is the third function; goals may be explicit or implicit. The fourth function is that of integration, maintaining the morale and emotional solidarity of the group. In Parsons' analysis, any social system must perform all of these functions. Particular institutions are especially relevant for one of these needs. Government is reckoned to be specially important for the attainment of goals. Since systems of action are analytic units, Parsons is able to write at a very high level of generality about the political system, or, as he prefers to call it, the polity. This he does from time to time in books that are readily available to those specially interested in his approach.[14]

As a device for empirical analysis, Parsons' scheme has considerable shortcomings. In his own writings, references to politics tend to involve simple or even banal generalizations.[15] Even the most sophisticated applications of Parsonian-type analysis to important historical questions concerning economic and political development in Britain, France, and Asia leave me feeling uneasy, for I am not quite sure on what grounds empirical material is put into particular conceptual boxes.[16] Nowhere are we given reliable criteria by which two different observers could decide independently of each other that a particular political institution has one function rather than another. For example, it is not clear how to tell whether a system is performing adaptive functions or pattern maintaining functions. Yet the distinction between change for its own sake, change in order to preserve, and the appearance of change without its substance is crucial in English society. The problem of telling one Parsonian function from another always reminds me of the story of the American newspaper reporter who made up for his lack of grammar by a considerable enthusiasm. He was once accused of not knowing the difference between *who* and *whom*. 'Sure, I do, sure I do,' he replied. 'One of them is singular and one of them is plural, but I can never remember which is which.' Incidentally, the subject of this anecdote did not remain forever a reporter. By the time I came to know him he was manager of a symphony orchestra.

David Easton's scheme of system analysis is more political than that of Parsons, although it is only 25 per cent as discriminating, for it is concerned with one function only, the persistence of political systems. On this simple base, Easton erects a very elaborate framework for analysing political activity in terms of things that, by imputation, must be done if the system is to survive. The emphasis upon the inter-relation of government and electorate and of politics and other social phenomena is couched in rather general terms. Easton seems much more interested in what happens outside government than in what goes on inside that 'black box'. In an era when the collapse of regimes is a frequent if not predictable feature of political life, Easton has further limited the relevance of what he writes by not considering what, if anything, happens when a government is overthrown or, as he might say, when forces so challenge the workings of the system that critical variables are 'pushed beyond what we may designate as their critical range'. Easton literally and figuratively assigns such awkward political systems, in an uncharacteristically clear and Dantesque turn of phrase, to 'a limbo'.[17] Perhaps, inscribed over the portals of the place populated by most of the regimes known to history, is the motto: 'Abandon all hope for further analysis, ye who enter.'

A less abstract but still highly general description of the functions of government can be found in the writings of Gabriel Almond. A decade ago, he posited that the chief political functions in all societies were: political socialization and recruitment; interest articulation; the aggregation of interests; political communication; rule-making; rule application; and rule adjudication.[18] Unless some group of people, working through formal or informal institutions made sure that each of these things was done, there could be no state or government. It is sometimes argued that the terminology is neologistic, e.g., that the distinctions between rule-making, rule-applying and rule-adjudicating refer to nothing more than our old friends, the legislature, the executive and the judiciary. This is not the case. If one starts by postulating the importance of a legislature as an institution, inevitably this leads to a place such as Parliament. If one starts out from Trafalgar Square by asking the question—where are the rules made in Central London?—Parliament is likely to enter the picture at a late stage and in a relatively subordinate place. To my mind, Almond's categories are more political, and therefore more relevant than very general conceptions such as those of Parsons, or sociological theories that assume one can infer everything of importance politically from a little data about occupational class. Almond's approach leaves such things as the political importance of class open to empirical analysis. The chief weakness is that the concepts employed are not derived systematically from a formal theory nor are they welded together to form a coherent theory of politics. The categories do have an intuitive kind of unity, but Almond does not demonstrate why these seven and only these seven functions are important in political analysis.[19]

The interesting thing about Almond's work is that instead of making his categories more formalistic and more abstract, he has turned his attention to the more concrete activities of government. Almond and Bingham Powell suggest that politics involves a government's capability to extract resources from subjects, to regulate their behaviour, to distribute benefits to them, to provide symbolic gratifications, and to respond to popular demands.[20] Each of these activities is of some social and political importance in itself. They are not derived from a tight logical model, but rather, from a general concern about the potential importance of government to society. The approach is more congenial to the political philosophy of a *dirigiste* state than to that of a liberal state. But since most governments now want to be *dirigiste*, rather than govern on *laissez faire* lines, this does not discredit the emphasis; it makes it more relevant to the concerns of policy makers.

As an alternative to studying government in terms of abstract and imputed functions, one might begin by looking in the most simple and material way at what governments do with their own resources. Since nearly all governments summarize their activities in the form of annual budgets of manpower and money, this approach offers much to ponder. If use of these figures errs in the direction of reducing government to materialist indices, this may compensate for the social science tendency to describe government in terms verging on the ethereal, and the politicians' habit of describing actions in ways that often do not add up.

One way to approach the problem is to look at the numbers of people that government has in its employment, and at the things its manpower is meant to do. A head-counting exercise will not tell us what effects government has upon society, but a *sine qua non* of government intervention in social affairs is the presence of personnel to intervene.[21] In America, for instance, it is revealing to note that Fair Employment Practices Committees under Presidents Truman, Eisenhower and Kennedy had staffs no larger than 32 persons, including a dozen typists. Yet their task was to end discrimination against millions of Negroes in a continental labour force of about 75,000,000. In Britain, staffing for race relations is better—five headquarters staff, plus 7 clerical workers and 7 field staff—if only because the much smaller number of coloured people lowers the ratio of staff to people in potential need.[22] The most glaring British example of understaffing in recent years comes from the Treasury, which for many years managed the nation's economy with a staff of less than a dozen professional economists.[23]

The basic figures for public employment in Britain and the United States are set out, in summary fashion, in Tables VII.1 and VII.2.[24]

TABLE VII.1—PUBLIC EMPLOYMENT IN THE UNITED KINGDOM

Year	(A) Total Labour Force [000's]	(B) Total Public† Employment [000's]	(B) as a % of (A)	Armed Forces [000's]	Post Office [000's]	Central Gov't Civilians [000's]	Local Gov't [000's]	Education [000's]	Nationalized Industries [000's]
1891	14,682	554	3·6	249	(Not available)	110	175	40	—
1911	18,509	1,274	6·9	343	189*	271	660	214	—
1921	19,604	1,959	10·0	475	179*	508	976	257	—
1931	21,256	2,064	9·7	360	201*	441	1,263	276	—
1950	23,068	5,597	13·9	690	322	1,102	1,422	330	2,383
1961	25,057	5,754	23·0	474	350	1,302	1,782	422	1,846
1967	25,413	6,043	23·8	417	407	1,458	2,233	457	1,528

SOURCES: 1891–1950 figures—Moses Abramovitz and Vera Eliasberg, *The Growth of Public Employment in great Britain*, Princeton: University Press, 1957, pp. 25, 40–41.

1961 and 1967 figures—(a) *National Income and Expenditure*, London: HMSO, 1968, p. 15. (b) *Annual Abstract of Statistics*, No. 105, London: HMSO, 1968, p. 122; (c) *Ministry of Labour Gazette*, lxxvi, 1968; (d) *Employment and Productivity Gazette*, lxxvii, 1969; (e) *International Yearbook of Education*, xxiii, 1961, pp. 424, 427; (f) *Statistics of education*, vol. iv (1966), p. 117; vol. vi (1966), p. 103; pp. 108–109; vol. i (1962), pp. 30–31.

*Figures for 1914, 1918 and 1933, instead of 1911, 1921 and 1931.

†Total public employment, 1891–1931 inclusive, is the sum of the figures for armed forces, central government civilians and local government. The other columns report employees subsumed under these categories. In 1950, the total also includes nationalized industries; in 1961 and 1967, it includes nationalized industries and the post office.

TABLE VII.2

PUBLIC EMPLOYMENT IN THE UNITED STATES

Year	(A) Total Labour Force [000's]	(B) Total Public* Employment [000's]	(B) as a % of (A)	Federal Civilians [000's]	Military [000's]	Defence Civilians [000's]	Post Office [000's]	State and Local Gov't [000's]	Education [000's]
1929	49,440	3,326	6·7	500	300	—	—	2,500	1,100
1939	55,600	4,365	7.8	900	400	200	300	3,100	1,300
1948	62,898	7,100	11·3	1,900	1,500	700	500	3,800	1,600
1954	67,818	10,100	14·9	2,200	3,400	1,000	500	4,600	2,000
1962	74,681	12,100	16·2	2,300	2,800	1,000	600	6,800	3,400
1968	82,585	15,691	19·0	2,706	3,767	1,096	708	9,521	5,100

N.B. 1929–1962 figures—F. C. Mosher and O. F. Poland, *The Costs of American Government: Facts, Trends, Myths*, New York: Dodd, Mead, 1964, pp. 168–69.

1968 figures—(a) *Employment and Earnings and Monthly Report on the Labor Force*, xv:1 (1969, U.S. Dept. of Labor, Bureau of Labor Statistics), pp. 33, 55. (b) *Monthly Labor Review*, lxxxxi, 7 (1968, U.S. Dept. of Labor, Bureau of Labor Statistics), p. 88. (c) *Statistical abstract of U.S., 1967*, p.263.

*Total public employment=Federal civilians plus military personnel plus column of state and local government employees.

The figures substantiate the popular belief that the number of government employees (pejoratively, 'bureaucrats') has been growing greatly through the years. The number has risen more than four times in America since the Great Depression, and by three times in Britain, where the figure is increased by the post-war nationalization of coal, the railways, electricity and other major industrial employers. The economic significance of government as an employer has increased too. In America, the government now employs about two in every 11 people in work, as against one in 15 forty years ago. In Britain, the figure has risen from about one in ten to one in four.

The distribution of public employees shows some major differences through time and across continents. In America, the number of people in the armed services has increased more than 10 times in 40 years. In Britain, the numbers have risen only 17 per cent in a comparable period, and have been declining in recent years. In both countries, the growth in public employment has meant a centralization of manpower. In Britain, local government employed three-fifths of all government workers in 1931; now it employs less than two-fifths, even though the absolute number of people working for local authorities has almost doubled. In the same period, the size of central government has grown from about 880,000 in 1931, to about 3·8 million people. In the United States, the trend toward centralizing government has been less marked. The numbers of civilian employees in the federal government has grown from 534,000 in 1929 to 3,464,000 in 1962, an increase of more than six times. Employees in state and local government have grown even more in absolute terms, but because of the greater size of the lower levels of government initially, the increase in percentage terms, has 'only' been 280 per cent. Even when the military are included as federal employees, state and local governments still remain the major public agencies in America, employing 9·5 million people, as against 6·2 million in federal services. The bias in America toward truly local government is shown by the fact that its staffs are three times the size of those working at the state level.

The centralization of British government is geographical as well as legal. Approximately half of all central government white collar workers are employed in the London area. Only one of the other nine regions of Britain has a disproportionately large number of civil servants. In addition, more than half of all recruits to the administrative class civil service have been educated in the London area.[25] The Treasury and the Foreign Office, generally considered the most important and prestigious departments, are especially concentrated in London. The fact that the Foreign Office and Treasury both have many contacts in the capitals of other nations only intensifies the significance of their concentration. These departments speak for Britain in the world, but their first-hand contacts with the country are confined to one small corner of it. When the Treasury arbitrates disputes concerning home affairs, it may at times give more weight to overseas opinion than to domestic views, because these are the ones most immediately accessible to it.[26] In the United States, the Department of State is similarly concentrated, but this handicap is partly offset by a wider geographical basis in the recruitment of foreign service officers and by the relatively greater importance of defence and defence interests, remote from the capital, in the army camps of the South and in the defence industries of the Middle West, South West and Far West. The American Treasury maintains more regional contacts too: for example, the Federal Reserve Bank is divided into regions in a way that the Bank of England is not. The concentration of government employment, especially of high-level staff, is an expression of the necessity of easy access between agencies of government.[27] In America, this exists notwithstanding the fact that Washington, D.C., has never been considered an attractive metropolis, apart from government work. In Britain, as in most European countries except Germany, the capital of government is also the centre of the nation in a social sense. This makes it easier for government officials in London to identify the city in which they work with the entire nation. By contrast, many Washingtonians, especially those from further up the East Coast, spend their spare time asserting that Washington as a city is not the equal of various other places where they used to live. In both countries the departments with the most employees and regional branches outside the capital tend to be lowest in status, reaching bottom in the most decentralized of all departments, the Post Office.

Judged in terms of types of employment, the chief difference between Britain and America is the importance of productive workers in Britain. Notwithstanding the scorn sometimes directed at people employed in nationalized industries, there is no denying that they do make the electricity, and dig such coal and run such train services as Britain has. The nationalization of these industries was intended to give and does give government more influence upon the lives of its people, as well as giving it more power in the economy, for better or for ill.[28] In the United States, the federal government's massive defence budget makes it indirectly an important agent of employment. In addition to some 3·5 million men in arms, there are, even excluding circumstances like the Viet Nam war, an estimated 6·5 million persons employed in private industry in jobs created by the expenditure of federal funds, either for overtly military supplies, such as boots and bombs, or for defence-related expenditure, such as space research, or for civilian facilities such as federal highways. Except for these differences, other patterns of employment are much the same. For instance, education is the most important cause of public employment in local government. Education is a peculiarly labour intensive industry. Notwithstanding efforts by the British Treasury in the 19th century and the Ford Foundation in the 20th century, it remains difficult to apply labour-saving devices in modern schools.

The chief limitation upon the use of gross employment figures as an assessment of what government does is the fact that no allowance is made for the distinction between routine and non-routine work. The numbers and proportion of high level civil servants is small in both societies. In Britain, the administrative class civil service totalled only 2,700 of a staff of 850,000 in 1967, and the number of important people outside this category would be of the order of a few thousand.[29] An American study of the higher civil service defined the group as numbering about 16,000 men out of a total federal civilian labour force of 2·4 million.[30] Most political scientists would assume that one higher civil servant was more important than two dozen officials doing routine work, say, in a local employment exchange. In terms of the influence of one individual upon total governmental resources, this is undoubtedly true. Yet in terms of *aggregate* influence, it is less easy to say how much more one economist concerned with employment policies in Washington does to maintain employment than two dozen men in the field. From the viewpoint of people being governed, the civil servants they meet in the field *are* the government.

Another conventional way to describe government activity is in terms of money expenditure. To say this is not to argue that everything that government does is, or should be, costed by economists. The provision of justice for a single individual is worth a considerable amount of time, money and inconvenience, or so old-fashioned liberals would argue, and new policies too, such as racing to the moon, can also be undertaken without cost-benefit analyses. I wonder whether we would have more confidence in a government if it said it was promoting education because it was good for the economy, or promoting education because it was good for the people being educated. With such qualifications in mind, there is no reason why civilized Western materialists should scorn to look at figures drawn from bookkeepers as well as phrases drawn from books. Moreover, governments provide copious if not always convenient amounts of information about their budgets, and within recognizable limitations, this data can be used for comparisons across national boundaries and across time.

The pattern of government expenditure in Britain and America shows similar trends in both countries.[31] (See Tables VII.3 & 4). The trend has been up. In America, total public expenditure rose from $1,700 million to $263,000 million between 1902 and 1967. In Britain, between 1890 and 1967 total government expenditure rose from £123 million to £16,380 million. Reckoned in terms of dollars and £ of constant value, the changes are still great. In constant prices, public expenditure has increased by more than eleven times in this century in America, and by more than six times in Britain.

Because the government's expenditure has increased it does not follow that the burden of government expenditure has increased proportionately. When the economy can grow faster than government commitments or the population, then public officials are in the happy position of providing greater benefits at proportionately less cost than previously. In Britain, population has been relatively static in this century, increasing by only one-quarter; the gross national product has been relatively dynamic, increasing in real terms by one and one-third times in the same period. Because governmental expenditure has grown faster still, the cost of government per head has increased about 5 times in real terms; expressed as a proportion of the gross national product the cost has gone up about four times. In America, the population has increased by approximately

TABLE VII.3

PUBLIC EXPENDITURE IN THE UNITED KINGDOM

Year	Population (Mn.)	G.N.P. (Mn.) (A)	P.E. in Current £ Mn. (B)	(B) as a % of (A)	P.E. *per cap* [Current]	*Social Services *per cap* [Current]	Defence *per cap* [Current]	Central Gov't in Current Mn.	Local Gov't in Current Mn.
		£	£		£	£	£	£	£
1890	37·5	1,468	123	8·4	3·2	0·6	0·9	73	50
1910	45·0	2,143	258	12·0	5·7	1·8	1·5	128	130
1932	46·3	3,973	1,138	28·6	24·6	11·0	2·4	736	402
1951	50·2	12,926	5,217	40·4	103·9	44·5	26·2	4,018	1,199
1961	52·8	23,701	8,955	37·8	169·6	80·1	33·8	6,560	2,395
1967	54·4	34,292	16,380	47·8	301·1	72·7	41·4	12,370	4,010

SOURCES: 1890–1961 figures—Jindrich Veverka, 'The Growth of Government Expenditure in the United Kingdom since 1790', *Scottish Journal of Political Economy*, x.1, 1963, pp. 114, 119.

1967 figures—*Annual Abstract of Statistics*, London: HMSO, No. 105, 1968, pp. 262, 265, 278.

*Social Services include National Insurance.

TABLE VII.4

PUBLIC EXPENDITURE IN THE UNITED STATES

Year	Population (Mn.)	G.N.P. (Mn.) (A)	P.E. in Current Millions (B) $	(B) as % of (A)	P.E. *per cap.* [Current]	Insurance Trust Fund *per cap.* [Current]	Defence *per cap.* [Current]	Non-Defence *per cap.* [Current]	Federal Gov't *per cap.* [Current]	State Gov't *per cap.* [Current]	Local Gov't *per cap.* [Current]
		$	$		$	$	$	$	$	$	$
1902	79·2	21,600	1,700	7·9	21	0·00	4	16	8	1	13
1913	97·2	39,100	3,200	8·2	33	0·00	5	28	10	3	21
1922	110·1	74,000	9,300	12·6	84	0·90	22	62	33	9	41
1932	124·9	58,000	12,400	21·2	99	1·60	18	80	32	16	50
1938	130·0	85,200	17,700	20·8	136	4·60	16	115	58	22	52
1948	147·2	259,400	55,100	21·2	374	17·70	179	177	220	47	90
1958	174·9	445,500	134,900	30·3	771	82·90	321	367	405	94	189
1962	186·6	554,900	175,800	31·7	942	115·70	349	477	477	114	236
1967	198·7	803,900	263,184	32·7	1,324	205·70	353	766	651	170	303

SOURCES: All figures from Frederick C. Mosher and Orville F. Poland, *The Costs of American Government: Facts, Trends, Myths*, New York: Dodd, Mead, & Co., 1964, pp. 155–156, except for 1967, from: *Statistical Abstract of the U.S., 1967*, Washington: U.S. Dept. of Commerce, 1967, p. 5; *United Nations Monthly Bulletin of Statistics*, xxii.11 (Nov. 1968), p. 186; *Statistical Abstract of the U.S.*, 1967, pp. 386, 387, 390, 391; *Statistical Abstract of the U.S.*, pp. 390–91.

one and one-half times since the beginning of the century. The gross national product has increased in real terms by almost three times. Government expenditure per head has increased eleven times; expressed as a proportion of the nation's wealth, it has risen from 7·7 per cent in 1902 to 32·7 per cent in 1967, an increase of almost the same size as that in Britain. In America, as in Britain, the major portion of increased expenditure has required new taxes. About one quarter of the increase in public spending in each country could be financed by economic growth.

In both societies, the growth of government expenditure has been matched by the centralization of expenditure. In the United States, direct expenditure by local government accounted for 57 per cent of all government expenditure in 1902, and 23 per cent in 1962. In the same time period, the federal share increased from 38 per cent at the turn of the century to 65 per cent, including spending from social insurance funds such as old age pensions financed partly by contributions from employers and recipients. Centralization in the United States is still only a matter of degree. Spending by local governments has increased more than four and one-half times in this century in real terms, and state and local governments together still retain substantial revenue powers, as well as important primary responsibilities in such fields as education and police powers. In Britain, local authorities are not as independent as American local authorities in raising revenue and exercising powers. Central government's share of total public expenditure has increased from 50 per cent in 1910 to 75 per cent in 1961; it also provides the grants for another 11 per cent of public expenditure channelled through local authority offices. In real terms, while local authority spending independent of central grants has doubled, central government expenditure has increased by almost nine times, exclusive of its subsidies to local government.

War and national defence costs have accounted for most of the increase in public spending. In America, defence related spending has increased by 20 times in real terms between the two peace-time years, 1902 and 1962. In Britain, defence spending (including servicing the national debt inherited from past wars) has increased by nearly six times between the peace-time years of 1910 and 1961. In America, the change represents an increase in the share of total public expenditure from 20 per cent to 32 per cent. In Britain, there is a fall from 26 per cent to 15 per cent. The reduction in defence spending in Britain may be regarded as a melancholy reminder of the country's decline in great power status, or as a bonus for its disengagement from a central position in international relations.[32] Judged in terms of total national burdens, American defence consumed 11·7 per cent of the gross national product in the relatively 'normal' year, 1962, seven times more than at the turn of the century. In Britain, defence spending now takes less of the national budget than it did sixty years ago.

In domestic policy—assuming that the guns piling up are for use outside the country—a few services command large sums of money in both countries, but most services involve a relatively small expenditure of public funds. Many welfare benefits are partially or chiefly financed by insurance-type arrangements, even though the actuarial bases may be suspect, with benefits regulated more by electoral considerations than cash reserves. The value of these payments in relation to the total pattern of government expenditure is greater in Britain than in America. The trend upwards is greater in the latter country because social insurance schemes were not introduced in America until the 1930s, whereas they had begun before the First World War in Britain. In both societies, education makes a major and rising demand upon public expenditure in response to a common pattern of welfare pressures—a rising birth rate, an increase in the amount of education received by each child, and an increase in the quality and cost of the education received. A number of the public services are not directly comparable cross-nationally. For instance, the National Health Service is a major burden on the British budget, with costs nearly matching those of education. In America, public spending for health and hospitals, even before Medicare, had doubled since the war; it is still only one-quarter that of education. In Britain, housing has been a field for major central and local government subsidies. In America, by contrast, spending on highways and air transport have been major environmental charges. The country's housing conditions have, by European standards, been unusually good, but its continental distances have made the costs of communication high.

A reasonable conclusion is that the things that governments spend their money on are generally similar in the two countries. To note this is not to argue that differences in degree are not important. The degree of resources invested in health and education in the two countries differ in ways that underscore the contrasting values of the two cultures. Stated bluntly, it is better to be ill than ignorant in Britain, and better to need education than medical treatment in America, unless you are as rich as a doctor. The extent of similarities suggests that the processes affecting the activities of government are not unique to one society or to one political party.

Many things that the government does cannot easily be quantified in terms of cash budgets or manpower budgets. Intuitively, we feel that there is a big difference between a government decision to drop an atomic bomb and a decision to drop frequent garbage collection in a suburb of wealthy hypochondriacs. This would remain so even if the number of men employed and the marginal cost of frequent garbage collection is greater than the cost of firing a nuclear missile that is constantly depreciating in value. Many books reflect this intuition, for much more attention is given to decisions about war and peace than those about routine municipal services. For instance, in *The Power Elite*, C. Wright Mills concentrates attention upon five decisions of post-war American military diplomacy. It so happens that constitutionally power ought to be and is concentrated in very few hands when matters of war and peace are at stake.[33] One would only be justified in generalizing from these cases, if nothing else that the government did was of significance. I would not accept Mills's implication that the United States government did nothing much between dropping the atomic bomb in August 1945 and the decision to fight in Korea in June 1950. In Britain, the development of in-depth reporting of crisis activities in government has produced the tautological but journalistically convenient assumption that any decision involving the Prime Minister is a big decision and that the Prime Minister takes all the big decisions. Both academic and journalistic practices make one wonder whether there is not some sort of ego-identification between author and subject: I am writing about a big man who takes big decisions. Therefore, I must be a big man too. Given the extreme language sometimes used about politicians, the appropriate clinical term might be father-identification—with or without a desire for parricide.[34]

Budget figures and journalistic accounts of government differ in that the latter look at government as a series of big decisions—'to govern is to choose'—and the former depict government as a continuing process, maintaining more-or-less routine services, subject to marginal alterations. In the last analysis, the importance of world war as against public health or public libraries cannot be stated in terms of common units of measurement. The crisis event, by definition, is big as well as atypical. Yet anyone who has ever contemplated the problem of changing government routine knows that fighting routine is a major task, precisely because no one at any particular time is capable of taking a decision that will quickly resolve matters. For example, in America a great change in race relations cannot follow simply from a Presidential act. It can occur only through a whole series of non-routine conflicts, routine adjustments in public services, and changes in the cultural norms of blacks and whites. In Britain, individual Chancellors may take decisions with some immediate effects upon the £, but no one, whatever the party in office, can take a decision that will quickly alter the structure of an ageing industrial economy and the obsolescent cultural norms of workers and managers. By contrast, a military emergency is simplicity itself. It puts immediate power to act—e.g., to move troops or planes or missiles—in the hands of a few persons capable of getting a quick response when they push their buttons.

When a person asserts that what happens in the White House or in Whitehall is more important than what happens in Kalamazoo or Widecombe-in-the-Moor, the great problem is: how can this choice be justified? It is noteworthy that justification is usually expressed in quantitative language. The decisions taken by central government are said to be 'bigger'. Yet how is magnitude to be measured? It is hardly suitable to rephrase the answer, and say that 'fundamentally' these decisions are more important. This avoids commitment to quantitative measurement, but it still implies the ability to know when we have got to the bottom of the matter. On balance, it seems better to think in terms of magnitude rather than in terms of some essentialist property. People are never likely to agree on what is most essential, and there is no way to compare degrees of essentiality, without wandering into quasi-mystical language about levels of essence. By contrast, discussions couched in terms of magnitude easily permit comparison. One may not be able to measure precisely how big the First World War or the Second World War was, but at least one can make the important comparative statement that these events were bigger than decisions to licence colour television.

If we try to estimate the magnitude of government decisions, the next problem is magnitude in terms of what? Lives risked or lost? Money spent? Manpower? The energy employed by leading politicians in combating one another? Or, influence upon the lives of subjects? The varying standards have contrasting implications. Magnitude assessed in terms of lives lost would in this century refer to wars, and in more peaceful times, to public health measures. A judgment based upon the energies expended by politicians, something that could easily be observed in a community study, might lead to pride of place being given to an occasion which affected few citizens, but intensely concerned the rules of the game by which politicians gained office. It seems to me that the best standard to use, if one is concerned with the relation of government to society, is the importance of government actions for people being governed, and not their significance for the governors.[35]

The first criterion of importance could then be the *scope* of a government activity: how large a proportion of the population is affected by its action in a given field? The thing that makes decisions of war and peace important nowadays is that we are in an era of total war, i.e. wars affect civilians as much as soldiers, whether civilians remain working at home or are driven out of their homes by bombs or enemy troops. Now that education is universally compulsory, it too is an activity of equal scope in Britain and America at least, if not yet in Nigeria or the Congo, where war has more scope than education. Many of the activities of government are intentionally limited in scope, such as provisions for subsidizing geographical regions or sectors of the economy.

A second criterion is the *intensity* of the impact of government activities: how much importance is attached to it by the people who fall within its scope? Military crises are important because, if things go wrong, the consequences will be felt intensely by those involved in the subsequent war. At the other extreme, while the postal services also affect nearly everyone, their ups and downs affect few people intensely. Educational services might fall in between these two extremes, since schooling, *on average*, is likely to be of some importance, but not of highest importance, to those in receipt of public education.

The significance of government decisions is also modified by the *frequency* of their impact: how often or how long are people affected by certain actions of a government? Transportation is now a significant activity of government since people need to move about frequently, and their movements are no longer confined to familiar village paths, but follow highways, buses, trains and other services that governments underwrite or regulate. By contrast, wars happen infrequently, and this reduces their significance. Many things that governments do have intermittent effects, or their effects are limited in duration. For example, parks and other recreational facilities are used more on weekends and during summer holidays than at other times, and schools are used more at certain periods of a life-cycle than at others.

Probability is the fourth criterion: how likely is it that a person will be affected by a government policy? The probability that a child will be affected by state policy on education is very high in Britain and America. By contrast the probability is very low that someone in London, even Mac the Knife's London, will be affected by the retention or abolition of capital punishment. People manage to remain calm in the face of all the disasters that *might* befall them through government action by reckoning that the probability of trouble is very low. An extreme example is the procedure intended to reduce to nil, or virtually nil, the accidental firing of thermonuclear weapons.

Since each of these four criteria involve statements about magnitude—how large? how much? how often? how likely?—it is possible to state of two activities that one is more than, less than, or equal to the other. An important consequence is that one can then make some crude comparisons between private power and public power. For instance, one might assess the scope, the intensity, the frequency and the probability that activities of automobile manufacturers would influence a society. This could then be compared with similar judgments made about the influence of public officials appointed to regulate automobile manufacture and use. Since any government decision, judged by the foregoing criteria, would be more important to the manufacturers than to an individual motorist, private firms will have strong incentives to use their private means to influence public policy.[36] The criteria can also be applied to things that the government does not do, but might do. Insofar as it is possible to assess the probable impact of the hypothesized decision upon those being governed, then it is possible to compare the relative significance of a decision actually taken to build new schools, as against one that was never discussed, for example, a decision to nationalize the banks. For example, if the community in question was a rural community with schools still meeting effectively the demand for education by farmers, then the marginal significance of improving schools would be small on each of the four criteria. If privately owned banks, however, were charging high rates of interest and often threatening to foreclose farm mortgages, a policy that a nationalized bank would not be reckoned to pursue, then nationalization of credit would be more important than improving education.[37]

It is not possible to assign precise numerical values to each of these four criteria. It is easiest to try to measure the scope of a government's actions, that is, the number of people *directly*[38] affected by what is done. One might, for example, count the numbers of people using schools, highways or whatever during a stipulated period such as a year. Probabilities can be stated in numerical terms for most governmental actions. For example, the probability that a person will be affected by a rise in the tax on cigarettes or gasoline is a function of the probability that he is a smoker or runs an automobile. In some cases, such as the use of public highways, the probability is virtually 1·00 that this policy will be of some significance to any individual. The frequency with which government policies influence individuals can be reckoned in two different ways. Some government services affect people continuously, such as sewage disposal or the manufacture and distribution of electricity. Some influence people only intermittently, such as the use of snow ploughs to keep public highways clear. Other services such as education are significant with a varying frequency through a lifetime. Intensity is the criterion which is least suited to quantification. At a minimum, one can distinguish five degrees of intensity—life-or-death, very high, not so high, low or minimal. The nil point registers reaction to government policies on such things as the size and style of government letterheads, and the maximum, feelings about atomic war or, for some people, race relations.

The value of thinking about activities of government in this way is heuristic. The exercise does not lead to any simple solutions that can be readily applied to societies as different or as similar as two members of the British Commonwealth, or as America and Alabama. It does, however, make one realise how many things are implicit in statements about the importance of government actions. Since implicit assumptions are even more powerful than explicit assumptions, it is well to make clear how difficult it is to justify our intuitions about these things. Each reader can immediately check this by trying to state, by intuition or by application of the preceding criteria, which are the most important among the following activities: atomic war, preventing crime, education, highways, housing, military conscription, pensions, racial discrimination, racial violence, taxation and town planning regulations.

Assessing the importance of a single political problem is a problem to people who are not social scientists too. From the point of view of a voter, how much importance should he assign to particular issues, if he is interested in weighing up considerations before casting a vote? In 1968, an American might have reckoned Mr Nixon more likely to end the war in Viet Nam but more likely to increase race riots at home, and Hubert Humphrey better at keeping the peace at home than in South-East Asia. In Britain, as one cross-pressured economic journalist has described matters, the Labour Party could be thought better at libertarian and humanitarian policies, and the Conservatives better at economic policies; this offers him no choice but the horns of a dilemma.[39] Men in government, too, must weigh the importance of issues explicitly or implicitly, in the priorities they set themselves.

These priorities not only involve the things that the government will try to do, but also the things that busy men, especially men at the top, decide to ignore. Most politicians make an entirely intuitive assessment of which issues are important. Perhaps this explains why, after a term of office, a number seem to have got their priorities wrong.

Any attempt to measure the magnitude of political problems not only shows the difficulties of quantifying judgments, but also the difficulties of making non-quantitative judgments. If author and readers disagree about weighing problems when the foregoing *relatively* clear criteria are used, the chances are that they will disagree even more if they compare subjective intuitive judgments, for there are no criteria by which these can be rationally compared or justified. Paradoxically, the difficulty in quantifying the importance of government activities becomes a strong common sense argument for the exercise, since the prospect of reaching reliable and valid conclusions is even less when implicit, subjective criteria are used.

Whatever methods are employed, it is certain that government actions will be shown to be heterogeneous. Governments do many different things, and agencies of government often do different and sometimes contradictory things simultaneously. While varied, the activities are not infinite. Government would not work if every activity was unique in all its major respects; there would then be no basis for routinization. It is routinization, often described pejoratively as 'bureaucratization', that makes it possible for governments to start new ventures as well as to maintain established activities with little effort. An innovative measure, such as the establishment of a national health service or agencies to combat poverty in big American cities, involves many problems, e.g., personnel matters, accounting practices, etc., etc., which can be handled by routine procedures. At times, the procedural routine may conflict with substantive governmental goals.[40] On balance and in the long run (two qualifications as disheartening as they are important) the existence of some common features in many problems makes it possible for government agencies confronted with a new task to concentrate attention on its non-routine aspects, while handling many things still by its normal bureaucratic routines.

Constructing a general typology of the different things that governments do is very important, for once a general typology is at hand, then it is meaningful to ask that studies of power should make very clear the types of decisions that they concentrate upon. The most comprehensive studies would be those that examined a representative cross-section of problems. If the general typology stipulated four different types of government actions, then at a minimum, four cases would be needed for generalization; if 24 different types were stipulated, then the requirements for data would be proportionately greater. Ultimately, the number of case studies is less important than the representativeness of these studies. After all, a person who watched hundreds of cases being handled in a local employment office, or in the Whip's office in the House of Commons or the United States Senate, would have only a very partial idea of what governments do.

The four criteria outlined above provide a logical framework for categorizing public activities. If one simply stipulates that any problem may be high or low in terms of scope, intensity, frequency or probability of affecting people, then there are at least 16 different types of government activities. They range from those of maximum importance, high on all four counts, down to those of maximum triviality, of little importance even to the few people who occasionally by an offchance become aware of them.

The most important activities of government, those high on all four criteria, do not include war, for war is a matter of limited frequency. Governmental efforts to try to manage the national economy are the best example, for economic problems concern nearly everyone a lot almost continuously. Community power studies have devoted little attention to this form of power, though the relation between political power and economic power has been of considerable interest for centuries. The omission probably arises from the fact that there is no such thing as a community economy in modern New Haven or in Newcastle-under-Lyme. Business is conducted across great distances. Insofar as one may speak of a community of economic influentials, this group would lack geographical concentration. In America, the category would include a disproportionate number of people resident in Washington and New York, but also people in Boston, Chicago, Detroit, Texas and California. In Britain, a study of the community of economic decision-makers would include the historically autonomous City of London as well as government offices in Whitehall, and a few people from industrial centres such as Birmingham and Manchester. However such a study was defined, it is unlikely that it would end, as Dahl's did, with the generalization that the chief elected office holder was the most important person. Instead, one would more likely envision a situation in which no one had his hand on Ariadne's thread. This is certainly the lesson that studies of the postwar British economy suggest. Studies of public budgeting in America also emphasize the importance of impersonal determinants in economic affairs.[41]

The second most important category of public affairs are activities important on three of the four basic criteria. The maintenance of law and order is important in terms of scope, intensity and frequency of effect. In England, there has been a limited probability that anyone would be seriously affected by this service, in view of the generally peaceable nature of English society in the recent past.[42] When law and order cannot be taken for granted, as in Northern Ireland or bi-racial parts of America today, then the probability that police activities will affect most people rises, and this problem becomes as important as the government's role in the economy. Notwithstanding the importance given law and order, at least since Hobbes' writings in the light of the English Civil War, political scientists have shown little interest in studying the chief institution by which this is done, the police. This is specially surprising in view of the prominence of the police in community affairs, not least in cities such as Chicago, the site of two of the best community power studies.

The provision of health services is also important on three criteria—the scope, intensity and the probability that nearly everyone will at some time need medical care. Health services are not, however, frequently in demand by the majority of the population, thus making the problem not so important as economic affairs. Whether or not a government spends large sums of money in providing subsidized health services is a matter of policy. A commitment to avoid expenditure is just as important politically as the decision to establish a publicly financed national health service. Nowadays, it is harder to avoid some form of public medical care than to launch a programme. Even the United States government provides roughly one-quarter of all funds spent for health purposes, though it has preferred to do this good by stealth.[43] Studies of campaigns for health services in Britain and America have to date drawn sharp contrasts between the two countries. In America, such studies have emphasized the strength of a small, prosperous pressure group, the doctors, whereas in Britain studies have emphasized the strength of political, and more specifically, party and ministerial influence, as against the private power of doctors. My impression is that intensive studies of the hospital service in Britain today would emphasize the inequality of power as between the Ministry officials responsible for hospitals and the Treasury, responsible for giving or withholding funds for such purposes. In American cities, a community study that compared the calibre of public health care with private care would conclude that there were great disparities of influence, and illustrate how government can affect people by deciding to do very little or nothing.

Education and defence are almost as important as health. All are high in scope and in the intensity of their significance. The frequency with which education affects people is at least as great in a lifetime as the impact of health services. The probability that health care will be important is very high, since it can be a life-and-death matter for everyone. There is not the same probability that education will be of high importance to those exposed to it. On average, one might hazard the judgment that there is a 50-50 chance that it will be very important. Any estimate of the probability that defence forces will be used is even more prone to error. The strategy of deterrence leads military men to argue that the greater their forces, the lower the probability of their use. That model of conflict which regards the piling up of arms as a prelude to war implies the opposite. On historical grounds, one can say that military force is used intermittently; defence forces are not constantly in action, but they are 'not infrequently' in use.

Activities limited in scope but intensely important, frequent, and highly probable to influence a limited but discernible minority are familiar in the contemporary and classical literature of politics. In Britain, the entrenched powers of the House of Lords long provided an absolute bulwark against legislation that would affect the aristocratic minority. Similarly, in America, the system of checks and balances within federal government and between federal and state government has made it relatively easy for minorities to compensate for their lack of numbers in other ways, as well as important to explicate the significance of their behaviour for theories of majority rule.[44] When minorities are otherwise privileged, as has been the case of peers or Southern plantation owners, it is unlikely that they will be greatly oppressed by specific majoritarian measures. When minorities are otherwise weak, there is less assurance that government actions will take them into due account. In Britain, an example of an important minority are people needing basic welfare grants to subsist. In a time of full employment and rising wages, this group is limited in size, but it still includes 5 million or more people for whom welfare payments will probably be matters of intense and frequent importance. In America, there are also the chronically poor. Racial discrimination, involving people who are often poor as well as black, remains the most prominent example of a problem limited in scope but very high in the intensity, frequency and probability of effect upon black Americans.

Post office services are high on three of the four criteria of public importance: scope, frequency of use and the probability of getting mail. The intensity of feeling aroused by the postal service is, by comparison with other things previously discussed, relatively low. It is interesting to consider whether low intensity of itself makes the post office an unimportant government activity. It could be argued that the cumulative significance of small irritations in the postal service is considerable. In Britain, the nationalization of industries dealing with millions of consumers further increases the opportunity for people to feel small irritations with government services. While people dissatisfied with their meat still blame the butcher, people dissatisfied with their coal now blame the government. On balance, government-owned services with many consumers appear of medium importance, less significant than education but clearly more important than things low on at least two major policy criteria, e.g., regulations for licensing pets.

In view of the importance given the study of issues in *Who Governs?*, it is important to note that none of the three issues studied there—education, urban renewal or the nomination of partisan candidates—ranks high on all four measures proposed here. The changes in the New Haven schools were of medium importance, for they primarily concerned buildings. Nothing there would compare in significance with conflicts about racial integration in the schools, paying public funds to church-supported schools, or changing the management of schools to give more influence to local minority groups, the issue which led to bitter school strikes in New York City in 1968. The urban redevelopment programme is another issue of medium significance. It would be important to businessmen and to residents of the area being redeveloped, but it would be hard to argue, even in America, that rebuilding commercial facilities in a city centre is the most important thing that local government does. Decisions about the nomination of party candidates are low in significance; they have limited scope and intensity, occur infrequently and rarely concern citizens directly. The choice between Tweedledum and Tweedledee gains a little, of course, if ethnic conflict makes it competition on the Democratic side between Patrick J. O'Tweed and Tony Tweedodello, and on the Republican side, between John Winthrop Tweed and Herman Tweedenhaupt. It is possible to suggest that the political problems studied in *Who Governs?* were not meant to be evaluated for their significance or representativeness. The book, like many other studies by political scientists past and present, is much more concerned with *how* decisions are made by those who govern, than with *how much difference* they make to the people being governed.

At a time when public issues are becoming increasingly difficult and increasingly grim in America, there is much to be said for political scientists giving more attention to the content of government policy.[45] There are signs that this is happening. For instance, politicians and political scientists both show an interest in what defence decisions are made as well as in the process of strategy-making. Sociologists have given a fair amount of attention to problems of race relations and the lives of the very poor, and American political scientists are slowly beginning to follow this path. Of course, generalizations drawn from studies about people with problems will not necessarily fit more conventional issues. One might even suggest that an important task for students of politics today is to examine, under what circumstances and to what extent, governments making decisions affecting poor people or black people work differently than they do when taking decisions affecting missile manufacturers, bankers or trade union leaders.

NOTES—CHAPTER VII

1. For discussions of some basic concepts that might be used, see e.g., G. A. Almond, 'Introduction', to Almond and J. S. Coleman, *The Politics of the Developing Areas* (Princeton: University Press, 1960); Robert A. Dahl, *Modern Political Analysis* (Englewood Cliffs, N.J.: Prentice-Hall, 1963) and, for a more conservative approach, Samuel Beer, 'The Analysis of Political Systems', in Samuel Beer and A. B. Ulam, editors, *Patterns of Government* (New York: Random House, 1962 edition).
2. See e.g., such often reprinted books as Wilfrid Harrison, *The Government of Britain* (London: Hutchinson, 1960, 6th edition), and Lord Morrison's *Government and Parliament* (London: Oxford University Press, 1964, 3rd edition).
3. For a critique of American textbooks, see Theodore J. Lowi, 'American Government, 1933–1963: Fission and Confusion in Theory and Research', *American Political Science Review* LVIII:3 (1964).
4. *Parliaments* (London: Cassell, published for the Inter-Parliamentary Union, 1962) pp. 256–57, 285.

5. Cf. the famous New Deal Supreme Court case invalidating the National Industrial Recovery Act, Schechter Poultry Corporation *v.* United States, 295 *U.S.* 495 (1935).
6. The illustrations are taken from the *Congressional Directory*, 85th Congress, 1st session (Washington: Government Printing Office, 1957). I doubt whether American government has got any simpler or smaller since then.
7. Cf. Douglass Cater, *op. cit.*, and D. Nimmo, *op. cit.*
8. Cf. three articles on the Bank Rate and the Bank of England by Ely Devons, H. J. Hanham and Tom Lupton and C. Shirley Wilson, in the *Manchester School of Economic and Social Studies* XXVII:1 (1959). The article by the last two authors, 'The Social Background and Connections of "Top Decision Makers" ', is reprinted in Richard Rose, editor, *Policy-Making in Britain* (London: Macmillan, 1969).
9. Admittedly, the 100th anniversary edition, with a picture of monarchs of the period, including, chivalrously, Edward VIII. *Whitaker's Almanack*, 1968 (London: J. Whitaker, 1967).
10. See e.g. Malcolm Moos and Francis Rourke, *The Campus and the State* (Baltimore: Johns Hopkins, 1959). No comparable political study has yet been published of English universities. A good starting point for information at almost any time would be the letters column of *The Times*.
11. The concept of 'political system' is often used in place of 'government'. It is discussed in more detail in Ch. 8. Systems theorists would expect most of the functions discussed here to be performed primarily through the machinery of government in Western societies.
12. See Leslie Wolf-Phillips, *Constitutions of Modern States* (London: Pall Mall, 1968) p. 53.
13. *Op. cit.*, Part I. Cf. Kingsley Davis, 'The Myth of Functional Analysis as a Special Method in Sociology and Anthropology', *American Sociological Review* XXIV:6 (1959).
14. The simplest and most relevant introduction to Parsons can be found in W. C. Mitchell, *Sociological Analysis and Politics: the Theories of Talcott Parsons* (Englewood Cliffs, N.J.: Prentice-Hall, 1967). The book contains a detailed bibliography. See also, Mitchell's *The American Polity* (New York: Free Press, 1962).
15. See e.g., ' "Voting" and the Equilibrium of the American Political System', in Eugene Burdick and Arthur J. Brodbeck, editors, *American Voting Behavior* (New York: Free Press, 1968 edition).
16. See e.g., the major efforts of Robert Holt and John Turner, *The Political Basis of Economic Development* (Princeton: Van Nostrand, 1966) and Neil Smelser, *Social Change in the Industrial Revolution* (London: Routledge, 1959).

17. *A Systems Analysis of Political Life* (New York: Wiley, 1965) pp. 24, 223.
18. See G. A. Almond, 'Introduction'.
19. For instance, in my own application of Almond's categories, *Politics in England*, it was necessary to expand the seven categories to 11 chapters.
20. G. A. Almond and Bingham Powell *Comparative Politics: a Developmental Approach* (Boston: Little, Brown, 1966). The capabilities are discussed as variables indicating a society's political development by their increase.
21. The absence of large masses of trained civil services gives special importance to the problems of public administration in developing countries. See e.g., Joseph LaPalombara, editor, *Bureaucracy and Political Development* (Princeton: University Press, 1963).
22. See Paul B. Norgren and Samuel E. Hill, *Toward Fair Employment* (New York: Columbia University Press, 1964) p. 157, and *Report of the Race Relations Board for 1967–68* (London: H.M.S.O., 1968) p. 12.
23. Cf. Samuel Brittan, *The Treasury under the Tories* (Harmondsworth: Penguin, 1964) pp. 25ff., and *The Civil Service*, Vol. 4, pp. 86–88 and Vol. 5 (1), pp. 39–42.
24. The discussion in the following section draws principally upon M. Abramovitz and V. Eliasberg, *The Growth of Public Employment in Great Britain* (Princeton: University Press, 1957) and F. C. Mosher and O. F. Poland, *The Costs of American Government* (New York: Dodd, Mead & Co., 1964).
25. See Edwin Hammond, *An Analysis of Regional Economic and Social Statistics* (Durham: Rowntree Research Unit, 1968). Tables 2.7.2, and 2.7.3.
26. Cf. Samuel Brittan, 'The Irregulars', p. 338, in Richard Rose, editor, *Policy-Making in Britain.*
27. Cf. David Stanley, *The Higher Civil Service* (Washington: Brookings, 1964).
28. No up-to-date comprehensive study of the nationalized industries now exists. But cf. W. A. Robson, *Nationalized Industry and Public Ownership* (London: Allen & Unwin, 1966 edition) and A. H. Hanson, *Parliament and Public Ownership* (London: Cassell, 1961).
29. Cf. F. M. G. Willson, 'Policy-Making and the Policy-Makers' in Richard Rose, editor, *Policy-Making in Britain.*
30. See David Stanley, *op. cit.*, p. 1.
31. In addition to Mosher and Poland, and J. Veverka, cited in Tables VII.3 and VII.4, see also, Alan T. Peacock and Jack Wiseman, *The Growth of Public Expenditure in the United Kingdom* (Princeton: University Press, 1961).

32. Cf. Harold and Margaret Sprout, 'The Dilemma of Rising Demands and Insufficient Resources', *World Politics* XX:4 (1968).
33. See Daniel Bell's lucid discussion, *op. cit.*, pp. 52ff.
34. For psychological studies of attitudes towards Presidents see, e.g., Fred Greenstein, 'Popular Images of the President', *American Journal of Psychiatry* CXII:5 (1965) and 'The Benevolent Leader: Children's Images of Political Authority', *American Political Science Review* LIV:4 (1960) and Robert Hess and David Easton, 'The Child's Changing Image of the President', *Public Opinion Quarterly* XXIV:4 (1960).
35. Cf. Nelson Polby, *op. cit.*, p. 96, where criteria are presented which cut across these boundaries.
36. Cf. Murray Edelman, 'Symbols and Political Quiescence', *American Political Science Review* LIV:3 (1960).
37. For a case study of the problems of economics, farming and power, see, e.g., S. M. Lipset, *Agrarian Socialism* (Berkeley and Los Angeles: University of California Press, 1950).
38. Indirect effects are much more difficult to quantify. One might even argue that indirectly, everything affects everybody. This is the tendency of systems analysts, who stress the interdependence of phenomena.
39. See Samuel Brittan, *Left or Right: the Bogus Dilemma* (London: Secker & Warburg, 1968).
40. See e.g., Harry Eckstein, 'Planning: a Case Study', *Political Studies* IV:1 (1956).
41. Cf. e.g. Samuel Brittan, *The Treasury Under the Tories, 1951–1964* and Aaron Wildavsky, *The Politics of the Budgetary Process* (Boston: Little, Brown, 1964).
42. Peacefulness is not a long enduring constant of English society, and is subject to change. Cf. Geoffrey Gorer, 'The Psychological Role of the Police in England', in his *Exploring English Character* (New York: Criterion, 1955) and Jenifer Hart, 'Some Reflections on the Report of the Royal Commission on the Police', *Public Law* (Autumn, 1963).
43. The trend in the United States can be studied in the annual editions of the Statistical Abstract of the United States (Washington: Government Printing Office). See e.g., the 82nd edition, 1961, Table 81.
44. See Robert Dahl, *A Preface to Democratic Theory.*
45. The controversy about the role that policy studies should have in the new, highly self-conscious science of political science is most easily followed in the pages of *P.S.*, the house organ of members of the American Political Science Association.

Eight

Enduring Change

When the earliest written record of man's observations on his fate is discovered, it will probably be a reflection upon the problem of political change. After years spent trying to decode the strange symbols, archaeologists may find, to their embarrassment, that the sentiment expressed is only too familiar. My guess is that the inscription will have one of three possible translations: 'Every day the world is getting better,' 'Every day the world is getting worse,' or 'The world is in a continual state of flux.'[1] Conceivably, the inscription will be in a language so subtle that it can be translated in all three ways. Probably the most appropriate translation will refer to flux. Our problems are hardly better or worse to live with than those that confronted our ancestors, whether they were King's men or Cromwell's Roundheads, or rode with General Washington or General Lee.

Remembering our past does not make the difficulties of an uncertain present any less real for ourselves or for the people who affect and are affected by what we do in a world in which mutual influence, if not mutual understanding, continues to enlarge. Near at hand, every community nowadays faces the problem of how to expand or how to avoid decay, how to maintain its own autonomy while sharing fully in a modern economy, and how to train the next generation to meet a more complicated future. At the national level, the leaders of British government are trying to adapt economic and political institutions successful in past generations to a world in which Britain is increasingly vulnerable to actions outside its national boundaries. In America, national leaders face incipient civil strife between black and white, and simultaneously, responsibility for peace in a far from stable balance of power. In the euphemistically named 'developing' countries, the dispiriting events of the past decade remind us that stagnation or decay are possible alternatives to development. Leaders there may march with the baton of Lenin or Mao Tse-tung in their knapsacks, but, while many begin the march, few are likely to finish it.

Academic social scientists are also challenged by problems of political change. Aristotle was able to outline a theory of political change from democracy to tyranny, but the study of this branch of politics seems to have been going downhill since. Until recently, the conventional wisdom of political science made little allowance for changes in people or institutions, except perhaps to assume movement at an uncertain pace toward the universal goal of liberal democracy. The upheavals of the Soviet and Nazi revolutions made most of us aware that some political changes are not for the better. The end of colonialism has shown that changes can start from economic levels and cultural outlooks even less advantageous than those of Czarist Russia or Nazi Germany. While the world is changing thus, social scientists have difficulty in giving names to the changes taking place; because of this, they have trouble understanding the changes of which our lives are a part.

There are many motives for trying to understand the nature of political change. A modest academic might feel that efforts to define the nature of political change would at least make us aware of our ignorance of contemporary trends. A more ambitious academic would regard theories explaining change as more sophisticated than theories about static conditions. The practical argument for studying change is that change is the stated aim of many politicians; this is as true of Hailie Selassie as it is of Harold Wilson.[2] Sometimes, political changes are an end in themselves, and sometimes a means of improving national social and economic conditions. Without goals or some model of change, politicians involved in trying to bend events to their will will not know where they are going or what they are trying to do. A study by Robert Packenham of the justifications for foreign economic aid used by officials in Washington shows how practical politicians can be confused about aims. Packenham found that some officials thought American overseas aid was of limited economic benefit, but would have desirable political consequences; others believed the programmes made political conditions worse, but would have desirable economic consequences.[3]

In trying to understand the nature of political change, the British and American peoples are curiously situated. Few nations have experiences analogous to ours, yet the course of history in the two countries is fundamentally different. There is no *prima facie* reason to believe that conclusions drawn from the study of industrialization in Britain 150 years ago will fit a primitive African rural economy, nor that generalizations from the last 200 years of American history would necessarily fit the last or next 2000 years of an Asian society. Yet, if we cannot be conscious of our own past and its particular significance, the chances of generalizing accurately and shrewdly about the rest of the world are less than good.

British historians are sitting on a fortune, although many do not realize this. As the first European society to undergo a modern political revolution, in the middle of the 17th century England faced unprecedented problems. In the event, the great difficulties of Civil War and Restoration were quickly and happily resolved. J. H. Plumb succintly summarizes the change in *The Growth of Political Stability in England, 1675–1725*:

> 'In the seventeenth century, (English) men killed, tortured and executed each other for political beliefs; they sacked towns and brutalized the countryside. They were subjected to conspiracy, plot and invasion. This uncertain political world lasted until 1715, and then began rapidly to vanish.'[4]

Stable 18th-century political institutions were increasingly subject to pressure, as England experienced from the 1760s the first Industrial Revolution. The interplay between government and economy stimulated men as diverse as Adam Smith and Karl Marx to generalize; it continues to provide a source of theoretical stimulus to those who appreciate that it is easier to test theories of change in the past than in the future.[5] In socio-economic terms, England became a modern society more than a century ago. It is less certain when or even, perhaps, whether it gained a fully modern set of political institutions, for many values and institutions have persisted from the past. To note the relative antiquity of major changes in British politics is not to imply that no changes have occurred since the middle of Queen Victoria's reign, or that all changes since have necessarily been for the better. In the first 14 years of this century, disputes about women's suffrage, about the House of Lords' place in the Constitution, about industrial relations and, above all, about Ireland, threatened grave internal disorder.[6] The outbreak of the First World War did not save the country from all domestic upheaval; it simply turned the war by which Ireland gained independence into a minor sideshow.

The most frustrating thing in British historical scholarship is not the presence of detail or the absence of broad generalizations or new concepts. Any good historian uses a set of implicit assumptions to order his materials, and any critical reviewer can elucidate these. The historian's concern with the concrete and with types of information that cannot conveniently be put on IBM cards is a useful caution against the social scientist's weakness for formulating statements that apply to everything in general, but not to any thing in particular. My complaint is that British historians do not continue their narrative to the logical conclusion: the present. We probably know and understand more about political changes in the middle of 19th- or 18th- or 17th-century Britain than we do about events in the middle third of 20th-century Britain. The reason for this is not the unavailability of manuscript materials, for one does not need access to Cabinet documents to study recent public opinion, or social and political changes in industrial areas. The great attention given to events of the distant past would not be bothersome if a few historians undertook the task of explaining how we got from there to here. Perhaps some day a course in British history might start at the present and work backwards as far as needed to understand the political conditions of Britain today. Inquiries would probably extend back to before the Norman Conquest, but it would be good for a change to have students rush through the period A.D. 700 to 1066 at a gallop, instead of flying through the period since 1918.

Americans are fortunate because they do not have to extend their studies far back in time. Occasionally, students of American history must trace events back across the Atlantic when studying the slave trade or government in the colonies.[7] The fact that the United States was settled in a virgin land free from an inheritance of centuries of earlier civilization has meant that Americans could claim to be born free of Europe's feudal past. Moreover, as Louis Hartz has argued, the most important changes in American society may be those things that have made the immigrant fragment different from the European societies from which they became detached.[8] The cascade of immigrants into 19th-century America not only created a society with polyglot traditions, but also meant that differences between America at the time of the Revolution and the contemporary United States are far greater than those in Britain in the same period. While Britain's land area was shrinking a fifth by the loss of 26 counties in Ireland, the area of the United States quadrupled from 1800 to the present. In population, Britain has grown fourfold since 1790, while America's population has increased 50 times. The political institutions developed since the late 18th century in America are intrinsically interesting and important, but they do not seem suitable for generalization to other societies. Founders of new states seem to draw more direct inspiration from Britain, the French Revolution or the Soviet Union than from the United States. The few that have tried under American sponsorship, such as Liberia and the Philippines, are not particularly good advertisements for the transferability of American political arrangements.

One general conclusion that can be drawn from a review of British and American history is that the definition of change is itself no easy task. What do we mean by change? When we speak of political change it is usually unclear whether we are thinking about changes in kind or some other type of alteration. When we go to a *bureau de change* and change English or American money into French or Swiss francs, the act involves a change in kind. But if one changes citizenship and is no longer governed by the American presidential system or the British parliamentary system, but by de Gaulle's Republic or the Swiss Confederation, what exactly has been changed? A change in the label given a constitutional system is not a guarantee that the parts of each differ. The same is also true when constitutions change within a single country. Typically, the civil service and the organization of the army are little affected by this.

The political changes that we observe are partial, not total, whether viewed in terms of institutions or the persons running them. A political revolution can begin overnight, but it takes more than a generation to complete. In countries as static as the United States and Britain, it would be foolish to assert that everything political had been transformed in the past century, yet it would be highly tendentious to claim that 'fundamentally' nothing has changed. The very vagueness of the word change makes it usefully neutral. It avoids the disturbing overtones of such words as revolution, and the soothing ease of labels such as adaptation, which imply that all changes are gradual, painless, necessary and desirable.

Students of politics have a particularly difficult time in studying change, because there is no agreed answer to the question: *What* changes when political change occurs? When we hear an economist talking of economic change, the meaning is easy to understand and to measure. He may mean a change in the quantity and the character of the gross national product, in the distribution and types of industries, or in the use of resources. When we hear a sociologist talking of social change, the meaning is relatively clear and measures are at hand. We think of changes in class structure and in status relations, of urbanization, and higher literacy. Given a stated set of indicators, it is then possible to define with considerable precision when changes take place in an economy or in a society. For instance, applying James S. Coleman's criteria for socio-economic change to Britain leads to the conclusion that Britain had changed sufficiently to be regarded as a modern economy and society by about 1850. The functionalist criteria of political change offered by a sophisticated social scientist such as Coleman are not susceptible to ready quantification. They are high-level abstractions. In the case of Britain, this means that there might be as much as 100 years disagreement in dating 'system' changes reckoned to have occurred in the recent past.[9] Some awkward individuals might even argue that a key characteristic of Britain, or of any society, is the particular mix of old-fashioned and new attitudes. Even in a society building space-ships for the moon, there remain some people bringing up the rear by plane, train, bus, island ferry, on horse or on foot.

Changes in the formal institutions of government are fewer and more subtle than one might expect. Only monarchies seem to disappear completely from the political landscape, and in England even this has failed to occur. Many offices and titles seem to have remarkable staying powers. Some of the offices of British Cabinet Ministers today, such as that of the Chancellor of the Exchequer, have medieval origins, and the government's own accounts were not formally recorded in English with Arabic numerals until 1821. Even in the 1960s, efforts to change the government's machinery for keeping track of the economy involve a Bagehotian interplay of substantive alteration and the theatrical appearance of change.[10] In the United States, most of the major institutions of government are entrenched in the Constitution. The chief exceptions are the political parties, but the Democrats and Republicans, in spite of a number of inward transformations, together constitute the oldest unchanging party system in the Western world.[11] Changes that do occur in such institutions as the British Treasury or the Presidency typically involve alterations in informal arrangements or in the consequences of actions, rather than changes in offices *per se*.

From the viewpoint of the individual citizen, the most important changes that can occur are those that affect his opportunities to influence government, or the influence that government has upon him. The modern political history of England and America is often cast in the form of a chronicle of the gradual development of institutions of popular representation through the reform of franchise laws and the development of political parties.[12] After securing liberty from government interference and freedom to interfere in government, popular political groups began to demand that governments benefit them by providing the services that now constitute the welfare state. From the viewpoint of individuals, changes in pensions or health service benefits are more likely to be thought important than changing an indirectly elected to a directly elected Senate, or a bi-cameral Parliament to one in which the House of Lords is of little influence.

The most striking illustrations of the way in which political change can affect individuals are found in the lives of ex-colonial peoples. Often the changes are disturbing. In a traditional society, where little or no change occurs, both leaders and followers know their place and what to expect from authority. Once this position is threatened or disrupted, then people lose many cues to behaviour. They must adapt their lives to a society where guidelines are often novel, complex and conflicting. Choosing the standards by which one lives is especially a problem for the leaders of a traditional society, since political change is usually induced by contact with foreigners in a colonial or dependent relationship. As Lucian Pye has shown in a study of Burma, changes in authority can disturb a man's personality. First, the individual may over-identify with imperial cultural values and then reject these for an idealized version of traditional values, or vacillate uncertainly between the two.[13] In Britain, the phenomenon is most familiar in the Indian politician with a Cambridge or London School of Economics degree, first asserting himself in European terms and, if threatened with defeat, then asserting superiority in terms of traditional Hindu values. In America, the most familiar examples of persons disturbed by change are found among leaders of the Black Power movement, proclaiming allegiance to a black myth while simultaneously trying to maximize power within a predominantly white society. Politicians whose lives have been deeply affected by social change are interesting to listen to, but disturbing to try to do business with.

The most general and fashionable term used today to describe political phenomena—the political system—is ill suited to the analysis of change. In David Easton's definition, it is 'a set of interactions, abstracted from the totality of social behaviour, through which values are authoritatively allocated for a society. Persons who are in the process of engaging in such interactions, that is who are acting in political roles, will be referred to generically as the members of the system'.[14] The definition makes at least one thing clear: this analytic construct is totally abstract. While it has uses in studying a society at one point in time, it is less helpful in studying changes through time. There are few benchmarks by which one can tell whether interactions are changing, and if so, how. One can only confidently say they continue or they stop. Unfortunately, Easton seems uninterested in exploring less extreme examples of changes. His own writings devote attention to the ways in which political systems maintain themselves, by a process known technically as a static equilibrium, and capable of being caricatured colloquially as 'going around in circles'.[15] Since a political system is a composite entity, *par excellence*, it is always possible to analyse changes in parts of the system. When this is done however, it is not clear what happens to the whole.

The ideal theory of political change would identify the most significant objects that must alter for pervasive changes to be set in train. It would also identify the long-term and some of the short-term factors likely to cause these changes to occur and specify the probable social consequences of these changes. For such a theory to be fully fashioned (or fully fashionable), it should be suitable for the study of political changes at all times and in all places. In practice, most of the generalizations launched in ambitious analytic schemes are likely to fit somewhere, sometime. Often, they seem to fit only one country really well, the land of *Weissnichtwo*, described in Carlyle's *Sartor Resartus*. It is appropriate to recall that the best known savant there was Diogenes Teufelsdrockh, the Professor of Things in General.

People who feel the impact of political change in their own lives do not need to worry about labelling the things they feel. The key questions that concern them, questions with broad social science relevance, are: Where are we going? What are the things driving us on? The first question expresses a desire to find some meaning in changes that are often disturbing or disruptive in the short run. The desire to understand the causes of change may reflect the curiosity of an engaged but objective intellect. It may also be the response of a practical politician, groping for a set of ideas which promise him the chance of influencing the course that his people are following.

The greater the change, the greater the likelihood that it will be disturbing. The greater the disturbance, the greater the desire of politically conscious people to rationalize their harrowing experiences, that is, to find an ideology. Lucian Pye has been among many suggesting that persons questing for meaning might resolve their tensions if a national leader can propound, out of his own experience, an ideology which gives meaning and value to the trials of a people. Malcolm X sought to do this for American Negroes, and Gandhi to do this for Indians. The development of a new ideology, proving that the weak are or shall be strong, can be therapeutic for an individual, as well as politically threatening to the *status quo*. While many leaders seek a following for such charismatic visions, few succeed. As Weber notes, if a leader 'is for long unsuccessful, above all, if his leadership fails to benefit his followers, it is likely that his charismatic authority will disappear'.[16] Pye also suggests as an alternative that disturbed individuals with leadership potential seek occupational fulfilment. By showing professional skills internationally accepted by teachers, lawyers, physicists, administrators or politicians, they could gain a secure place as individuals.[17] This presupposes that non-Western nations have a disproportionate number of mute inglorious Keynes or Einsteins, a dubious proposition. Moreover, since the goals that Pye recommends are made in the West, if not overtly ethnocentric, his prescription might be taken to imply that the psychological characteristics of professionals in Nixon's America, Harold Wilson's England or Charles de Gaulle's France approximate some universalistic standard of good mental and political health. It may well be that the best thing for a non-Western leader and his people is to follow traditional values. It may be easier to live with Hinduism or Mohammedanism, as one's ancestors have done for centuries, than cope with World Bank economic criteria or apply in guerilla warfare the training received from Russian or American military advisers.

Just as there is no single direction in which individuals may go, so there is no necessary direction in which nations need head when faced with political problems likely to confront all societies sooner or later. Six of these crises have been particularly emphasized by the Committee on Comparative Politics of the American Social Science Research Council.[18] The crisis of identity arises when subjects of a state must decide whether they see themselves sharing a sense of nationhood or are divided in contrasting or mutually exclusive ways. The crisis of legitimacy concerns basic questions about the authority of the regime claiming voluntary obedience. The degree of penetration affects whether the regime has the skilled manpower to make its regulations effective throughout its territory. In turn, this influences the resolution of the crisis of participation. How people are integrated in a political system can be considered yet another crisis. Last, and in the eyes of modern Western people not least, is the problem that arises when governments are challenged to redistribute goods and honour in a society. Such a catalogue of crises gives some order to knowledge. For example, one can compare the way in which different countries have coped with such things as the crisis of political participation in Europe in the 19th century, and see the differential consequences of contrasting responses. No particular rate or direction of change is implied in this framework. This strength is also a major limitation, for there is no rationale justifying the special importance of these crises, or indicating the causes or likelihood of different courses of resolving them. Moreover, the language of crisis suggests that each problem is capable of a once-for-all solution. In fact, disputes about the distribution of wealth, about participation, or about the legitimacy of a regime can occur. France is the most obvious example of a European society with persisting and recurring crises.

If one assumes that political conditions are largely determined by social and economic conditions, as a number of writers do, then it is possible to gain some sense of direction, although at the cost of some freedom of choice. Once one ascertains the details of social and economic conditions and the rate at which they are changing, the future political events are then thought to be predictable. Implicit in this approach is the belief that one can affect a country's political future by influencing its economy or social conditions. It remains to be seen whether these forces are more amenable to purposeful government influence than are things more immediately under the control of politicians.

Facts of social and economic change can be found in census data and international economic reports. In most parts of the world, there is a clear tendency for literacy, urbanization, gross national product and other measures of modernity to increase rather than remain stable or decline over time. It would, after all, take considerable political skills to drive city people back to the countryside, or to depress an economy operating at subsistence level. While the direction of these changes is clear, the annual rate of change is limited. Karl Deutsch has shown, for example, that in countries such as Turkey, Chile and Ghana, somewhere between the depths of poverty and the heights of industrialization, annual rates of growth for the economy, for literacy and communications, and for urbanization, are of the order of a few per cent, and sometimes less than one per cent.[19] Population increases heavily discount the *per capita* value of economic growth. A small percentage increase in a small national product or in the urban population of a predominantly agricultural society is a token of socio-economic change; it is not proof that a transformation is well advanced. In the long run, perhaps the people of Honduras, Thailand, or Nigeria will be just as modern as the more cosmopolitan inhabitants of London or New York, but this news is of little comfort to those in the countries concerned. In their official capacities, politicians, even more than the peasants of such societies, have short life expectancies.

The political significance of environmental changes is difficult to discern. Deutsch is clearly on good grounds when he argues that present socio-economic changes will break down old commitments and communities. It is less certain what kinds of government will emerge in their place. Indices of change are much more easily calculated for social and economic phenomena than for politics. In the *World Handbook of Political and Social Indicators*, published in 1964, only 20 of the 75 characteristics tabulated there concerned explicitly political phenomena. If one assumes that political conditions are predominantly determined by socio-economic conditions, then this is not a major limitation. It is worth noting, for example, that all of the 14 countries with the highest gross national product *per capita*, the High Mass Consumption Societies, have free elections.[20] Yet among the seven countries just below the entry point to this category, four—East Germany, the Soviet Union, Venezuela and Czechoslovakia—lack free elections. It would require considerable analytic skill as well as optimism to show that each of these countries will automatically have free elections when it reaches some specified level of economic wellbeing. A different type of inference can be drawn from data on the military, and central government expenditure as a proportion of national income. Average figures do not alter as one goes from High Mass Consumption societies to Industrial Revolution societies and then to Transitional societies, even though the gross national product of the least of these, Iran, is only 1/24th that of the United States, the highest ranking country. The major contrast is between these three groups of countries and the 26 classified as 'Traditional Primitive' or 'Traditional Civilizations'. In the latter places the military is on average only half the size of that in more advanced societies, and proportionate central government expenditure is a third less than in more advanced societies. This emphasizes the importance of a minimum socio-economic standard if a government is going to extract money and manpower from its nominal population. It tells us little, however, about causes of variations among the 81 countries more prosperous than Haiti, the best off (*sic*) of the traditional civilizations. One possible interpretation of the enigmatic facts is that there is no common set of political consequences arising from any type of socio-economic change. The stimuli of change may produce different political responses in different societies.

A sense of direction is given to the discussion by those social scientists or policy makers who believe or hope that higher living standards and better social conditions will promote democracy. Phillips Cutright sought to test this hypothesis with data from 76 countries.[21] Cutright scored countries by the degree of political competition in their legislature and the number of years in which the executive head of government was chosen by free election. He labelled this an index of 'national political development', confusing development with democracy. The social condition that correlates most strongly with democracy is good communications. It is more important than the national level of urbanization, education or agriculture. The Anglo-American and Scandinavian countries, plus Switzerland, show the highest scores on both these characteristics. It is also noteworthy that Ireland ranks very high on democratic government even though it is disproportionately low on communications; probably, this is because of its former British connections. While Cutright's finding is plausible, Deane Neubauer has shown how a different definition of the key political variable can lead to a contrasting conclusion.[22] Neubauer defined democracy in more complex terms, using a set of eight criteria originally outlined by Robert Dahl. This measure puts Britain first and the United States 16th, beneath Italy, Japan and West Germany as well as below Sweden, Norway and New Zealand. The low score for America arises in part from the importance Neubauer gives nation-wide newspaper circulation as a guarantee of competing sources of information. America is one of the few countries with hardly any newspapers with a nationwide circulation. It is also low because in the North as well as the South, restrictive electoral registration laws effectively disfranchise a substantial number of whites as well as many Negroes.[23] No strong relationship is found between socio-economic conditions and democracy, as measured by Neubauer's index. Neubauer concludes that while a minimal level of development is necessary for democracy, there is no tendency for a country to become more democratic as it becomes richer and socially more advanced. From these exercises, the optimist might conclude that economic growth and social change will some day make it possible to develop democracy in countries that are now poor, backward, and undemocratic. The pessimist would emphasize the distance that countries have to travel before they reach the socio-economic threshold for democracy.

The desire to find an ethically neutral way in which to describe how the world is going has led many social scientists to write about 'political modernization'. Sometimes the word political development is used instead, to describe the process by which nations are said to become politically modern. This can happen under Communist, democratic or other types of governments. A political system becomes more modern as its capabilities increase and its characteristics become more rational, i.e., consistent with the logic of large-scale organizations. There is no agreement among social scientists about the precise criteria of political modernity. Lucian Pye has catalogued ten different meanings for the term 'political development'.[24] The most succinct definitions are usually the most abstract. For example, David Apter defines development as 'the proliferation and integration of functional roles in a community'.[25] The more general the definition, the less it is likely to be implicated in a single set of cultural values, but the less helpful it is likely to be empirically. A definition of 'modern' which brackets in one category America, England, Canada, Germany, France and, now or in the near future Russia and Japan, implies that there is nothing 'essentially' different in their politics. Such a proposition is a matter far too important to be settled by definition.

Implicit in the literature of political modernization is the assumption that stronger means better. This is not unreasonable, given the importance of power in theories of politics. But those of us who live in societies that became strong long ago face special problems. If one assumes that change is continuous and that our modern political systems have not achieved some sort of metaphorical consummation, one must ask: What are the chief features of the post-modern politics toward which we are heading?[26] Trying to decide such criteria calls attention to value considerations often ignored in what social scientists write about the rest of the world. A military strategist might reckon that a post-modern political system was extra-terrestial, capable of extending its earthly power into space. An economist might see further change as an increase in the character or magnitude of national resources. Sociologists would probably expect a different type of class structure. Socialists might argue that post-modern politics would come with the redistribution of wealth and status. Humanitarians might hold that once modern goals are achieved, governments advance by giving more humane treatment to the backward, the unbalanced and even the criminal. Race militants look optimistically to a future that is indeed black.

Some of the intellectual problems that arise from stipulating that change occurs in a single direction can be solved by hypothesizing two attractive but conflicting alternatives. This doubles the sophistication of an analytical framework and more than doubles the intensity of the leaders' problems. Faced with a choice, they must decide in which direction to head as well as how best to move. There is no guarantee that the choice will be easy. David Apter's study of *The Politics of Modernization* illustrates this approach; he makes choice central to his analysis, emphasizing its moral character. The chief alternatives, Apter argues, are the politics of reconciliation and the politics of mobilization. In a reconciliation system, governments are responsive to the demands of social groups, trying to maintain or increase social harmony, even if nothing else gets done. In a mobilization system, governments try to change society to achieve economic, military or ideological goals; in the short run, this can increase conflict with its subjects. A reconciliation system is best suited to a modern industrial society. In Britain, for example, politicians proclaiming modernization (or re-modernization) still have to listen to the men on the factory floor and in the board room. This may frustrate politicians, but it is doubtful whether the wool merchants of Bradford or their Pakistani mill hands think that economic conditions in Britain are so bad that they must sacrifice the delaying powers of representative government. In America, active Presidents may curse Congress, the institutional locus of representation and obstruction, but few Americans, whatever their colour, would wish to abolish Congress and trust a President elected by plebiscite. In non-Western societies, mobilization may appear the only practical strategy in the absence of the cultural prerequisites for bargaining to reconcile differences. As Peter Nettl succinctly notes: 'Extensive self-discipline, civic devotion, etc.—the qualities required for an efficient reconciliation system—do not grow on trees.'[27] Unfortunately, mobilization systems work through centralized controls, and in economically backward countries effective central bureaucracies are equally difficult to pluck from trees. In theory, a leader could try to balance between the extremes. The penalty for failing to walk a tightrope successfully is a brutal fall.

Both directions of change suggested by Apter are movements forward, for either choice is an effort to gain more of something: economic goods or social harmony. Yet it is also possible to think of governments diminishing or even disappearing altogether. Samuel Huntington has been notable in arguing that the most important political dimension of change is institutional development *or* decay. As David Rapoport points out, the history of Rome, from the perspective of today's theories, can be regarded as a movement from 'the early period as modern, the middle as modernizing and the last as underdeveloped!'[28] Intuitively, the concepts of development and decay are easy enough to grasp. Unfortunately, Huntington's definition is diffuse and vague. To him, the level of institutionalization in a political system is 'defined by the adaptability, complexity, autonomy and coherence of its organizations and procedures'.[29] A particularly important feature of Huntington's analysis is that in some circumstances rapid economic and social development tend to lead to political decay. Specifically, he suggests that this will occur if political participation increases as a byproduct of socio-economic change at a faster rate than can be given direction and contained by the institutions of government and of the governing party. Huntington cites considerably data from several continents in support of his hypothesis.[30] The leaders of developing nations are thus confronted with a harder choice by Huntington than by Apter. The latter implies that whether political leaders try to change a society or to reconcile conflicting views, something is gained. Huntington suggests that the very attempt to change a society, if undertaken without prudential allowances for the infirmities of government, will lead to the downfall of the men trying to make the change.

At this point, the reader may begin to think that more than the collapse of a government is at stake. If the changes taking place around the world only lead to the collapse of regimes, in what sense is it meaningful to speak of political development? Although a number of the intellectual edifices of scholars are not durable enough to withstand the stress of great events, they can still be useful as temporary buildings, providing concepts and a sense of order as temporary shelter. Whether one regards ambitious schema as idealistic or Promethean,[31] ignorant or comical, or occasionally as a mixture of all these things, it seems to me the effort is useful. In the short run, it is better to have our assumptions about change made explicit, whatever their ultimate accuracy, rather than think in unwitting ways things that we would reject if our assumptions were made explicit.

One way to avoid the faults of generalization on the grand scale is to try to explain why political changes have occurred in one particular country. After all, if we cannot do this, then the chances of making accurate large-scale generalizations are not promising. England is an especially good country to look at in this context, because its history is well known and, by the standards of modern America, France or Germany, relatively straightforward. Many of the political changes in England during the past century have been a response—sometimes prompt and sometimes delayed—to social and economic changes in the environment. Viewed comparatively, domestic welfare legislation does not appear as a consequence of the activities of particular reformers, or parties and pressure groups, but rather as a consequence of industrialization and democracy. Even countries without strong Socialist parties have enacted a wide range of welfare measures. It is also noteworthy that party initiatives have not been all-important in making decisions about welfare principles or other matters. As late as the Second World War, major crisis decisions were usually taken by coalition governments formed across party lines, a practice going back at least to the first part of the 19th century.[32]

The military and diplomatic achievements of British government in this century are even more clearly a story of a government reacting to the initiatives of Continental powers. The nation's strong insular position made 'wait and see' policies practicable, and allowed time in which to compensate for the mistakes that were made. Indirectly, major wars of this century have also caused reactions with important consequence for domestic welfare legislation. Peacock and Wiseman argue that many welfare measures have been adopted in post-war periods because the peace-time cost of defence declines so rapidly that still high war-time rates of taxation leave the government with a surplus of revenue. Instead of surrendering all this revenue, governments use it to finance welfare programmes for which there was not sufficient income previously.[33] These programmes are more palatable to former opponents because many continue principles accepted as necessary by coalition governments in wartime emergencies. The explanation does not fit the pattern of rising welfare expenditure in the 1960s, but it is at least consistent with protests about the level of peacetime taxation imposed to meet the costs of these programmes.

The role of individual great men in changing a nation's history seems strictly limited. On occasions when there is a fine balance between two very different outcomes, then it is possible to argue that a great man, or the weather, or any of 101 things might have tipped the scales. It so happens that the margin of England's victory in the two major wars of this century was a narrow one. Therefore, it is entirely reasonable to argue that without David Lloyd George or Winston Churchill the country would not have been on the victorious side. In peacetime, political events usually happen incrementally. Hence, the weight of any group or individual is not magnified out of proportion. In such circumstances, it is very difficult to argue that any one person was himself decisive in effecting a political change. One can rarely say that if X had never lived, the measures he advocated would never have been thought of or adopted in his country. One might mean that if he had not lived, the measure would not have been adopted in just that way and in just that time in a country. One can make the point most dramatically by asking historians to provide accounts of men powerful enough to prevent the introduction of compulsory education, state pensions or minimum housing standards in a modern industrial society. To note this is not to denigrate the efforts of individuals to influence the rate, the tempo or the content of particular public policies, but to see their efforts in historical perspective.

Explaining change in a non-Western society is no easier, though the value of attempting to explain the unfamiliar may be greater. A good example is a comparative analysis of *Political Modernization in Japan and Turkey*, edited by a Japanese specialist, Robert Ward, and Dankwart Rustow, a specialist in Turkish affairs.[34] It attempts the simplest type of generalization, that embracing two countries. While thousands of miles apart, Turkey and Japan have some things in common. Both began to establish modern economic, social and political systems in the late 19th century. Both have always had self-government; neither was directly subject to colonial rule. Until about a century ago, both had limited contact with Western societies; they then began to change in response to Western intervention. Not least, a number of generations have passed since change commenced. To point out these similarities is not to assert that Japan and Turkey are identical, but that, in the imperfect laboratory that this world provides, they are more alike than most pairs of countries. The aim of the Ward and Rustow study is to explain why the Japanese have succeeded so much more than the Turks.

After carefully outlining the specific indicators of social, economic and political change that are important, the editors present articles by individual experts on the bureaucracy, the mass media and other social and political institutions in each country. Some 420 pages later Ward and Rustow face the task of drawing conclusions. Their principal conclusion, though not their sole one, is phrased as follows: 'It becomes apparent that we are dealing with two very different societies.'[35] In the great *gleichschaltung* of comparative studies, it is chastening to be reminded that sometimes comparison requires the explanation of contrast.

The difficulties that experts have in generalizing about countries that they know well is instructive. As Joseph LaPalombara, an American student of Italian politics, notes:

> 'Political scientists are loath to make high-flown generalizations about the American political system (the one about which we have the greatest amount of information) while they will at the slightest stimulus generalize about large-scale societies in Africa, Asia and Latin America, concerning which our lack of historical and contemporary information is perhaps the most striking thing we can say.'[36]

British academics do not make this mistake. Instead of generalizing about the world in ethnocentric terms drawn from their own experience, there is much respect for things that make each country different. This leads to the vice of reducing each country's past, present and future to a set of highly particularistic anecdotes, often stories that imply that while this is the way foreigners act, things are ordered differently in Britain.

My own efforts to find something of general significance in a mass of particulars have led to a different course. Instead of trying to compare every country in every way with every other, I have concentrated upon a single problem—the authority of regimes.[37] A regime is defined as a set of institutions co-ordinating and controlling the civil administration, the police and the military within a state. Different types of regimes—parliamentary, military, Communist, etc.—are familiar. The government of a regime consists of the group of people who, at a given time, hold the most important positions. For example, one speaks of the Labour government of Harold Wilson, or in America, of the Johnson or Nixon Administration. A change in regime is usually more important than a change in the party forming the government. The institutions of a regime may be tolerably well described by a written constitution, but as England illustrates, a regime can exist without benefit of legal titles or legal fictions. Regimes are important because they claim more or less successfully to have a monopoly of the use of force within the boundaries of their state. Any political group that wants to induce social and economic change must first gain control of the regime, or else overthrow it and establish another one.

The type of authority that a regime exercises is determined by whether its subjects have a cultural outlook supporting the regime, and whether they obey all laws affecting its maintenance. This definition enables one to typologize regimes according to the way in which they combine compliance and support. Compliance emphasizes the *de facto* power of a regime; support, the voluntary basis of obedience. We normally think of Britain and America as regimes with high support and high compliance; such regimes may be called fully legitimate. A regime able to force its subjects to comply with its major laws but without support, like East European Communist satellites, would be a fully coercive regime. In theory, we could conceive of a fully isolated regime, with high support but little compliance. Ethiopia may approximate this type. A regime completely without support and compliance is fully repudiated. Since it belongs to the historic past, one can more confidently generalize about it. Many regimes are in some intermediate category. Because they have partial support or partial compliance, one cannot say they are fully legitimate, fully coercive or fully repudiated. The interesting thing about such divided regimes is: in what direction are they heading?

Politically, the most important thing is whether or not a regime is heading toward repudiation. The events of 1968, from the riot cities of Chicago and Washington to Paris, Prague and Berlin, have made many comfortable people realize that no regime is totally safe against a loss of support and compliance. How long do regimes survive? Before one could confidently assert that a regime is likely to last a while—with or without the support of those whom it claims to govern—at least two conditions should be met. First, the regime should have had time enough to socialize at least one generation of adult citizens to support it, and to try to re-socialize those who originally learned to accept the authority of its predecessor. Since people begin to develop a sense of regime loyalties or disaffection in childhood, one must allow 30 to 40 years before confidently asserting that the majority of a nation's adult population had been subjected to a full set of socialization experiences in support of a regime. A second condition is that the regime should survive a succession in leadership, thus showing that its existence is not the byproduct of support for a particular man or ruling clique. Among Western European nations, France, Spain and Portugal have yet to show that once their current leader goes, a second leader can maintain the regime he established. In such countries as Germany, Italy and Austria, one party has always been in office since the post-war establishment of new regimes there. None of these countries has yet managed a complete alternation in party government. The difficulty of succession is emphasized by Rustow's international study, which concludes that the political leadership of a country is more often changed by actions which also cause the repudiation of a regime than it is by measures which bring in new men, but leave the institutions of power unaffected.[38]

One can only make statements about the duration of regimes by examining those states that have a past. While long histories exist in many Afro-Asian societies, few have regimes with a history of any length, for most of these societies have been incorporated as independent states for one or two decades at most. Europe and Latin America are the only two areas where many states have long had an independent existence. Here, it seems best to concentrate attention upon the familiar case of Europe. Latin American regimes are hardly likely to be more durable. Unfortunately, Anglo-American scholars have tended to think about Europe in terms of the three most populous countries of *Western* Europe—Germany, Italy and France. There is a common-sense justification in devoting more attention to big countries than small countries, but the general significance of an intellectual conclusion is not directly proportional to the size of the country described. If this were the case, anyone writing about China or India would be likely to draw conclusions two or three times as important as statements about American government, and ten times as important as those about British government. It seems safest to define Europe in a strict geographical sense, with boundaries stretching from Iceland and Spain to Russia and Turkey, since Turkey has historically been governed from the European side of the Bosphorus. One could argue that Iceland, Spain, Turkey, Russia or even England, are not 'really' a part of Europe. The more restrictionist the argument, however, the more nonsensical it becomes in geographical terms. There is, for example, no other continent to which England could conceivably be assigned. This definition has the practical advantage of increasing the number of cases available for study, as well as including a large portion of the countries of the world which have been independent for more than two decades.

The majority of European regimes are neither new nor long-established. Six—Britain, Iceland, Ireland, Russia, Sweden and Switzerland—have been governed without interruption since before the Second World War and have successfully survived a change in government. They are distinguished on both counts from Germany, Italy and Austria. Three regimes—France, Greece, and Turkey—have been established in recent years by *coups*. Two regimes established by force, Spain and Portugal, have yet to pass any test of succession. It is arguable whether the Eastern European regimes have faced problems of succession. It is indubitable that the majority have faced challenges to compliance, and none confidently claims the full support of its subjects. These regimes have survived since the war, but they lack full legitimacy and the direction in which they are tending is a matter for expert debate.

An alternative way to estimate the duration of regimes is to ask: how many regimes have the states of Europe had in the not so distant past? The year 1900 is a convenient date to choose as a starting point, for it spans a time within the living memory of the oldest generation of Europeans. No common pattern of regime changes can be found among the states existing in Europe at the beginning of the century. Four states have had only one regime—Britain, Iceland, Sweden and Switzerland. Eight states—Albania, Bulgaria, Finland, France, Germany, Greece, Rumania and Spain—

have had at least four regimes each, at a conservative estimate. Four states recognized in 1900—Austria-Hungary, Montenegro, the Ottoman Empire and Serbia—have ceased to exist at all. One can, of course, say that if it hadn't been for the First and Second World Wars, the number of regimes would have been far less than those counted here—an average of 2·7 for each country surviving through the period. This is true, but if one takes away the two great wars of this century, the political conditions that caused them and the political consequences that they have had, there is not much left to study in modern Europe. Moreover, Latin American states, where state boundaries have altered little and where continental wars are unknown, is hardly a better example than Europe of durable regimes.

Given the record of regimes in Europe in this century, any analysis of the authority of regimes should start with a pessimistic rather than an optimistic bias. Statements of general significance about the authority of regimes, should show a bias toward explaining why regimes are repudiated or, at least, why regimes do *not* become fully legitimate. While it may be interesting to ask why the regime in New Zealand enjoys full support and compliance, it hardly seems relevant to the problems of France, Czechoslovakia, or nearer home, to the problems of Northern Ireland, Quebec, Harlem and Mississippi.

The importance of war as a means of repudiating regimes is indubitable in modern Europe. The end of the First World War saw 11 new states and regimes created, and the disappearance of four regimes by the abolition of their statehood. The end of the Second World War saw fewer changes in regimes arising from alterations in state boundaries. Three states—Estonia, Latvia and Lithuania—lost their independence, but only one new state of a sort, the East German Democratic Republic, was created. The implication of this for new states created from former colonies is that states themselves are vulnerable to aggression from neighbouring powers or from internal war.

The Second World War brought about the repudiation of many regimes through invasion. Of the 20 European countries invaded and occupied by one or more armies from the date of the Austrian *Anschluss* in 1938 until V-E Day, only four—Belgium, the Netherlands, Norway and Denmark—might claim that the post-war regime was a restoration. Yet in at least three of these countries, as well as resistance groups, there were collaborationist groups prepared to accept the war-time regime.[39] Typically, invasion brought to a head deep divisions within the occupied society. In extreme cases, such as Yugoslavia and Poland, civil wars were fought simultaneously with wars of resistance. In each instance, the differences were not ones that could be resolved by free elections, and a change of regime rather than restoration occurred after the war. The advance of Western and Russian armies provided an opportunity for the settlement of old antagonisms that had divided pre-war regimes. Some groups stayed put, while others fled or were expelled. It is a cruel but relevant fact that those tribes of Poles, Hungarians, White Russians and other refugees, familiar in Paris, London and New York, are making a contribution to the survival of the regime in their native land by being in exile from it. History seems to imply that much opposition to regimes in non-Western states may only be removed by violent means. A sophisticated African could even argue that civil war and police state tactics were evidence of Europeanization, rather than retrograde steps. For instance, the measures by which the Nigerian government has sought a final solution to the Ibo problem in Biafra have recent European parallels.

The well established political traditions of European societies are a reminder of the influence that the past has upon the future of every regime. The leaders of a new regime cannot control their precursive conditions and precursive conditions can be fatal congenital defects. The stronger the traditional culture, the more likely a regime is to be repudiated if it tries to deviate from traditional norms by introducing social and economic development plans intended to change society. The more divided a society is in its pre-existing cultural loyalties, the less likely any regime is to achieve full legitimacy. The most it can hope to do is to have the approval of one sub-culture, hopefully a majority large enough to compel compliance if not support. The degree of cultural fragmentation remaining within contemporary state boundaries is indicated by the fact that in only 50 of 131 states in the world do nine-tenths of the population share a common language. Divisions are worst in black Africa, where 23 of the 33 states have populations where no single language is spoken by as many as half of its people.[40] The greater the precursive pool of civil administrators, the more likely a new regime will be to obtain compliance. This is true whether administrators previously owed loyalties to their opponents or to an Imperial power. Events in

20th-century Germany and Russia show the willingness of civil servants to serve successive regimes, whatever their policies.

Pre-existing socio-economic conditions affect the course of a regime in at least two ways. The greater the aggregate national resources, the more likely a regime will be to have a pool of administrators able to demand compliance. Even if most of the people are poor, countries with large aggregate national incomes can do things that small, prosperous countries cannot. China and India, for example, are tied for 101st in the world in terms of *per capita* gross national product, but they rank fifth and eighth respectively in terms of total GNP. This in turn makes it possible for India to rank third and China fourth, just after America and Russia, in total numbers of pupils in higher education.[41] Total wealth also affects communications, and communications make it possible for a regime to gain or lose support quickly, since most of its subjects will quickly become aware of what its actions are. The experiences of a new regime's leaders prior to taking office can influence their capacity for survival. Ideally, one might reckon that a new regime would combine men with the skills of conspirators, agitators, soldiers, party organizers and civil administrators. Yet so varied a group of people would form a coalition difficult to hold together. Given the many precursive obstacles to support and compliance, it is hardly surprising that so many regimes at the time of their collapse, and some at their origins, appear to be born losers.

The founders of a new regime have considerable influence upon the circumstances leading to its creation, whether they are colonial agitators, granted power more or less peacefully by a retreating Imperial authority, or Latin American colonels, executing a *coup d'état*. The unity that can be created to expel foreign rulers, as in Afro-Asian independence movements, need not survive long into the life of a new regime, when leaders have only each other to quarrel with. The collapse of the unity of resistance groups in Europe quickly after the Second World War is a cautionary example.[42] In a society in which a *coup d'état* is a recognized means of changing governments, the use of force in seizing the national capital need not prejudice the life of a new regime. The limited scope of a 'palace' revolution, however, means that its activities are unlikely to constitute a social revolution without considerable additional labour. In the short run, at least, it would seem that the greatest security for a new regime in a culturally divided society is likely to be victory in a very bloody civil war. The bloodier the war, the more likely the outcome is to be accepted as decisive by the losing side. Badly beaten opponents of the regime in Ireland since the 1920s, Spain since 1939, Yugoslavia since 1945, and the American South since 1865 have shown little desire to fight again, given the costs involved. For instance in Northern Ireland, defeated Catholics are against a recurrence of violence by a majority of more than 6 to 1. The reason most often given is to the effect that 'Innocent people (i.e. we) will only get killed'. In a complementary fashion, a willingness to fight again for their regime is shown by a majority among Protestants, for they have enjoyed the fruits of success in trial by combat.[43]

The leaders of a new regime have considerable latitude, in the short run at least, in the course that they attempt to follow. In terms of this analysis, we can distinguish four alternative strategies. A regime might seek to be popular, valuing both support and compliance. Alternatively, its leaders might follow an authoritarian course, trying to maximize compliance without regard for popular support. A regime which puts support ahead of compliance is weak, effectively letting authority devolve into other hands. In some countries, regimes may be arbitrary, with leaders interested neither in support nor compliance, but only in exploiting the population for their own personal advantage. In theory, it is difficult to hypothesize which strategy should prove best, for so much depends upon particular local conditions. It is also difficult to tell what strategy a new regime's leaders actually follow, for often an attempt is made to mask the effective machinery of authoritarianism behind the dignified appearance of popular support, as in such curious events as the Albanian election of 1962.[44] All but ten of 889,875 registered electors had their votes counted, and the Communist National Front won, 889,828 to 37.

The obstacles to survival that leaders of new regimes face—whatever course they try to follow—can be crudely grouped under three headings: security problems arising from threats of external aggression or internal subversion; problems of maintaining whatever support and compliance they have; and problems of developing greater support and compliance. Developing greater support or compliance is not the same as economic or social development. Rapid economic growth may upset a regime rather than 'buy' support, especially when the dividends of a 4 per cent growth rate to individuals are not likely to be as great or immediate as the psychic payoff it provides economists. Economic change, moreover, imposes costs upon peasants and workers who are the objects of change. Even in England and America, the psychological cost of industrialization was very considerable. Given the extent of parochialism in such relatively developed countries as Italy and Mexico,[45] it is unlikely that the mass of population in more backward countries is actively pressing demands for economic development. The rhetorical assertions about the so-called revolution of rising expectations perhaps tell us more about the salience of economic issues to social scientists, including their ex-pupils now in key government jobs in Afro-Asian societies, than they do about their salience to subject and parochial masses.

In a perfect universe, each regime would be conceived in circumstances in which the precursive obstacles to survival were few, and the chances for economic development favourable. But the world is imperfect. Everyone does not have the good fortune to be born a white or black American, or some kind of Englishman, even if only of the Irish variety. Most European societies have now reached a kind of political *modus vivendi*, but the costs have been great, even for the most spectacular example of rapidly and simultaneously building support, compliance and an economy, the Federal West German Republic. No one would wish that another country would take the course that Germans have followed in their search for political order. Perhaps India is a more typical example of a non-western regime in the course of change. It has inherited considerable precursive advantages, some indigenous and some the legacy of British rule. It has also inherited considerable precursive disadvantages, most of which are indigenous. At any given time, the leaders of the regime face security problems from Chinese or Pakistani aggression, as well as internal subversion organized by communal or linguistic groups and, conceivably, by Communists. The job of maintaining existing levels of support and compliance is no mean one given the rate of population growth. All of these great problems must be faced simultaneously. The leaders of a new regime are, like an American president, in Neustadt's phrase: 'The prisoners of first-things-first, and almost always something else comes first.'[46]

One conclusion that might be drawn from the changes that occur in regimes can be summed up in the following hypothesis: the greater the number of precursive influences and the greater the difficulty of contemporary problems, the less likely a regime is to survive. Unfortunately, the regimes with the severest loads also tend to be those with the least capabilities. One would, of course, hypothesize that the greater the obstacles to survival, the greater the opportunity for creative responses by leaders of a new regime. This statement recognizes the possibility that political leaders can make a crucial difference to the course of a regime. Postulating the possibility of an event is no guarantee, however, of its occurrence. The probability seems greater that leaders of a new regime will be overwhelmed by great challenges than that they will master them. For many leaders, the most realistic goal may be to 'tread water', avoiding repudiation without establishing a fully legitimate or fully coercive regime.

While Western social scientists are quick to assume self-interest as the basic motive of men when studying their own countries, few impute self-preservationist ends to political leaders in other parts of the world. Perhaps many of these leaders have reached their political eminence because they gambled, heedless of risks, and won against the odds. But experience of office teaches men many things. It is not unreasonable to assume that the role-expectations of a man in office differ from those of the same man when he was an agitator in the streets. Men in power may have an interest in political change, but they also have an interest in preserving what they have already got. If Western politicians are expected to maximize short-term benefits, then how much greater an allowance should be made for leaders in states where the risks of a regime failing are much greater, and the penalties for loss far higher. These conclusions may strike British and American readers as gloomy. This does not necessarily make them untrue. It seems to me that the experience of Britain and America is very different from that of most European states, let alone states elsewhere in the non-western world. With the best of intentions, it is therefore hardly sensible for Anglo-American social scientists to project their faith in a happy history upon people whose own stories give less grounds for optimism.

Instead of contributing further to the literature of myth, social scientists might turn to another branch of literature, that of tragedy. One does not need to go back to the time when a King named Lear may have ruled in England. Americans can turn to the rural but hardly bucolic novels of William Faulkner's Yoknapatawpha County, Mississippi, or Arthur Miller's early plays about the hard realities of New York City. Reserved Englishmen, troubled by what E. M. Forster once described as the problems of an 'underdeveloped heart', have only problems of class to nag at them. If they wish to sympathize with those who suffer worse, they might turn to modern Ireland. O'Casey and Yeats there reflect a sense of violence almost great enough to make Englishmen understand how passionate people can be in their politics. For what it is worth, my own expectations of the world are perhaps best reflected in Chekhov's *The Cherry Orchard*. The commissars of drama may take this as a hymn to the future, and the reader with fond memories of the *ancien regime* as a lament for its passing. From my middle-aged perspective, it appears to be a testimony to the variety of life, a variety so full of surprising combinations that events happen randomly. Chekhov saw the play, as his subtitle indicates, as a comedy, not a tragedy, for random events can be funny or joyful as well as sad. In the circumstances, the ending is almost happy. Madame Ranievskaya will lose her estate, but she returns to Paris. Lopahin, a type who will always do well, gets his prompt reward. Feckless Waffles wins 20,000 undeserved roubles in a lottery. Even old Firs, the faithful servant, gives evidence at the end that he is safe against the future, for he will soon die. Such an ending can hardly be celebrated in the superlative language of American motion picture advertising; it might better be described by an English locution: 'not too pessimistic'.

Invoking authors from the humanities in support of political assumptions is useful as a means of reminding us of the nature of social scientists and their subject matter. In writing books, social scientists sometimes place themselves as men apart from the events discussed. Emotional detachment can be reinforced by physical detachment. This striving for detachment is understandable and justifiable, as long as its limitations are kept in mind. The most obvious limitation arises from the fact that no matter how hard one strives, one can never be value free. Every social scientist necessarily puts something of himself into what he writes. Computers print out tables or even books without feeling pleasure in their results, or concern about the implications of what their lineprinters say. But social scientists are different. Ultimately, they have more in common with the politicians and voters they study than with the apparatus of science; they too are but people in politics.

NOTES—CHAPTER VIII

1. Cf. *The Gospel According to St. John*, III:8 and the Venerable Bede on the Synod of Whitby, in *Ecclesiastical History of the English Nation* (c. 700 A.D.) Bk. II, Ch. 13.
2. Cf. Robert Levine, 'Ethiopia: Identity, Authority and Realism' in Lucian Pye and Sidney Verba, editors, *op. cit.*, and Paul Foot, *op. cit.*
3. Robert Packenham, 'Political Development Doctrines in the American Aid Program', *World Politics*, XVIII:2 (1966).
4. *Op. cit.*, p. xviii. But not in Ireland.
5. For recent efforts by American social scientists to mine meaning from the British past, see e.g., W. W. Rostow, *The Stages of Economic Growth* (Cambridge: University Press, 1960); Everett E. Hagen, *On the Theory of Social Change* (Homewood, Illinois: Dorsey, 1962) Ch. 13; Robert Holt and John Turner, *op. cit.*, and Neil Smelser, *op. cit.*
6. Cf. George Dangerfield, *The Strange Death of Liberal England* (London: Constable, 1936).
7. See e.g., Bernard Bailyn, *The Origins of American Politics* (New York: Knopf, 1968) and J. R. Pole, *Political Representation in England and the Origins of the American Republic* (London: Macmillan, 1966).
8. Louis Hartz, editor, *op. cit.*
9. Cf. J. S. Coleman, 'Conclusion', in G. A. Almond and Coleman, *op. cit.*, pp. 532ff., and Richard Rose, 'England: a Traditionally Modern Culture', pp. 86ff.
10. Cf. Emmeline W. Cohen, *The Growth of the British Civil Service* (London: Allen & Unwin, 1941) p. 49, and W. J. M. Mackenzie, 'The Plowden Report: a Translation', in Richard Rose, editor, *Policy-Making in Britain.*
11. Cf. the analyses of the changes in relationships in what nominally remained a continuing two-party system in William N. Chambers and W. Dean Burnham, editors, *op. cit.*
12. Cf. Stein Rokkan, 'Mass Suffrage, Secret Voting and Political Participation', in *European Journal of Sociology* II:1 (1961).
13. *Politics, Personality and Nation-Building* (New Haven: Yale, 1962).
14. *A Framework for Political Analysis*, p. 57.

15. Easton has lately begun to take up the problem of disruptions. See his 'The Theoretical Relevance of Political Socialization', *Canadian Journal of Political Science* 1:2 (1968).
16. *The Theory of Social and Economic Organization*, p. 360.
17. *Politics, Personality and Nation-Building*, pp. 287ff.
18. For discussions of these crises, see e.g., Sidney Verba, 'Conclusion', in Lucian Pye and Sidney Verba, *op. cit.*, and Lucian Pye, *Aspects of Political Development* (Boston: Little, Brown, 1966) Ch. 3.
19. Karl Deutsch, 'Social Mobilization and Political Development', *American Political Science Review* LV:3 (1961) pp. 507 ff.
20. Bruce Russett *et al.*, *ibid.*, pp. 294–98.
21. 'National Political Development', *American Sociological Review* XXVIII:2 (1963). Note the criticisms of this article in Neubauer, cited *infra*, footnote 22.
22. 'Some Conditions of Democracy', *American Political Science Review* LXI:4 (1967).
23. Cf. *Report on Registration and Voting Participation.*
24. 'The Concept of Political Development', *The Annals* Vol. 358 (March, 1965).
25. *The Politics of Modernization* (Chicago: University Press, 1965) p. 67.
26. Cf. Richard Rose, 'Modern Nations and the Study of Political Modernization', in Stein Rokkan, editor, *Comparative Research Across Cultures and Nations* (Paris: Mouton, 1968).
27. J. P. Nettl, *Political Mobilization* (London: Faber, 1967) pp. 245–46. For further comments on Apter, see reviews by Arthur Stinchcombe, Robert Rotberg and Robert Bellah in the *American Sociological Review* XXXI:2 (1966) pp. 266–69.
28. 'The Corrupt State: The Case of Rome Reconsidered', *Political Studies* XVI:3 (1968) p. 413.
29. 'Political Development and Political Decay', *World Politics* XVII:3 (1965) p. 394.
30. Samuel P. Huntington, *Political Order in Changing Societies* (New Haven: Yale, 1968), especially Ch. 1.
31. For a figure such as Max Weber, the Promethean imagery is not out of place. Cf. the quotation from Rilke that stands as the epigraph to Reinhard Bendix's *Max Weber: An Intellectual Portrait* (New York: Anchor, 1962).
32. See Reginald Bassett, *The Essentials of Parliamentary Democracy* (London: Macmillan, 1935) Part I.
33. Cf. *op. cit.*, and Thomas Marshall, *Social Policy* (London: Hutchinson, 1965).
34. (Princeton: University Press, 1964).

35. *Ibid.*, p. 463.
36. Joseph LaPalombara, 'Macrotheories and Microapplications in Comparative Politics', *Comparative Politics* I:1 (1968) p. 63.
37. Much of what follows is drawn from Richard Rose, 'Dynamic Tendencies in the Authority of Regimes', *World Politics* XXI:4 (1969).
38. 'Succession in the Twentieth Century', *Journal of International Affairs* XVIII:1 (1964) p. 107.
39. See e.g., Werner Warmbrunn, *The Dutch under German Occupation, 1940–1945* (Stanford: University Press, 1963).
40. Cf. Dankwart Rustow, *A World of Nations* (Washington: Brookings, 1967) p. 287.
41. See UNESCO *Statistical Yearbook 1965* (Paris UNESCO, 1966) pp. 249–66.
42. Cf. Derek Urwin, *Western Europe Since 1945* (London: Longmans, 1968) Ch. 1.
43. Data from a survey study in Northern Ireland undertaken in 1968, and to be analysed in a forthcoming book by the author.
44. *A Review of Elections, 1961–1962* (London: Institute of Electoral Research, 1964) p. 52.
45. G. A. Almond and S. Verba, *op. cit.*, Ch. 3.
46. *Presidential Power*, p. 155.

Epilogue

In times of uncertainty and trouble, the desire to do something is strong in many people. Given the complexities of life and the distance between individual intention and social consequences, it is difficult to say what one person can do. Concern with the style of politicians suggests that it is easier to decide how to behave than to determine what to do.

One motto that seems particularly relevant to me was spoken by a man who was neither a successful academic nor a successful politician. He was a drop-out from law school, a minor official in a major government, and three times a candidate for office but twice a loser. He failed to achieve even the limbo of success that his grandfather had reached. The words were spoken of a woman whose start in life could hardly have been less auspicious: a gawky girl orphaned before she was ten by the death of a belle of a mother and an alcoholic father. After a painful adolescence in the hands of a grandmother who never understood her, marriage to a charming socialite promised release, but he was then half-paralysed. In a memorial tribute, this man, Adlai Stevenson, said of this woman, Eleanor Roosevelt:

'She would rather light a candle than curse the darkness.'

Index